1971

1971

The
BEGINNING OF INDIA'S CRICKETING GREATNESS

BORIA MAJUMDAR
GAUTAM BHATTACHARYA

Harper
Sport

An Imprint of HarperCollins *Publishers*

First published in India in 2021 by Harper Sport
An imprint of HarperCollins *Publishers*
A-75, Sector 57, Noida, Uttar Pradesh 201301, India
www.harpercollins.co.in

2 4 6 8 10 9 7 5 3 1

P-ISBN: 978-93-5422-306-8
E ISBN: 978-93-5422-311-2

Typeset in 11.5/15.7 Sabon LT Std at
Manipal Technologies Limited, Manipal

Printed and bound at
Thomson Press (India) Ltd

To Jagmohan Dalmiya

*One of the best administrators the game will ever see,
and someone we considered family.
Wish we could have tea together and hand a copy of this
book to you, Jagguda.*

Contents

Preface

Thank God there was 1971.

2020 was perhaps the worst year in centuries, with stress and anxiety levels reaching new heights in India due to the COVID-19 pandemic. The coronavirus caseload in the country is in crores now—lakhs of people have lost their lives, and the situation is still far from normal. Besides COVID-19, there are several other issues the country faces. We saw the worst of the media in the Sushant Singh Rajput case, and it challenged the very idea of the unified India that we stand for. In Delhi, the political rhetoric is perhaps the worst it has been in a while. Communal tensions have been on the rise, and scepticism about the economy and its continual slowdown has raged unabated. Amid all this negativity, sports and, more importantly, this book have been a source of sustenance for us both.

Life and sports as we knew them before 2020 have changed drastically. The International Cricket Council (ICC)

Women's T20 World Cup final between hosts Australia and first-time finalists India saw a record 86,174-strong crowd on 8 March. Towards the close of the year, Naomi Osaka, the young Japanese tennis star, stood in solidarity with victims of systemic racial discrimination by wearing masks at the US Open with the names of the victims on them. Poland's Iga Swiatek won her country's first Grand Slam singles title as she became the youngest women's champion at the French Open since 1992. Young leaders from sports emerged elsewhere, too. Para-badminton world champion Manasi Joshi, one of *Time* magazine's 'Next Generation Leaders', became the first Indian para-athlete to have a doll modelled to her likeness as part of the Barbie 'Sheroes' family. The shift in narrative around female athletes continued while the emergence of bio-bubbles in the wake of the coronavirus pandemic marked a new era in the practice and organization of sports worldwide. We witnessed Board of Control for Cricket in India (BCCI) President Sourav Ganguly do his best to stage the Indian Premier League (IPL) in the UAE and badminton guru Pullela Gopichand work tirelessly during the months-long lockdown to spread the message of physical literacy in India. Amid all these victories against seemingly insurmountable odds, the essence of 1971 came to the fore – the perfect underdog story that ended in triumph. A story of hope, resilience and ecstasy. And with the fiftieth anniversary of the twin tours of 1971 upon us, we wanted to document the stories of that memorable year. So here we are with our labour of love—a work of cricket literature that helped us get through COVID-19 and allowed us to retain some semblance of normalcy during the lockdown, making us believe that not all is lost yet.

In the last major cricket event of 2020, the Women's T20 World Cup, sixteen-year-old Shafali Varma, who once had to dress up as a boy to get an opportunity to play among the kids in her state, Haryana, donned India colours and lived her dream. In the IPL, we witnessed many more like her do the same. Teen batsman and 2020 Under-19 World Cup star performer Yashaswi Jaiswal, for example, bought by the Rajasthan Royals for ₹2.4 crore, is the next big thing in Indian cricket. Devdutt Padikkal, who in his debut IPL season showed immense character when batting with Virat Kohli for the Royal Challengers Bangalore, is as promising. Sports, in these times of despair, remains a ray of hope. It brings with it an optimism that inspires confidence in the idea of India we stand for and believe in, and remains a true mirror of our democracy. And each of the men and women mentioned above carry a history that is a testament to the greatness India can achieve in the years to come. That's what makes 1971 relevant. Padikkal and Jaiswal are very similar to Sunil Gavaskar. Had there been no Gavaskar, one wonders if the likes of Padikkal and Jaiswal would have pursued the sport. The year 1971 was the foundation on which the present superstructure of Indian cricket was built. It allowed us to believe in Gavaskar's sacrifices and successes, and even inspired Sachin Tendulkar to play the game. And that we can produce a Tendulkar, whose family was anything but rich, underlines something inherently good about India. As Tendulkar once said, 'Very rarely does the whole country unite on something. That's what sports is able to do.'

At a time when the idea of India is being challenged at every step and politics has become all about personal slander, animosity and violence, the 1971 story comes as a breath of fresh air. And that's why we hope you will welcome this book. We cannot escape the reality that is primetime television news in India; as a society, though, we can already see signs that suggest it could do more harm to the fabric of our democracy than good. As the idea of the real India continues to be mutilated in the fight for television ratings, stories about the victories achieved by the Indian men's cricket team in 1971 can make a difference. At least we believe they can. In 1971, did the people of India care about the religion or economic background of the cricketers who made up the national team? Perhaps not. Instead, each time Gavaskar scored a century, all of India collectively celebrated his and the team's feats. Political parties across the spectrum enjoyed the success of Ajit Wadekar and his boys, and corporate India, most likely for the first time, came together to applaud the new champions. The national rhetoric, despite the backdrop of the war over Bangladesh, was one of achievement and success about what India could do rather than what was wrong with the country. And to read and recreate this story for all of you when our sensibilities were being challenged every day was a huge relief. To us, this is more than just a book. This project helped us move on with life and gave us reasons to believe that a relook at our history could help us envision a better future for India.

Introduction

Renaissance at Midnight:
1971 and the Beginning of Greatness

Never before had India won a Test match against the West Indies. And in what was a fateful tour to the Caribbean in 1962, India almost lost its captain, Nari Contractor, forever to a vicious Charlie Griffith bouncer. While Contractor survived the threat, his cricket career was over. Shaken by the incident, a 0–5 defeat against the likes of Wes Hall and Charlie Griffith wasn't a surprise. With new captain Mansoor Ali Khan Pataudi forced to take charge and no one wanting to open the batting in the aftermath of what had happened to Contractor, the tour ended up being a poor misadventure for the Indian team. Given the reputation of lethal fast bowlers operating on surfaces conducive to pace with no limit on the number of bouncers coupled with the, relentless earfuls doled out by the hostile crowds, touring the

West Indies was considered the ultimate test for a cricketer in the 1960s and 1970s. While it is true that the 1971 team that faced India did not have fast bowlers of the quality of Hall and Griffith, it was still a West Indies team led by Sir Garfield Sobers, and included batsmen like Clive Lloyd, Rohan Kanhai, Roy Fredericks and Sobers himself. To even suggest that it was a series win of modest significance is to miss the point altogether.

To the Indians, it did not matter. For them, what really mattered was the series win. The embarrassment of 1962 had been avenged and they had taken giant strides in establishing themselves as an evolving power in world cricket. Sunil Gavaskar was hailed the world over as a new phenomenon and captain Ajit Wadekar's support for Dilip Sardesai stood vindicated. Sardesai, who had made it to the team because of Wadekar's confidence in his abilities, played the best he ever had in his career.

That this victory had struck a chord with fans back home was evident when thousands turned up at the Santacruz airport in Bombay (as Mumbai was known at the time) to welcome the players back. This was also a sign of things to come—television had not yet become a mass medium of communication in India, and all the fans had to rely on was radio commentary and newspaper reports that were a day old because of the time difference.

There was, however, a section that remained unimpressed. The West Indies, it was argued, was no England, and Wadekar's real test would come two months later when the Indians toured the UK. England, fresh off an Ashes victory under Ray Illingworth and a come-from-behind victory against Pakistan, was widely accepted as the best team in the world at the time, and most did not give the Indians a chance. India's poor away record in England—lost 0–5 in 1958 and 0–3 in 1967—was repeatedly cited in the media to keep a lid on people's expectations. A drawn series, it was felt, was as good as a win in English conditions. Former India players, while praising the team for winning the away series in the West Indies for the very first time, were also wary of India's chances in England. In the absence of a good crop of fast bowlers and a stable middle order, India was always going to struggle against the likes of John Snow, Derek Underwood, Geoffrey Boycott and Ray Illingworth.

While the Indians missed out at Lord's and got a tad lucky in Manchester because of the rain, it all boiled down to the third and final Test match at The Oval in London. With a record of fifteen defeats in nineteen Tests at the ground going into the match, Wadekar's team needed something extraordinary to happen to change their poor track record at The Oval. This was more so after England managed a 71-run first-innings lead and appeared to be in firm control of the contest. With two days still left to play, India's breakthrough summer was gradually starting to get out of control.

And then, it became the Bhagwat Chandrasekhar show.

To Wadekar's credit, he attacked from the outset in England's second innings. The deficit of 71 runs wasn't something that had influenced his tactics, and the aggression fetched him immediate dividends, with England, reduced to 24 for 3 against the guile of Chandrasekhar. Chandra had picked 2 in 2 off the last 2 balls before lunch in five minutes of intense drama.

India kept up the pressure post lunch, and with Srinivas Venkataraghavan and Eknath Solkar backing up Chandra with excellent close-in fielding and catching, England was bowled out for 101—their lowest total against the Indians in the fifty years since India's Test debut at Lord's in 1932.

The job, however, wasn't done yet. India still had to score 172 runs for a victory, and the pressure of a first-ever series win against England in England could not be ignored. The nerves only multiplied when Snow got Gavaskar out LBW for a duck early in India's second innings. With India's best batsman out, the captain had to play one of the most important knocks of his career to set up the run chase. Wadekar, to his credit, was well up to the task. Losing Ashok Mankad had not deterred him, and with Sardesai, he lent the innings stability and India finished the day at 76 for 2, with less than a 100 runs required for history to be scripted.

Though he was run out at the start of the fifth day, Wadekar's conviction hadn't wavered and he immediately went to sleep in the dressing room. It was only when India had won that he was awakened by Ken Barrington with the news that the Indian summer had become a reality. Wadekar had successfully beaten the West Indies in the West Indies and England in England in a matter of four months, and, in doing so, had turned the tables for the game in India.

The victory against England against all odds in 1971 was arguably the best ever in the history of Indian Test cricket, only to be matched more recently by India's victory at the Gabba against Australia in January 2021. The team had exceeded expectations under Wadekar, giving the game a serious shot in the arm in India. For an erstwhile colony that had appropriated the British game at the close of the nineteenth century and made it their own by the early twentieth century, 1971 marked the completion of the turnaround. Indians were no longer exotic imports from the Orient to be represented in *Punch* cartoons and written about as subjects of curiosity in the mainstream media.

The 1971 cricket triumph was in every way comparable to India's landmark victory over England in hockey at the London Olympics in 1948, within a year of gaining independence in August 1947. For a newly independent India, the London Olympic Games of 1948 were more than a mere sporting event. When the Indian hockey team won gold at the London Olympics in 1948, defeating the English 4–0 in the final, much more than an Olympic victory was scripted. It was a newly independent nation's declaration against the forces of colonialism—retribution for the humiliation meted out by the English for almost 200 years and a statement to the world about the significance of 'sports' in an era of decolonization.

Cricket had done something very similar in 1971.

In this book, we celebrate the fiftieth anniversary of this victory, and also attempt to bring out the layers of grey which lay hidden under the surface but have forever influenced the 1971 narrative. Our attempt is not meant to be controversial for the sake of creating controversy. Rather, we are committed to documenting history in the manner in which it unfolded, while also attempting to showcase the deep-rooted complexities of Indian cricket. For example, Erapalli Prasanna, one of the best spinners India has ever produced, could never forget the humiliation of 1971, when he was overlooked in England, with Venkataraghavan preferred over him. Leaving out Prasanna, the architect of the Indian series win in New Zealand in 1967, wasn't easy and caused a major rift in the team. History has it that it marred the celebrations to a degree and also became a major controversy, with Prasanna eventually writing about it in his book, *One More Over*.

The other highlight of our book is the series of interviews with many of the actors involved in the drama, conducted at various times over the last four decades. We have included the interviews as a separate section at the end, for that makes room for an uninterrupted retelling of history without the reader having to gloss over the complexities often ignored in the existing narratives of 1971. Be it the uneasy relationship between Bishan Singh Bedi and Wadekar or the gradual breakdown of the team in 1974, the interviews provide a first-hand peek into what the protagonists of 1971 have felt over time.

Chapter 1
The Pecking Order

Why is the year 1971 significant and why do we call it Indian cricket's original renaissance? Did India not win a major away series before '71? They did; so why is it that '71 is labelled the breakthrough year in India's cricket history? Is it just because India beat the West Indies and England on their own turf in a span of four months, heralding a new era, or is there more to the story?

Detractors have said that the West Indies in '71 were half the team compared to what they were in the 1960s, so India's triumphs were no big deal. Others have said that India got lucky with the last day of the second Test at Old Trafford getting washed out, for if the weather had not intervened, India would have gone to The Oval 0–1 down. The impact of the mental scarring from a possible defeat is not something we can ever adequately analyse. We can't say with certainty if The Oval win would have been a reality had Ajit Wadekar's team stepped out to play the third and final Test 0–1 down.

But none of this explains the significance of the year 1971. India had already beaten New Zealand on their home soil in 1967–68; Erapalli Prasanna felt that Indian cricket's first renaissance had already occurred with that first win abroad, and '71 was simply a continuation. What really makes '71 the breakthrough year for Indian cricket is not simply the results achieved on the field, but what transpired off it, too. It is this synergy, a first in Indian cricket, that makes '71 a historic year.

In this chapter, we endeavour to explain how '71 was different by comparing it with every Indian tour of England undertaken until then, each of which had ended in defeat. By doing so, we aim to decode why '71 will always remain pivotal to the coming of age of Indian cricket.

Teams Divided

When the first Indian team travelled to England in 1932, the euphoria around the tour was often lost to the growing differences between two of Indian cricket's foremost patrons, the Maharaja of Patiala and the Maharajkumar of Vizianagram (better known as 'Vizzy'). When Vizzy lost to Patiala in the race for captaincy, he decided against touring, and was intent on focussing his energies to regain lost ground and mount one more strong challenge for the captaincy when the Marylebone Cricket Club (MCC) toured India in 1933. Patiala, never a player of repute, lost interest with Vizzy temporarily throwing in the towel, and withdrew from the tour. Instead, he made the Maharaja of Porbandar his nominee to lead the team to England. This in itself raised eyebrows because Porbandar was no match for someone of C.K. Nayudu's calibre; the latter had been nominated by

Wisden as one of the players of the year in 1933. Porbandar eventually withdrew in favour of Nayudu, who captained India in their first-ever Test match at Lord's on 25 June 1932. The differences, however, continued to play out in the background.

There were two groups of players with their allegiances clearly drawn: while one group supported Nayudu, others were more loyal to Vizzy. These differences came out in the open in 1936 when India toured England for the second time and Lala Amarnath, considered close to Nayudu, was picked on to send a stern message to the players. Amarnath, arguably the best player on the tour, was sent back to India on charges of indiscipline by Vizzy, a decision that made it amply evident who was in charge. Requests not to do so from the players did nothing to change the decision; it seemed that India's performance was considered secondary to the playout of power politics. Amarnath, while known to be hot-headed, had not done anything to deserve the harsh punishment he was handed, and it came as a shock to many in the team. Syed Mushtaq Ali pleaded with the management to reconsider the decision but they had already made up their minds. While Amarnath was the man in the firing line, the message was also directed—albeit implicitly— at Nayudu and his loyalists; they needed to toe the line or face the leader's ire.

Even after his return to India, the Amarnath drama continued. The final act in the saga was perhaps the most bizarre. Even after the board president, the Maharaja of Bhopal, announced to the press that Amarnath would rejoin the team in England and his cricket kit was reportedly put on the ship, he was instructed not to travel.

The following comment by Bill Fergusson, baggage supervisor of the Indian team at the time, illustrates the on-ground reality quite aptly: 'Vizianagram took with him thirty-six pieces of personal baggage, plus a couple of young servants, who were at the beck and call of their master twenty-four hours, every day. They slept on the floor by the door of his bedroom … just in case some marauder [read: player] might have ideas about disturbing their illustrious employer during the night … Vizianagram sometimes imagined I was also a servant, insisting that I should carry his coat, even dress him or look after the long hookah …'

One of the players who missed out on a possible Test berth in 1936 was Shute Banerjee, considered close to Nayudu. He was apparently asked to insult Nayudu over breakfast, failing which the Test spot was passed on to Baqa Jilani, who had agreed to carry out the captain's orders. While a number of these stories are probably apocryphal, what remains undisputed is the deep divide that existed between the players—something that was always going to impact the team's performance. Despite a few individual acts of brilliance, like the centuries from Vijay Merchant and Mushtaq Ali at Old Trafford, the Indians lost the series from which Amarnath had been expelled 0–2.

By the time the next tour came around in 1946, things had turned worse. On this tour, under the captaincy of the Nawab of Pataudi Sr, the Indians were confronted with a peculiar problem. Most of the inconvenience stemmed from food rationing, which, in 1946, still wrecked the lives of most in Britain. With the Second World War wreaking havoc, insufficient amounts of food for the players became a feature of the tour, and this created a deep distrust within the team of the BCCI back home. That the board wasn't able to take care of the basics did not go down well with the players. Finally, the imminent possibility of death by starvation was averted after an appeal was made in the press for help. This appeal caused cricket enthusiasts all over England to send gifts of their precious cheese rations, packets of tea and other such items to their favourite players. This helped a lot, although the kind of food offered was basic and often not to the Indians' taste.

In other ways, too, the tour was dispiriting. Writing to Nayudu, his mentor, Mushtaq Ali described his English experience in 1946 thus:

> Now Sir, in my humble opinion, this tour is worse than 1936, the same old trouble: no team work at all. Every member of the team is for himself. No one cares for the country at all ... Whenever a county player is set for a big score, you will find the Indian captain back in the pavilion. I am very much fed up with him, as are the other members of the team. Believe me Sir, the second Test match was ours after such a nice start. We collapsed because he sent in Abdul Hafeez at No. 3 instead of going in himself ...

In the same letter, which is now housed at the Fanattic Sports Museum in Kolkata, Ali accuses Pataudi Sr of being a poor captain and a divisive force within the team. Under an ineffective captain, the result was a foregone conclusion, according to Ali. This letter, candid in its language and content, was perhaps the most open letter ever written on tour. It goes deep into the psyche of the players and offers insight into matters that we hardly ever delve into. It is clear from the letter that the Indians did not really want to play; the team was disunited and there was no support for the captain among the players. In fact, the one statement—'He [Pataudi] is very much against the Indian players'—raises a lot of eyebrows in the context of what was happening on the political front: the bloodiest partition in history was a year in the future. Was Ali implying something that has never really come to light? Was there a class divide, or was there more to the letter, something that we will perhaps never know? For Ali to state, 'As Captain, he is worse than a school boy. I am very much fed up with him, as are other members of the team,' is far more explosive compared to what Greg Chappell said to the BCCI in 2005 about Sourav Ganguly. Imagine what would have happened had Ali written this letter with social media around! Primetime television anchors who love sensationalist rhetoric would have had a field day, and Indian cricket would have been labelled a cauldron of class and communal divide. Ali's last statement, 'I think Merchant is a far better captain than this fellow', would have been trending on Twitter and Instagram for days, with journalists hounding him, Pataudi and, of course, Merchant for comments.

Ali, fed up with the situation, subsequently decided to opt out of the touring team to Australia in 1947–48. Intrigue and machinations were par for the course in the game in India at the time, and the players were often pitted against each other for personal ends. This resulted in poor on-field performances, with the players playing as individuals and never as a united team.

Off the field, problems reached yet another high in 1952 when Vinoo Mankad, arguably the best player in the team, was left out by the BCCI for reasons very similar to what Farokh Engineer encountered in 1971, ahead of the West Indies tour. It all began when Mankad wrote to the BCCI in November 1951, informing the board that he had an offer to play as a professional for the Haslingden Club in the Lancashire League the following season. With India scheduled to tour England in the summer of 1952, Mankad's assignment as a professional was not looked upon with favour by the BCCI. However, given his reputation, the BCCI would have found it impossible to drop him and, accordingly, he was advised to fly back from England to attend the trials for the forthcoming tour. It was surmised that the board knew Mankad would have to rescind his contract with the Haslingden Club in order to come to India to attend the trials. Frankly, it was all a ploy to keep Mankad out.

Upon receiving the invitation, Mankad agreed on the condition that his selection be assured—by no means an unjust demand from one of the world's top all-rounders. It seemed reasonable because Mankad, under contract with the Haslingden Club as a full-time professional, would have to forsake his only source of income to make himself available for the trials. Mankad proposed to the board that he play in all four Test matches while assisting his club for the rest of the tour.

At first, the board responded with sympathy, urging him to join the trials and leading him to believe that his selection was a formality. On 16 February 1952, though, matters took a turn. After a board meeting, Mankad was told that he was not needed for the tour. One of the selectors decreed that Mankad was not special and Indian cricket had dozens of players of his calibre.

But as fate would have it, Vijay Hazare's team faced disaster at every step in England. The irony was Mankad's rousing form while he was playing for Haslingden in the Lancashire League. In his first appearance, Mankad was unbeaten on 71 in a score of 118 for 5, and even before the first Test at Leeds, played from 5–9 June 1952, Hazare was forced to turn to Mankad for assistance. This was after two players, Ghulam Ahmed and Dattu Phadkar, were injured. However, their injuries were not serious, and it was almost certain that both would be fit for the first Test. Even if they weren't, Chandu Sarwate and Ramesh Divecha, both part of the touring party, were available for selection. Given these circumstances, the team management's SOS to Mankad seemed awkward. On its part, the Haslingden Club was apprehensive about releasing Mankad, knowing it would affect both the club's championship prospects and its revenues. Accordingly, it initially refused permission and India was forced to play the first Test without Mankad. They lost by seven wickets.

Before the start of the second Test, the club, under intense pressure, reversed its decision. Mankad's release, it was surmised, may have been facilitated by Sir Herbert Merrett, a leading Welsh industrialist and president of the Glamorgan County Cricket Club, who made a cash offer to Haslingden. This, he said, was to demonstrate to the Indians how much the Welshmen admired their pluck as cricketers. While Merrett's gesture was greeted warmly by the Indian manager, Pankaj Gupta, the BCCI president, J.C.

Mukherjee, expressed his ignorance about the attempt to bring Mankad back. Referring to the news that Merrett had made a cash offer to Haslingden, Mukherjee felt such a move would not be appreciated in India and that the board would most likely refuse to have Mankad on those conditions. Against Mukherjee's wishes, Mankad was included in the team for the second Test, with Haslingden consenting to release him for the rest of the series.

The second Test, which India lost by eight wickets, is still best known as 'Mankad's Test'. He scored 72 and 184, and took 5 for 196 in the first innings. Even after what was an impressive performance, the BCCI did not honour Mankad and he was forced to return to Haslingden later in the month. The club wanted to give him a hero's welcome, but Mankad, disappointed by the treatment in India, turned down the offer of a red-carpet reception.

Back home, the *Times of India* expressed disgust at the manner in which the BCCI and the team management had conducted themselves on the Mankad issue: 'Principles have gone by the Board, solemn decisions which were based on the experience of past tours have been blithely ignored, and the manager of our side has not only condescended to accept for Indian cricket what is tantamount to pity and charity but also, to all intents and purposes, demanded that consideration.' As for Mankad himself, saddened at the treatment meted out to him, he confirmed his decision to retire from Test cricket at the end of the English season. Hearing this, the board acted promptly and persuaded him to change his mind in what was considered an urgent act of damage control.

The unfortunate reality of 1952 was repeated yet again in 1958, when India ended up having four different captains for four Test matches in what was a deeply divided team. There was serious distrust among the players and no one really knew what was going on. Pankaj Roy, who captained the team for one of the Test matches, had mentioned in personal circles that a group of players had conspired against him and spread the rumour that Roy was having difficulty sighting the ball and, as a result, was no longer good enough to play Test cricket. This was an attempt to push him back in the captaincy pecking order which, till then, was the monopoly of players from the western and northern parts of the country. In such circumstances, the result could only go one way.

While things were a tad better in 1966–67, India was still no match for England. To win a Test series against England in their backyard was still a far cry, and that's what makes the triumphs of 1971 such an important milestone. To borrow from Steve Waugh, it was India's final frontier at the time, and coming on the heels of beating the West Indies on their home soil made the achievement all the more special. Not only did the twin victories surprise critics back home, but they also added much to cricket as a brand, an entity that's since grown exponentially.

It is best to go back to Sunil Gavaskar to understand the importance of 1971 better. '[The year] 1983, to me, will always remain the highest point of my career. We were world champions, you see,' Gavaskar told us during a chat in 2020, the excitement in his voice palpable. It made for an interesting conversation because it made us all feel positive at a time when the rising global numbers of COVID-19 cases and deaths had injected despair into everyday life. In fact, even before we could go further on about '71, Sunny bhai stopped us to say, 'There can only be one world champion team and that's a very different feeling. Immediately after 1983, I will keep 1971 on my list of achievements, because to win Test series against the West Indies and England away from home was huge. We had never beaten the West Indies before, and never won a Test match on English soil. It was a pivotal moment for all of us, and helped the game go forward in India.'

That's why 1971 is right up there in our pecking order. In fact, we tend to agree with Gavaskar that it comes right after 1983 and perhaps 2011 on India's list of achievements. The two World Cup wins are ranked higher simply because they were world tournament wins, but in terms of the sheer scale of accomplishment, 1971 was certainly no less. And only recently have we added Mission Australia 2021 to this list.

Chapter 2
Pataudi and Merchant

While we might never find out what Vijay Merchant may have felt about the appointment of Pataudi Sr as captain in 1946, there is plenty of evidence to suggest that it was done in a manner that wasn't exactly 'cricket'.

Would it be fair to say, then, that Merchant never forgot this humiliation and eventually retaliated against Pataudi Jr when he had the opportunity to in January 1971, preferring Ajit Wadekar to the former? Was Merchant's casting vote in favour of Wadekar, which decisively changed the course of Indian cricket, a result of what had happened a quarter century earlier? Was it simply Bombay asserting its dominance over the rest of India, and did Pataudi Jr pay the price for what was done to Merchant by India's cricket mandarins in 1946?

Merchant, many believe, was the greatest batsman to play for India in the 1930s and 1940s. While his first-class average of 71.64, second only to Sir Donald Bradman, underscored how good he was, there are several eyewitness accounts that draw attention to his exceptional batting skills. A legend, Merchant, many argue, was also an efficient captain and had been groomed by Anthony De Mello, the founding secretary of the BCCI, to take over the reins of the team in the 1946 tour of England. He had already captained India against Lord Tennyson's Englishmen in 1937–38, as well as against Lindsay Hassett's Australian Services team in 1945–46. For all practical purposes, Merchant's appointment as captain against England in 1946 should have been no more than a formality. However, it was still the era of the British Raj and Pataudi Sr, a royal who had previously played for England, was considered a force to reckon with despite not having played sufficient domestic cricket since his return to India from England. Pataudi Sr, who had scored a hundred in his debut in the 1932–33 Bodyline series against Australia, had neither played in the Bombay Pentangular, the foremost tournament in colonial India, nor in the Ranji Trophy. He had, however, tactfully aligned himself with the Maharaja of Bhopal, a former BCCI president, and De Mello, a former mentor of Merchant's and one of the most powerful figures in the BCCI. It was De Mello, under the instructions of the Maharaja of Bhopal and in partnership with Pankaj Gupta, a key figure in the Cricket Association of Bengal (CAB), who pulled the rug from under Merchant's feet and handed the reins of the captaincy to Pataudi Sr in 1946.

While Merchant was the overwhelming favourite going into the selection committee meeting, having secured mandates of most state associations, De Mello was a true master of astute politics. Having played a part in setting up the BCCI in 1928, he was aware of its workings better than most, and the majority support for Merchant was never really a concern for him. He knew the mandates would mean little if he were able to convince and win over the state representatives who would eventually cast their votes in the all-important selection meeting.

As reported in the contemporary press, De Mello had found two useful allies in Karmakar and Pankaj Gupta, who represented the Baroda Cricket Association (BCA) and the CAB respectively. Gupta also held the proxies for the Bihar and Orissa state cricket associations, which meant he alone counted for three votes in the election. Although Gupta and Karmakar had been mandated by their associations to vote for Merchant, last-minute negotiations and offers of gratification from the opposition camp swayed them in favour of Pataudi Sr. A report published in *Sportsweek* in the 1970s, which looked back at how the tables turned, described this development as the most stunning act in India's cricket history, and suggested that its impact was even greater than the appointment of Vizzy as the captain of the Indian touring team to England in May–June 1936.

Within days of switching sides, Karmakar was appointed assistant secretary of the BCCI, a position he held for the next twenty-five years. Gupta, meanwhile, took charge as the manager of the Indian touring team to England under Pataudi Sr, a post he was reinstated to two years later as India toured Australia for the first time in 1948. Merchant, who had been nominated to take over the captaincy for the tour of Australia, wasn't able to do so on account of a groin injury, and the mantle of captaincy was eventually passed on to Lala Amarnath.

Gupta, who played a decisive role in Indian cricket in the 1940s and 1950s as the Indian team manager and a senior BCCI administrator, was never fully pardoned for this act of 'treachery' by members of the CAB. As a result, he was never again allowed to represent the association at the national level. However, in an age of proxies, the snub mattered little to Gupta, who had already secured the support of the Bihar and Orissa associations and continued to attend BCCI meetings as a representative of one of these two state cricket bodies.

It remains a matter of conjecture whether Merchant hadn't fully forgotten the humiliation of 1946 and if, in 1971, he felt it was payback time. Either way, it is impossible to dismiss the backstory of what had happened in 1946 or underestimate its impact on the developments in 1971, when Merchant used his casting vote to seal Pataudi Jr's fate. Merchant, who stood for the shift in power in cricket from the Raj to the educated middle classes, may have inadvertently also ended the dominance of the Raj by doing what he did in 1971. What may have been an acutely personal act had wider ramifications for Indian cricket, which in the long run changed the direction of the sport in the country.

To how Merchant pulled it back in 1971, we now turn.

The Dutta Ray Saga

The Merchant versus Pataudi Jr episode would have been a non-starter had it not been for Manindra Nath (Bechu) Dutta Ray, a veteran cricket administrator from Bengal. Dutta Ray, it can be said, was a polarizing figure who knew the backstage of Indian cricket well. For those who knew him, he was both the devil incarnate and a pragmatic genius rolled into one. Chuni Goswami, one of the most revered stalwarts of Indian football, confirmed to us that Dutta Ray was reviled at home as well. 'He would be served his food and to show their repulsion for him, the family would also place a plate of ash next to the food each time he sat down to eat,' Goswami once said. He continued: 'Dutta babu, however, was unflustered. All he would do was just move the plate of ash to one side and continue eating.' Goswami also emphasized that Dutta Ray had held positions of prominence in the BCCI for years—a kind of entitlement he had started to take for granted. While Bengal was never a powerhouse on the field and had made the finals of the Ranji Trophy only a few times, off the field, the troika of Gupta, Dutta Ray and A.N. Ghosh, the incoming BCCI president, managed to hold sway. As a result, when Dutta Ray lost in the BCCI elections in 1970, it was a shock for him. Had it been anyone else, he would have gracefully accepted defeat and moved on; but not Dutta Ray. In fact, soon after the election was over and Dutta Ray had been ousted from the selection committee by the casting vote of the BCCI president, Zal Irani, he gave an interview saying he 'vowed to return sooner than later'.

Immediately after losing the election, Dutta Ray met Ghosh to try and persuade the latter to give him a fresh opportunity. Ghosh, who had taken over as board president from Irani, was the opening Dutta Ray needed. Not one to give up, he had a compromise formula up his sleeve and proposed to Ghosh that all the new president needed to do was appoint him selector for a period of sixty days. Audacious as it may sound, Dutta Ray used his proximity to Ghosh to actually ask for a sixty-day window to set things right. He was willing to hand over his resignation to Ghosh, dated 30 November, which the president could invoke on that date. This, Dutta Ray argued, was a face-saver for him and was something he badly needed to redeem himself. Ghosh, who had worked with Dutta Ray and Gupta for years, had no option but to accede to the request. It is pertinent to add that Dutta Ray had also secured the support of a section of the southern Indian states, all of whom played a part in convincing Ghosh to reappoint him as selector.

Having successfully entered through the back door, Dutta Ray was not one to squander the opportunity. And as far as the BCCI goes, two months is a considerably long period. As the sixty-day period ended on 30 November, there was stony silence from him, and all queries from journalists were blocked with a terse 'No comment'. Moreover, he had actively started lobbying to get Keki Tarapore elected as the manager of the touring Indian team to the West Indies in 1971, going against the wishes of the very people who backed him in his comeback bid, and who were all supporting Colonel Hemu Adhikari for the post. Words of caution from his supporters failed to have any impact on Dutta Ray and, by the end of November, he had alienated most members who had supported his comeback bid. That's when the BCCI struck back. Eleven out of a total of twenty-seven voting members wrote to the president, objecting to Dutta Ray continuing as selector. Following the completion of his two-month term, BCCI members argued that he had no right to attend the selection committee meeting that was scheduled to be held on 6 January. Unless the president was firm with Dutta Ray, the members would move court to settle the issue.

Ghosh too was left with little option but to dump Dutta Ray, his long-term associate and ally. However, far from buckling under pressure, Dutta Ray, in complete disregard of the clamour for his resignation, continued to back the appointment of Tarapore as manager against the wishes of the majority of the BCCI members. This was intransigence; he was taking the BCCI head on, and there were bound to be consequences. After successfully winning Tarapore the vote by 11–9 on 6 January, Dutta Ray started to lobby hard for Pataudi Jr Livid to see him hold on to power and act against their diktat, the BCCI members had all but made up their minds to go to court with a copy of the resignation he had submitted on 30 September. Pushed to a corner, Dutta Ray to back off. Even when he left for Calcutta from Bombay citing high blood pressure, he was quick to check if it was possible for him to vote in absentia. Had there been a provision in the BCCI constitution to do so, Dutta Ray would have sealed the deal for Pataudi Jr. It was no secret that among the five selectors, Merchant, the chairman, and Amit Dani were in favour of Wadekar, while Gopinath, M.M. Jagdale and Dutta Ray were in favour of Pataudi Jr The division was out in the open, and it was known that Dutta Ray's was the deciding fifth vote. With the five selectors present and voting, it was always going to be 3–2 in Pataudi Jr's favour, Merchant and his opposition notwithstanding. In fact, had Dutta Ray not backed Tarapore, Pataudi Jr would have sailed through. It was only because of Dutta Ray falling foul with his mates in the BCCI that Merchant got an opportunity. And once he did, he did not let go of it. First, he stopped Dutta Ray from voting while the latter was away, citing the constitutional provision that the very purpose of the selection committee meeting was to ensure fair debate. If he wasn't present in Bombay, there was no way Dutta Ray could contribute to the deliberations. Second, he made sure that the selection committee meeting wasn't pushed back any further, cementing the window of opportunity. While Dutta Ray was sitting in Calcutta frustrated, Merchant completed the job. With Dani firmly in his corner, he pitted Wadekar against Pataudi Jr and, in a decision that divided the Indian cricket fraternity down the middle, cast his all-powerful deciding vote in favour of Wadekar to conclude the captain selection saga.

In a conversation with us, the nonagenarian C.D. Gopinath recalled that the meeting for the captain selection, unusually, took place in Merchant's office. 'I have been part of so many selection meetings,' Gopinath said, 'but I never saw anything similar to that meeting, where the name of the captain got debated over three hours.' According to Gopinath, Merchant and Dani had decided on Wadekar as the captain well before the meeting. 'Their logic was that the time had come for a change,' Gopinath said. He also specifically stated that Merchant had not wanted a casting vote situation: 'He was trying very hard to come to a unanimous decision in favour of Wadekar.' But with the situation in a deadlock among the selectors, the chairman's casting vote came into play.

Two days later, Ghosh, the BCCI president, clarified in Bombay that Dutta Ray hadn't resigned from the selection committee. He dismissed resignation rumours and said that Dutta Ray was unwell and recuperating in Calcutta. What is interesting, however, is that Dutta Ray travelled to Madras for the Special General Meeting of the BCCI on 13 January, casting doubts on the 'he is unwell' narrative. In Madras, he clarified what Ghosh had already said: he had not resigned from the selection committee. He also dismissed the conjecture that he hadn't attended the meeting in Bombay because of the threat of court action against him by a section of the BCCI.

The matter had not yet been put to bed, with Dutta Ray and Ghosh both keen on the former continuing as a member of the committee. As mentioned in *Sportsweek* in January 1971,

> Some of the Board members are actively considering calling a Special General Meeting to discuss the issue. The same could not be raised at the last meeting in Madras as it was not on the agenda. The members feel that Dutta Ray should officially go out of the selection committee and a new member be elected in his place so that the team for the England tour in July next could be finalized by a five-member selection committee.

While the last word on Dutta Ray can never be written, suffice it to say that there are few coincidences as pertinent as this. In 1964–65, Dutta Ray ensured the appointment of Pataudi Jr as captain by using his casting vote. Six years later, it was the very same casting vote, the use of which was made possible by Dutta Ray's absence from the meeting, that was used to unseat him from the highest position in Indian cricket.

Merchant: A Man of Strong Disposition

When we asked the affable Gundappa Viswanath if he remembers Merchant's role in the whole saga, we could sense a degree of discomfort in him. Viswanath, or Vishy as he is fondly known in cricket circles, all of a sudden looked a little apprehensive. Maybe he wasn't keen on revisiting the unpleasantness of what took place fifty years ago. When we further pushed him, saying it was important for readers to know what really happened, he opened up in a manner as though he was taking fresh guard while answering the question. He first asked if we wanted something to drink and subsequently ordered two glasses of fresh lime soda at the posh Karnataka Golf Association Club House in Bengaluru. To us, it was an attempt by Viswanath to compose his thoughts and then tackle the question. 'First, I will confess to you that I was disappointed that Tiger Pataudi wasn't appointed captain,' Viswanath said. 'Tiger was my leader and had backed me as a youngster, maybe a tad prematurely even. At the time I played Test cricket, in 1969, I was perhaps not fully ready,' he continued with a smile. 'As a result, it is only natural that I will forever have a degree of reverence for Tiger. Having said that, I will also say that Wadekar was a good captain, and it was Vijay Merchant who played the defining role in putting him at the helm. While I don't really know if it was out of a grudge or anything, what I do know is Merchant was always a person who spoke his mind regardless of whether anyone liked it or not.'

While Viswanath was clear that his opinion shouldn't be interpreted as a statement for or against Merchant and emphasized to us multiple times to put out a proper clarification, he did give us an example of how Merchant conducted himself, offering us a glimpse into the goings-on backstage. 'If you just take the story forward a little bit and consider what happened ahead of the England tour in the summer of that year, you will understand what Vijay Merchant was like as the chairman. When he met the members of the touring team, he singled out Chandra [Bhagwat Chandrasekhar] and said this was literally the last chance he was being given. Chandra, if you remember, wasn't part of the team to the West Indies, and was itching to make a difference in England. Much to everyone's surprise, Merchant told Chandra that he should be grateful for the opportunity and make it a point to prove himself, for it could well be his last tour for India. To be honest with you, Chandra was livid at being picked on. First, there was no reason for Merchant to speak to him in public. As a senior player, he could well have been spoken to in private, and that would perhaps have been better. He was the great Bhagwat Chandrasekhar and he had every reason to be upset and angry. Soon after Merchant left the room, Chandra burst out saying, "If he thinks I am not good enough, there is absolutely no need to pick me. I am not begging to get selected, nor am I dying to go to England." We hadn't seen Chandra that angry, and it was clear to us all that he had taken the slight personally. Maybe this was one of the reasons he bowled the way he did at The Oval. We tried to calm him down and asked him to move on. I am telling you this to give you a sense of how Merchant was as a man,' Viswanath said.

That Merchant was strong-willed is evident from every contemporary news report published on the issue. While Vinoo Mankad and Rusi Modi expressed dismay at Pataudi Jr being replaced as captain, Merchant stuck to his guns at every step and justified the casting vote in favour of Wadekar. This was much the same way that Merchant used to bat— not only was he technically correct and courageous, but he also had loads of patience, which was considered key to being a good Test batsman. A man of solid temperament, he was always one to put the team above himself, something that was evident in the way he had supported Pataudi Sr in the 1946 tour of England.

Speaking out in the 10 January 1971 issue of *Sportsweek*, Mankad described the decision as 'shocking', while Modi called it 'disgraceful'. While these comments were headlined on the cover as 'Stop Press', Modi, in the same issue, had argued in favour of Pataudi Jr as captain. While addressing the issue of captaincy, he was unequivocal in saying,

> My candidate is Pataudi. [Chandu] Borde's leadership does not inspire confidence. There is a move to appoint [Srinivas] Venkataraghavan as captain but, to my mind, he is rather inexperienced at the moment. The only yardstick in gauging the ability of a captain is when the pressure is on. I am aware of Pataudi's loss of form and the decline in his fielding but in the present circumstances, he is the best man for the job. He has a wealth of experience behind him and his batting methods are basically correct.

From Mankad's comments, it was apparent that Wadekar wasn't even considered a candidate for the job by some of India's best, so it was no surprise that his appointment was met with a sense of shock and awe. Mankad and Modi, both contemporaries of Merchant, were two of the most respected voices in Indian cricket, and their views were enough to influence public opinion against the chairman. Modi, it is important to remember, was the second most consistent run-getter for Bombay after Merchant for well over a decade, with multiple Ranji Trophy double hundreds against his name. In other words, the pressure on Merchant was mounting in the media, with fans, too, calling the decision 'outrageous'.

There were a large number of letters from angry fans that were published in the contemporary press soon after the selection committee meeting was over. Most of these favoured Pataudi Jr as skipper and targeted Merchant for what he had done. With time, however, experts like Mankad had moved on from their earlier position and, in fact, congratulated the selection committee for picking what was considered a very good team for the West Indian conditions. Mankad even went on record to say, 'The selectors deserve to be congratulated for availing the best available talent in the country. In fact, I think skipper Wadekar will have quite a problem on his hands in selecting his Test teams.' He concluded by saying, 'I consider the decision not to include a specialist pace bowler a good one, particularly since the selectors have strengthened the batting line-up with the inclusion of an additional all-rounder instead.'

Mankad's views found resonance in what Polly Umrigar and Bapu Nadkarni subsequently said to the media. While Umrigar called the team a 'very well-balanced side', Nadkarni stated that the 'selectors had been more than fair' to everyone.

Besides the appointment of Wadekar, the one other decision that rankled everyone was that of leaving Farokh Engineer out of the touring team. Going by form and quality, Engineer would have breezed into any Indian team at the time. In an interview given a few years later, a disappointed Engineer even said that he was tipped for the captaincy, and it was only because Merchant, who disliked his 'flamboyance', that he missed out on the job.

The official reason given was that Engineer, who played county cricket for Lancashire at the time, had not played any domestic cricket in India, and, as a result, could not be chosen to represent the national team. While this sounded unreasonable and dogmatic, more so because Clive Lloyd in the Caribbean too played county cricket at the time and not domestic cricket, it was a call that had the unanimous support of the BCCI. Engineer, too, played things down, knowing that anything inflammatory could have cost him his career. Speaking to the media just days after the selection while on his way back to England, he said, 'This was expected,' before going on to add that 'The West Indies, although not as formidable a side as it was a few seasons ago, is still a force to reckon with.' When he was pushed to comment on the BCCI's decision to leave him out and the unprecedented support he had received from fans, all he said was, 'I wish to thank them for their support and the concern that they have shown in the interest of Indian cricket, but I'd prefer to remain non-committal as I've been all along.'

In the midst of all this turmoil, Merchant had remained composed and resolute, before finally opening up to the *PTI* in an exclusive interview. He followed it up with another explosive interview to *Sportsweek* editor Khalid Ansari, which was the cover story of the magazine's 14 February 1971 issue. The headline in bold read: 'I'd rather have courage to use the casting vote—Vijay Merchant.' This one sentence summed up Merchant's mindset and the chain of thoughts he elaborated on in the interview. About Engineer, whom he said he had met in Bombay, he was quick to clarify that while there was no doubt he was a quality cricketer and that he would have made the team under normal circumstances, it was the BCCI's rules that prompted the selection committee to leave him out. At no point did he give any indication that the decision was based on any kind of personal vendetta. In fact, he went on to clarify that Engineer was not alone. Rather, the decision applied to Rusi Surti as well. While Engineer was the more accomplished and more versatile of the two, under normal circumstances, Surti should have also made the team had the BCCI's rule not been in place.

When it came to Engineer, Merchant was in denial mode. He was quick to emphasize that the decision to ban the inclusion of players settled abroad had not come from the selectors. In fact, none of the selectors had anything to do with it. It was a decision made by the board and was binding on the selection committee. He said that Engineer had been in Bombay a few weeks ahead of the selection committee meeting, and that Merchant had met him on 23 December and invited him to the selection committee room of the West Zone to ask why he was in India. Merchant also asked Engineer if he was available to play Ranji Trophy games in 1971, to which Engineer replied, 'I love the game so very much that I would like to play it all round the year, provided someone is prepared to pay my personal expenses to come down for Ranji Trophy matches.' This answer, Merchant argued, left a degree of ambiguity. Engineer hadn't really confirmed his participation and had laid down a condition, saying he would only come if his expenses were taken care of. It was this stand, Merchant argued, that forced the hand of the selection committee and pushed them to leave Engineer out of the team. 'I know he has not taken English nationality, but he admitted that he will play in England so long as he is good enough to play county cricket ... At the board meeting, when the above policy decision was taken, the names of Farokh Engineer and Rusi Surti were specifically mentioned. So, the Board members had more or less decided that these cricketers should not be included unless they play in local competitions. This does not mean being available for a match or two,' he explained in the interview.

Finally, he clarified that even after the selection committee meeting, the decision could have been reversed by the BCCI. In fact, the selection committee had indicated to the BCCI who to drop in case they decided to make an exception for Engineer, since he had not ruled out playing the Ranji Trophy. It was thus open to the BCCI, even at that late stage, to change the team if they felt that the selection committee had erred in interpreting the BCCI directive on non-residential players.

On Pataudi Jr, Merchant was clearly on the offensive. He termed the whole controversy unnecessary and blamed Pataudi Jr for triggering it, saying that had he informed the BCCI of his unavailability for the tour in time, the whole imbroglio could have been avoided. Pataudi Jr, it needs to be stated, claimed to have informed the BCCI of his unavailability through a telegram and a letter sent to the chairman of the selection committee. Countering these claims, Merchant declared that neither he nor the other selectors or the secretary of the board were aware of Pataudi Jr not being available. Stating that he had read it in the papers the next morning, Merchant went on to dismiss Pataudi's claims in the most scathing manner: 'In that report, Pataudi stated that he had sent a telegram to the Board or the Chairman of the Selection Committee. The only telegram that I received was dated the 12th instant and dispatched, according to my reading of the telegram at 00.25 a.m. on the 12th from New Delhi. It was delivered to me at the Cricket Club of India at 1.30 p.m., just as we were proceeding to my office for selecting the side. If there was already a telegram dispatched on the 8th [as had been claimed by Pataudi Jr], where was the necessity for this one?'

He further clarified that he had received a letter from Pataudi Jr on 13 January, dated 11 January, which indicated that Pataudi Jr wasn't available for the tour. However, neither the telegram nor the letter had offered any valid reason for him opting out of the tour. Yet again, Merchant questioned the need for this letter, and if previous intimations had been given by Pataudi Jr.

On stopping Dutta Ray from voting in absentia, Merchant was adamant. 'If there is no constitutional provision for voting by proxy, it technically means that such a vote cannot be exercised,' he said, outlining that had he allowed Dutta Ray to vote, he would be doing something unconstitutional and unethical. He also said that had Dutta Ray voted in favour of Wadekar, many on the board would have argued that Merchant agreed to this practice to get his own candidate elected as captain. 'I would rather have the courage of exercising my casting vote,' Merchant said, signing off.

Here was a man who meant business—he knew what he wanted and was confident of the team he had selected to represent India in the West Indies. Having played cricket at the highest level with distinction, Merchant was aware of what it would take to perform in the Caribbean and was desperate to reverse India's abominable record there. While conceding that India's opening attack lacked penetration, Merchant was totally at ease with having dropped Chandrasekhar from the touring team. He went on to suggest that he would have welcomed the inclusion of a wrist-spinner had there been one in good form. 'South Zone itself had dropped Chandrasekhar in the semi-finals and Kumar in the finals. No further comment is necessary,' he argued.

Finally, he dismissed insinuations that the touring team wasn't the best reflection of the talent available in the country at the time, and stated that while it was difficult to predict how India would fare against a relatively new-look West Indian side, much would depend on Wadekar's abilities as captain. 'Because our team is well balanced and has youth on its side, I have reasons to feel confident that they will render an excellent account of themselves. I have a lurking suspicion they will far exceed our expectations ... If our fielding gives that support to our spin bowling which our bowlers have a right to expect, the Indian cricketing public might be in for a surprise. I feel most optimistic—not because I helped select the team, but because I know what the team is capable of.'

History lends credence that Merchant was right. And in sport, the cardinal truth will forever be 'winner takes all'.

Chapter 3

The Caribbean: Hardly the Perfect Start

It is a well-known truism that some things are best left unsaid. That India and, more specifically, Ajit Wadekar, the captain, got lucky in the West Indies in 1971 is one such cliché. Delve deep and there it is—an all-pervasive rhetoric of denigration designed to deny Wadekar the credit he deserves for the series victory. It is argued that the West Indies team at the time wasn't good enough and, in their last four Test series, had lost twice to England, once to Australia and drawn a series against a low-key New Zealand side. Unlike the team of the 1960s, which had bowlers like Wes Hall and Charlie Griffith, the 1971 team did not have a single fast bowler with any experience to write home about. Sir Garfield Sobers, too, wasn't his usual self, with a lot on his plate after his visit to Rhodesia in 1970. Criticized for inadvertently supporting apartheid, Sobers, many argued in the local press, seemed disoriented. But while it is true that the West Indies were a team in transition and were trying out to a lot of experiments in the 1971 series, there is no denying that India had to overcome several adversities to get the result they wanted. From picking Dilip Sardesai against the wishes of many to dealing with the kit controversy on arrival to countering claims that Gundappa Viswanath had been chosen despite nursing a serious injury, things were never easy for Wadekar and his team after they left India for the Caribbean in February 1971.

The pressure had started to build on Wadekar within days of the final squad being announced. Writing in the *Times of India*, K.N. Prabhu, who accompanied the Indian squad to the West Indies and travelled on the same flight as the players, declared that '[Mansoor Ali Khan] Pataudi still commands support.' In his column, Prabhu argued that only a season ago, it had taken the selectors just two minutes to reelect Pataudi as captain for the twin tours of Australia and New Zealand. This time around, however, it had taken them two hours and 'a casting vote to dethrone him. That is some measure of the support he still commands in our councils.' Prabhu, who was present at the captaincy announcement, went on to describe the rather uncomfortable scenes at the Cricket Club of India in Bombay. 'His popularity among the followers of the game was evident from the uneasy stillness that descended over the assembly that heard the Board Secretary Professor [M.V.] Chandgadkar pronounce the final verdict on Friday night,' Prabhu wrote. 'It was received in stunned silence—as if someone innocent had been condemned to pay the ultimate penalty for the misdemeanours of others.' He added, 'It was a strange irony of circumstances that the casting vote, which had brought Pataudi to power, should have also been responsible for his downfall.'

Even as debates over this fiasco continued in the background, stalwarts started questioning the inclusion of Sardesai and Viswanath in the team—controversies that could have badly dented the team's morale as they left India for New York on their way to Jamaica. While it is safe to assume that had Pataudi made himself available, Sardesai would have missed out, the likes of Pankaj Roy and Dattu Phadkar openly canvassed for Ramesh Saxena ahead of the veteran Sardesai. While Roy was open to the idea of trying out Sardesai as an opener, he was quick to point out that as a middle-order batsman, 'I prefer Saxena, who plays well off the back foot.' His apprehension stemmed from the fact that Sardesai hadn't done anything stellar in domestic cricket in 1969–70, and was perhaps in the last leg of his career. Despite taking his experience into account, Roy argued that Sardesai had little left in the tank to offer the Indian team. He found support from Phadkar, who suggested, 'I would have liked Saxena in the side. He definitely gave an A-1 performance in the matches he played before the selectors. Saxena deserved a better "deal".'

If questions over Sardesai remained in the realm of murmurs, things around Viswanath turned distinctly hostile when the genial genius missed the first couple of matches of the tour. Labelled the 'Viswanath scandal', questions were asked in the press about whether Viswanath was 'smuggled into the tour party to the West Indies'. Some went on to say that reports emanating from the West Indies expressed serious apprehension regarding Viswanath's fitness and his ability to be a part of the team anytime soon, and this was proved by his omission from the team for the second successive game ahead of the first Test. It was argued that he was all but out of the first Test and was 'virtually a passenger through the first leg of the tour'. One of the reports even suggested that it was now up to the manager, Keki Tarapore, to complete the unpleasant task of sending Viswanath home and asking for a replacement. *Sportsweek*, for example, questioned what they called 'a really sad state of affairs' and asked if the board officials would care to explain 'why Viswanath was not made to appear before the Board's orthopaedic specialist in Bombay before the selection of the team was ratified at the Board's Special General Meeting'. Was he being given special treatment because he was from Karnataka and close to the board's senior vice president, M. Chinnaswamy? Other media sources were no less scathing, saying that it was all a cover-up and a case of Mysore flexing its muscles within the board. Most of the preferential treatment was attributed to Chinnaswamy, who, it was argued, had ridiculed the medical facilities on offer and said he had no faith in the board's specialist medical officer. He cited the example of Bhagwat Chandrasekhar, and how the BCCI had bungled in 1967–68 when the manager, Ghulam Ahmed, had sent Chandrasekhar back home halfway through the tour; according to Chinnaswamy, 'there was nothing wrong' with his 'so-called twisted ankle'. Chinnaswamy, it was argued, wasn't prepared to let Viswanath suffer the same fate as Chandra, and in ensuring this, went a tad too far. It was at his insistence that the BCCI decided on asking every player to furnish a medical certificate from an enlisted doctor under the aegis of their respective state associations. This went against the established practice of the BCCI getting the players examined by the board's medical officer.

Past incidents of mismanagement were raked up to justify this departure from the existing practice. For example, it was mentioned that in 1967–68, Hanumant Singh, who was a certainty for the tours in Australia and New Zealand, had to miss out on account of a thigh injury sustained earlier that year. Though his own doctor had passed him as fit and had categorically declared him available for the Australian tour, the BCCI's orthopaedic specialist overruled the reports and declared him unfit. The selectors, with no option left, had to overrule the requests of the Rajasthan Cricket Association, who had volunteered to get Singh examined by another specialist, and leave him out.

Conspiracy theories spread thick and fast. It was argued that an extra batsman was included in the touring 1971 team at the cost of a fast bowler to ensure Viswanath could be given additional time to recover. It was also mentioned that the selection committee had nominated Abbas Ali Baig as a standby in addition to Chandrasekhar, in case Viswanath had to come back. The selection of the extra batsman, some argued, had affected the team balance and was likely to cost Wadekar in what was to be a long, five-Test series, lasting for well over two and a half months.

Viswanath, however, dismissed these theories and was rather combative when we raised the issue with him. Anyone who knows him well will agree that aggression is against his nature, and it was rather surprising to see this very genial man lose his cool when we mentioned some of the media reports to him. 'You know me well enough to understand I would have declared myself unavailable if my injury was serious enough and if I knew that I wouldn't be able to play in most of the games,' Viswanath said. 'What these reports are saying is that I cheated my way into the team. That's not how I played my cricket.' Knowing him well enough, we are in full agreement with him, and must state in unequivocal terms that Viswanath was not one to hide an injury and sneak into a touring team. He, however, did make a confession. 'Yes, I was carrying an injury, and yes, everyone in the BCCI knew about it,' Viswanath said. 'However, it wasn't anything serious, and each one of us knew that I would miss the first couple of games of the tour. To say anything to the contrary is plain unfair and demeaning.'

Viswanath, by his own admission, had picked up the injury on the opening day of the Duleep Trophy final between South Zone and East Zone. He had twisted his knee and had not taken any further part in the game. In fact, he wasn't even allowed to bat, and Merchant had asked him to appear in front of Dr Arun Shamsi, the board's medical officer, for further diagnosis. Dr Shamsi, Viswanath mentioned, had asked him not to risk batting and further aggravating the injury, and instructed him to rest. Available records show that the BCCI had sent Viswanath to the orthopaedic centre of the KEM Hospital in Bombay on the third day of the game, and they even issued a statement in the evening stating that the injury was a minor one, expected to heal with a week of complete rest. The injury, Viswanath clarified, was a flare-up of an old one, and was something he had been nursing for the past few years. 'I was involved in an accident on a two-wheeler a few years earlier, and from then on, I had a problem with my knee,' he clarified. 'It was not new, and even in 1969, I had to manage the injury when it had flared up once or twice. At that time, I used to bowl a good number of overs in our local club games in Bangalore that were played on matting wickets. I used to bowl spin, and it often happened that I ended up bowling anywhere between 15–20 overs in a game. When I went to the doctor, I was asked to no longer bowl on matting wickets, for in doing so, I ran the risk of hurting my knee. Bowling, I can confess to you, was not something I was too keen on, and it wasn't a major decision to stop bowling altogether. It was a compromise I had to make, and I did so fairly early in my career. Once I stopped bowling, things started to get better and, even in 1971, it was only a matter of time before I was fully fit to play in the West Indies.'

While there was never any doubt in our minds about the truth of what Viswanath was saying, he was not done yet. 'Do you think Ajit would have taken me to the West Indies if he did not think I could play?' he asked. 'He had been appointed captain over Tiger [Mansoor Ali Khan Pataudi], and it was only natural that he wouldn't want an extra passenger to travel with the team. And while Tiger and I could be considered close, it was the first time that I was playing cricket under Ajit in any form.'

The allegation, we assured him, had been conclusively put to rest.

One thing, however, was clear from the very start of the tour—the Indians weren't in the best space mentally when they landed at JFK Airport in New York on their way to Jamaica. While on the one hand, they were expected to do well against a relatively young and inexperienced West Indies side, on the other, they were being picked on for reasons that had little to do with their cricket. To compound problems,

Sunil Gavaskar had been nursing a painful 'whitlow' in his finger as the team boarded the aircraft in Bombay and was in extreme duress by the time the flight touched down in New York. Gavaskar recounted, 'Soon after we reached the hotel, the manager, Keki Tarapore, took me to the hospital to get the finger checked. In the course of the flight, the swelling had increased considerably and the finger had turned so bad that the nurse who was assisting the doctor actually turned her face away on seeing the pus. However, the operation was eventually a minor one, and within ten minutes, I felt better. All I needed to do, I was told, was rest, and I would be good to go in about a week or so.'

With Gavaskar and Viswanath out with injuries, the Indians needed to use every resource in the two tour games leading up to the first Test in Jamaica, starting on 18 February 1971. After reaching the West Indies on 2 February, all the team had were two four-day games to fine-tune the final XI, with the first warm-up match slated to begin on 5 February in Kingston. This meant that the two days heading into the first practice game, 3–4 February 1971, were of utmost importance as far as acclimatization was concerned. However, calamity struck soon after the team landed in Kingston, with news coming in that the kit of almost the entire sixteen-member squad had not reached Jamaica. The Indians, it should be mentioned, had missed their scheduled connecting flight in New York, allegedly because of a mix-up by the airline staff—the team's luggage had to be offloaded at JFK Airport and could only be sent via the next available flight. It seemed incomprehensible to many that the kit hadn't been properly loaded the next day considering there was a near-twenty-four-hour gap between the two flights.

Seriously concerned over the non-availability of the kit, Tarapore, the manager, made multiple phone calls to the BCCI and the team's travel agents who were responsible for ensuring smooth passage between New York and Jamaica. Things turned dire when the travel agents informed the BCCI that the team's kit hadn't been found at the airport and that they had documents to prove it wasn't in New York. They circulated memos to show that the kit bags of all the players had left JFK Airport and had travelled to Jamaica on the same aircraft as the team. This sent the whole issue into a tailspin. With the team left to fend for themselves, Tarapore had no other option but to go back to the airport in Jamaica and ask the officials to check one final time if the kit had arrived from the US. To his amazement, he discovered that all the bags had been lying in the unclaimed baggage area at the Kingston airport for two days and, according to the officials, would have been removed had there been no claimant in the next day or so. The officials in Jamaica, it appeared, had goofed up, but were unwilling to own up to the mistake. It was just hours before the first game on 5 February that the Indians got their kit, making things that much more difficult for them to start with.

While a section of the Indian press blamed the BCCI for the 'mystery of the missing kit', as the incident came to be labelled, others suggested that the board should have been more proactive, learning from its 1961–62 experience. That tour of the West Indies nine years earlier had been disastrous, culminating in a 5–0 series defeat. Things had started to go south when, even then, the Indian team's kit did not reach Jamaica in time, leaving the players stranded in the city for the first two days without practice.

Prabhu, travelling with the team in the same aircraft in 1971, expressed surprise at how the entire team's kit could have gone missing. In his characteristic lyrical prose, he wrote, 'The night stopover at the Sherlock Holmes Hotel in Baker Street was interesting but of little use. On our onward journey, there was no trace of the cricketers' baggage for two days. This was certainly one where Dr Moriarty scored. One felt that James Bond would certainly have delivered the goods in more than one sense, pinning it down to one of Doctor No's henchmen in Kingston Town.'

Another issue, which affected some players more than others, was the growing political turmoil back home in states like West Bengal at the time of the tour. While the mounting unrest in Bangladesh, which finally resulted in the liberation of the country in December 1971, is formally documented to have started that year on 25 March, rising tensions in areas of Calcutta could be felt from January of that year. Rusi Jeejeebhoy, who was from Bengal and travelling with the team for the first time, was the hardest hit, with no communication from home adding to his growing anxiety. The following was reported in the *Times of India* on 23 February 1971: 'Indian cricketers have been distressed by the lack of news from home. This is particularly true of Rusi Jeejeebhoy as items on disturbances in Calcutta have appeared in the local press (in Kingston).'

The report went on to state that the BCCI, which had arranged for all correspondence to be directed through the West Indies cricket headquarters in Guyana, should think of a change in its stance, as the existing arrangement had been found unsatisfactory. None of the players had received any letters from home in their three weeks in the Caribbean—an issue that was considered unfathomable. The report quoted the players as saying it would be best if all mail was sent to the principal cricketing centres at the Queen's Park Cricket Club in Trinidad, the Kensington Oval in Barbados or the Bourda Oval in Guyana, calculating a margin of seven days from the designated arrival of the team in each of these venues.

It was against this backdrop of mounting pressure that Wadekar led his team into the first practice game against the West Indies Board President's XI in Kingston.

Unlike today, where practice games are hardly ever well-attended, the first two tour games in 1971 witnessed thousands of spectators coming to the stadium to watch the Indian team in action. The West Indians love their cricket, and, as Gavaskar has often said, 'These fans and the local media were an extension of the home side, making it that much more difficult for the touring team.' If the reports of the games are an index, the media did all it possibly could to add to the pressure on the Indians and push them on the back foot even before the first Test match had started. In a piece for *Sportsweek* titled 'No calypso ring in Wadekar's capers', one John Foster wrote, 'Ajit Wadekar and his boys might become unpopular with the enthusiastic crowds here. The Indians' scoring rate in the second innings nosedived to such an extent that the crowd which expects entertaining cricket from the Indians throughout the tour was sorely disappointed.' He singled out Jayantilal Kenia for his slow batting, saying he had taken more than four hours to score his half-century. The innings, according to Foster, had alienated even the Indian fans who had assembled at the stadium. The harshest words, however, were reserved for the captain. It was mentioned that Wadekar's declaration, which came really late in the day, robbed the match of a thrilling finish. 'The Indians batted in slow motion in the second innings and thereby lost whatever chance they had of securing a victory. Moreover, when the home side batted, the Indian bowlers sent down only 12 overs in the first hour, and this despite Bishan Singh Bedi being introduced into the attack quite early. The Indians' slow bowling rate coupled with arranging and rearranging the field at every possible opportunity wasted precious time on the last day.' The journalist went on to say that the slow over rate was actually a reflection of the mindset of the captain, who was intent on dragging the match on rather than trying to force a result. He finished off on Wadekar saying, 'If he persists with such tactics, he is bound to be very unpopular with the crowds here, who can be satisfied only by entertaining cricket and nothing else.'

Even the batsmen weren't spared. The media took potshots at Sardesai and Jaisimha, saying there was a desperate need to improve their running between the wickets if they had to bat for long periods with each other. Journalists cited the two run outs in the first innings of the tour game and said that Sardesai was already under pressure because he had twice been run out due to misunderstandings. This is where the experience of Sardesai worked to India's advantage. Not one to get ruffled and a typical 'khadoos', as Gavaskar would often say, Sardesai had worked himself into decent form in the tour games and was ready for the fight by the time of the first Test in Jamaica. What further helped Wadekar was the form of the spinners. With the wickets suiting their style of bowling, Bedi, Prasanna and Venkataraghavan had all worked themselves into good rhythm very early into the tour. Bedi had also won the prize for the best Indian performance in the match against the Board President's XI, which made him richer by 50 Jamaican dollars (INR 450 at the 1971 conversion rate). For a team that had never won a Test against the West Indies and had lost nine of the eighteen matches played between the two teams so far, all of this was essential to ensure that the Indians went into the first Test match on a positive note.

What may have also helped the Indians was the cramped schedule in the West Indies. While much is made in recent times of the lack of a gap between two Test matches, the Indians never had a gap of more than two days between matches in the Caribbean right through the tour. 'This meant we were never able to take our foot off the pedal,' said Viswanath. While it offered little time for players to recover, it also meant that the Indians were always in game mode in the absence of any significant gap between games. The first warm-up match was played from 5–8 February at Sabina Park, while the second match would start just two days later on 11 February at Montego Bay. Within a day of the second game ending on 14 February, there was a one-day game against the University of West Indies at Kingston, before the five-Test series got underway on 18 February at Sabina Park.

The months of January and February in the year 1971 weren't easy for Wadekar and the Indian team, but by the time of the first Test, they had been hardened enough to put up a credible fight and give a good account of themselves. Their 1–0 series victory was down to their hard work and hard work alone—a mantra that helped bind Wadekar, the captain, and Merchant, the chairman of selectors, together. It was also about winning the battle in the mind against the West Indian fast bowlers—an impediment that had weighed the Indian team down the last time they toured the Caribbean in 1961–62. And in doing so, the lead roles were played by Sardesai and Gavaskar, both of whom had their finest hours in the West Indies in 1971.

Chapter 4
Triumph in Trinidad

'It was tea break on day 2 of the first Test and Dilip Sardesai was batting extremely well to drag us out of trouble. After losing the first five wickets for just 75, it was the [137-run sixth-wicket] partnership between Sardesai and [Eknath] Solkar that changed things and lifted the gloom in the dressing room. While we were all feeling a little down at the loss of the first five wickets, this partnership was proof of what was possible. And that's when Sardesai stepped out of the changing room, looked at the ground and declared that these West Indian fast bowlers were nowhere close to [Wesley] Hall or [Charlie] Griffith. There was something in this statement and the manner in which it was said. Here was someone who was batting beautifully and had already managed to steer India out of trouble. Now he was telling us in the dressing room, with his usual swagger, that the bowling we were up against was mediocre and we had nothing to fear. It had the impact of giving every player the buoyancy they needed,' remembered Gundappa Viswanath, when asked about that rather eventful second day (the first day had been washed out) at Sabina Park in Jamaica in 1971.

A tour to the West Indies was all about playing fast bowling. In the 1961–62 series, India lost 5–0, having been blown away by the fast bowlers, mostly Griffith and Hall, and with the captain Nari Contractor suffering a debilitating blow to the head, which eventually cost him his career, things were dire from the very start of the tour. The team's morale, in the aftermath of the injury, had hit rock bottom. Mentally, the team had succumbed and just wanted the series to end. Anyone who has watched the documentary *The Test*, about the Australia men's cricket team in the wake of the Newlands ball-tampering scandal, can well imagine what it might have been like in 1962. In 2019, with all the protective gear that is now available, the Australian dressing room was in a state of panic when their premier batsman, Steven Smith, lay face down on the pitch at Lord's, having copped on the side of his neck a searing bouncer from England pacer Jofra Archer on the fourth day of the second Ashes Test. David Warner, in panic, walked up to coach Justin Langer and mentioned that Smith had been hit in the exact same spot as Phillip Hughes, an Australia Test opener with twenty-six first-class hundreds, who died after being struck on the neck in a Sheffield Shield match at the Sydney Cricket Ground (SCG) in November 2014. That you can die while playing the sport was one of the key takeaways from *The Test*. Back in 1962, things had been so much worse. There was no protective gear and emergency medical treatment was primitive compared to the advances of modern science today. It is no surprise that the Indian team suffered such a crushing series defeat in the aftermath of the Contractor injury.

'When your captain is struggling for his life in the hospital, there is very little you can do,' said the late Madhav Apte while speaking about the West Indian dominance in 1962. As we sat down over breakfast at the Cricket Club of India (CCI) a few years earlier, Apte, a true gentleman, tried to explain how hard it must have been at the time for Contractor. 'I played very little for India, but can tell you it was hard when I was left out of the team,' Apte said. 'And here, Nari was the captain and had just won a home series against England. All of a sudden, he had to come to terms with the realization that he would never play the game again. Imagine what an impact it had on him and the team.' With the exception of a few individual acts of brilliance (Polly Umrigar, for example, scored 56 and 172 not out in the fourth Test), India were never able to compete against the likes of Hall and Griffith. Sardesai, who was a part of the 1962 side, had experienced it all at close quarters—he had tasted defeat and knew that India had to take the fast bowlers on if they were to harbour any hopes of turning the tide. And that's what he did in Jamaica.

'When a senior player tells you that none of the fast bowlers are express pace and we can tackle them with ease, it helps a great deal,' Viswanath said. Most importantly, Sardesai walked the walk—during his 122-run ninth-wicket partnership with Erapalli Prasanna, he flayed the West Indian bowling to all parts of the ground and made a statement for every member of the team to take note of. When he was eventually dismissed for a career-best Test score of 212, India had achieved two things. First, they had recovered from their slump and posted a very respectable 387 in their first innings. Second, and perhaps more vital, was their new-found self-belief that made them realize that the opposition fast bowlers were not invincible. Sardesai's innings had completely changed the atmosphere in the Indian camp, and, by the time the West Indians stepped out to bat, there was an eagerness on the part of the visitors to take control of the game. 'With the first day washed out and with us having scored 387 in the first innings, there was little chance of us losing the game. On the contrary, we had everything to play for when the West Indies batted,' Viswanath mentioned.

'Sardesai batted beautifully in this Test match,' recounted a jovial Sir Clive Lloyd as we sat down to speak about the series at the Grande Hotel in Central London, with the majestic St Paul's in the background. 'He looked in control under pressure, and that one innings, like I have always told you, changed Indian cricket forever. It was proof that the Indians were no pushovers and, all of a sudden, had put us under pressure. Never had India taken a first-innings lead against us, and we needed to bat really well to keep this record intact.'

As he sipped his wine, Lloyd asked in jest, 'Why is it that every Indian journalist only wants to speak to me about 1983 and 1971? [Sardesai's] double hundred meant we had to bat well to stay in the game, and it was a tough ask against the Indian spinners like [Bishen Singh] Bedi, Prasanna and [Srinivas] Venkataraghavan.' With Lloyd, it is always straight talk. He played the sport with a degree of ruthlessness and presided over the most glorious phase of West Indian cricket. 'For a period, there was not one person born in the Caribbean who had seen us lose a Test series,' Lloyd said. 'We were proud cricketers and that's why, if anyone says to you the Indians were just lucky in 1971, it is plain nonsense. We played hard and, in 1971, they played better. You must give them the credit they deserve.'

With no play possible on the first day due to rain, the start of the series on day 2 couldn't have been more dramatic. Sent in on a moist wicket, India lost the first wicket with the score on 10 and the second on 13, exposing the middle order very early into the game. When Ajit Wadekar was out with the score on 36, and Salim Durani and Motganhalli Jaisimha subsequently departed with the score on 66 and 75 respectively, the West Indies, Lloyd said, '...hoped to bowl the Indians out for 150 or thereabouts.' However, Sardesai, Solkar and then Prasanna first managed to tire the bowlers out and thereafter launched a serious counter attack which shifted the momentum in India's favour.

With a big score behind them, the Indian spinners were brilliant right through, and had Prasanna not strained a muscle in the West Indian second innings to add to the finger injury he sustained, India could have won the game. 'The injury happened at a very important moment in the game. I was bowling well and could have won the game for the team,' recalled Prasanna. However, what the Indians successfully did was enforce the follow-on for the first time in the history of India–West Indies cricket.

'It had turned into a four-day game and, according to the rules, we needed a 150-run lead to ask the West Indians to bat again. Once they were all out for 217, Ajit informed us that he was going to ask Sir Garry [Garfield Sobers] to bat again. When he walked across to the West Indies dressing room to convey the message, Sir Garry felt Ajit was joking. He refused to believe we could enforce the follow-on with a lead of 160, and only when he was reminded of the rule did he realize what Ajit was asking him to do. This is what we wanted. It was a statement and we had managed to dent the West Indian self-esteem,' recalls Viswanath.

Enforcing the follow-on was a telling commentary of what the Indians had achieved. Never before in Test cricket had India managed to secure a first-innings lead against the West Indies, and here they had forced them to bat again in the opening Test of the series in Jamaica. Even though the West Indians came back strong in the second innings, with the No. 3 Rohan Kanhai scoring an unbeaten 158 and Sobers 93 at No. 5, India had secured a massive boost going into the second Test in Trinidad. The match ended in a draw, but India had emerged with bragging rights.

For one, there was the media rhetoric—hostile in the beginning, it had now changed dramatically. *Sportsweek* journalist John Foster, who had been extremely critical of Sardesai and his poor running between the wickets, was now singing high praises for the veteran. In a piece titled, 'Superb Sardesai', Foster wrote,

> Sardesai and Sabina Park. That's the association the Jamaica cricket fans will always hold whenever Indian cricket is discussed in this island on the Pacific coast. The Bombay batsman's magnificent double-century boosted India's prestige after the earlier batsmen had cut a sorry figure.

He went on to state that with the score reading 75 for 5, it was turning out to be the all-too-familiar story about India's batting, something Sunil Gavaskar attested to when speaking on how the series had started. Some even called the Indians a 'club side', and Gavaskar underlined, 'We needed to compete. At the time we had nothing else on our minds.'

The West Indies had seized the early initiative, and one more wicket would get them into the tail. It was just Sardesai who stood between them and an Indian collapse. But once he got in, things started to change. To go back to Foster, 'First, he retrieved lost ground with Solkar and ultimately thrashed the West Indies attack all over the park, with Prasanna for company.' The words lend testimony to the impact Sardesai had on the game. 'In a brutal assault, Sardesai did the bulk of the scoring, and 212 was his best [score] in Test cricket,' Foster concluded.

The confidence gained in Jamaica was on display as the team played its next tour game in St Kitts. Playing against the Leeward Islands, India decided on resting all three frontline spinners—Bedi, Prasanna and Venkataraghavan—and yet managed to bowl the opponents out for 147 in the first innings, with Jaisimha picking five. This was in response to the Indian score of 361 for 6 declared, an innings that saw Gavaskar bat for the first time on tour. 'If anyone told me at the start of the series that I would score 774 runs in the Test matches after missing the first Test and score more than 1,000 runs on the tour, I would have laughed it off. Of course, it exceeded my own expectations and that too by a country mile,' Gavaskar said. 'In fact, you know what? I wouldn't mind if I had scored 350–400 runs less in the Test matches and passed on the rest of the 400 runs to M.L. Jaisimha and Salim uncle. Jaisimha, as you know, was my childhood hero and it wasn't great to see him struggle and not score. Salim uncle was a very special man and I would have been happier if I could pass on the 400 runs between them, which would have ensured that the two of them made the cut for the England tour later on in the year.'

Gavaskar, always open and candid, spent hours discussing 1971 with us, a conversation that we have reproduced as a complete interview later on in the book. We have done the same for our conversations with Wadekar. These chats helped bring out fascinating details hardly discussed in the public domain.

Gavaskar, who had regained full fitness by the time the Indians had reached St Kitts, started the tour with a well-made 82 in the warm-up, an early indication of what he was capable of. With skipper Wadekar notching up a century, India was always in control of this game and was left with 57 to get off 12 overs to register their first win of the tour on the last day. That's when, as K.N. Prabhu reported, the crowd witnessed the free-flowing side of the twenty-one-year-old sensation. 'Gavaskar proved that he could open the innings in the orthodox fashion as we last saw him, and also bat like a gay cavalier,' wrote Prabhu.

> The six he hit off [Elquemedo] Willett put the issue beyond doubt for India. But a cover drive to a ball wide outside his off-stump was visually the most thrilling stroke of the day. He should go forth to his first Test match in Trinidad inspired by the same spirit that permeated his innings today.

In a subsequent dispatch titled 'India Has Reason to Feel Optimistic', Prabhu argued that the pitch at the Queen's Park Oval in Port of Spain, Trinidad, was likely to suit the

Indian spinners more than the West Indian quicks. Recent history was proof that off-spinners did well in Trinidad and the way the Indians bowled in Jamaica was a real blow to the opposition's confidence. He described the West Indian batting as having a 'strong body and a weak tail' and argued that once the Indian batsmen had cut through the top order, the lower half was likely to offer little resistance. He rounded off the piece by saying that Gavaskar, who was making his Test debut, had already proved his credentials and was going into the match with an average of over 100 in the series, something the West Indians would have been aware of.

When asked what his mental make-up was like ahead of his Test debut, an issue he had touched upon to a degree in his autobiography, *Sunny Days*, Gavaskar was unnaturally modest: 'I am no longer a spring chicken, you know. It has been fifty years, or will be in 2021,' he said. 'I hardly think back to my debut anymore.' Upon seeing that the two of us were unswerving, he started to open up. 'When we left for the West Indies, the chairman of the selectors, Vijay Merchant, had addressed the team at the Cricket Club of India,' he recalled. 'Much to my surprise, he picked me as the player he hoped would score a lot of runs in the Caribbean. I had not even made my debut, and here the legendary Vijay Merchant had reposed faith in me. It was both exciting and daunting at the same time. To be honest with you, there was a degree of apprehension in my mind because I had not played the Duleep Trophy before I played Test cricket. I had played school, college and university cricket and thereafter I was fast-tracked to play the Ranji Trophy for Bombay. What I had not played was the Duleep Trophy and, in those days, the best players always played in the Duleep Trophy. In the only opportunity that I had of playing the Duleep Trophy,

West Zone lost in the very first game in what was a knockout format, and it meant I had no further opportunity to test myself at the highest level back home. This had left me with a degree of apprehension as we travelled to the West Indies and, ahead of the Test match, I did think back to the question of whether I was ready to open for India at this level.'

Trinidad not only provided answers to Gavaskar himself but also to the rest of the world. His 65 and 67 not out in the first and second innings respectively were indications that India had finally found its successor to Merchant and, to echo Prabhu, someone who had the ability to be an all-time great of the game. While it was Sardesai, Gavaskar and Solkar who performed with the bat in Trinidad, Venkataraghavan, Prasanna and Bedi took centre stage with the ball, along with the indomitable Durani, in the West Indian second innings. Having managed a lead of 138 runs in the first innings, every Indian player was aware that they had a chance to register their maiden win against the West Indies. To do so, however, they needed to go past Sobers, Kanhai and Lloyd.

'We were having a drink in Ajit's room at the end of the third day's play when Salim Durani walked in,' recalled Viswanath, who had only just started to narrate the story when our curiosity got in the way. 'Did you hear Durani saying he would get both Sobers and Lloyd the next day?' we asked. Much had been written about Durani saying this, but we needed corroboration from someone who was actually in the room and had heard it himself. Viswanath paused, looked at us and sported a smile on his face. 'Yes, I did,' he said. The next few seconds felt like an eternity as he was intent on sipping his fresh lime soda, not seeming to notice that our excitement had started to peak. 'Salim entered the room and straightaway asked Ajit if he could have a drink,' recalled

Viswanath. 'He loved a drink or two in the evenings, and it was standard practice in the West Indies for all of us to assemble in Ajit's room and unwind. Just then, he said, "I will get you Lloyd and Sobers tomorrow in two overs." All of us were surprised and looked at him as he continued, "Just give me the ball when Lloyd is on strike, and even if someone else picks up the non-striker at that point, don't bother continuing with him and throw me the ball against Sobers." There was something in his voice and if you knew what Salim Durani was capable of, you would never doubt him.'

Viswanath went on to tell us the story of a game in India where Durani had squared off against Mansoor Ali Khan Pataudi. The game was played on one of the most docile of tracks and, according to Viswanath, there was every reason to believe Pataudi would score big on that pitch. He was in fine form and only the foolish would want to bet against him. 'That's when Salim came up to me and said, "I will get him tomorrow,"' recalled Viswanath. 'Seeing me amused spurred him on further, and he repeated what he had said, "Go tell Tiger [Pataudi] I will get him tomorrow," leaving me stunned. And, to be honest with you, the moment Tiger Pataudi came out to bat, Durani asked for the ball and, on a wicket where nothing was happening, all of a sudden a ball spun and jumped and Tiger was caught behind in the slips. At the end of the day, [Durani] showed me his finger and it was raw and bruised. He had given the ball such a rip that some of his flesh had come off.' Wadekar was aware of this incident and had blind faith in Durani's ability. 'No doubt he was temperamental, but he was also a genius,' concluded Viswanath.

The final word on these sensational back-to-back wickets in the Trinidad Test came from Salim Durani himself. 'I was casually talking to Jaisimha about how confident I was about removing them, and it was Jai who went and asked Ajit to get me to bowl,' Durani recounted. 'I had noticed that the wicket in the second innings had turned a bit slow, so you needed to bowl faster. There was a spot created outside the off stump that I had noticed earlier. I decided to capitalize on that. Sobers, after getting out, just couldn't believe [it]. He went away muttering, "Oh, Jesus!"' Durani said with a laugh.

Sport, as we have often argued, is about winning key moments. The moment Sachin Tendulkar hit Shane Warne over mid-wicket in 1998 on a turner in Chennai, the bowler having come in from round the wicket into the rough, half the battle was won. The moment Steve Smith hit the first ball for a six after coming out to bat at Lord's in 2019 in the aftermath of being hit by Joffra Archer, he had elevated himself to greatness. The moment Virat Kohli scored a hundred in the first Test of the series in 2018 in England after failing in every innings in 2014, we knew we were seeing one of the greats in action. In 1971, it was no different with Durani. True to his word, he first got Lloyd caught brilliantly by Wadekar, and thereafter bowled Sobers off the very first ball. While that very well may be all he did in the entire tour, there can never be any debate over his contribution to India winning the series for the first time in the West Indies. 'Salim uncle had set it up for us with Venkat doing the rest. We were confident 124 was chaseable on a good wicket, and even when we lost three wickets, self-doubt had not crept in,' said Gavaskar.

With Abid Ali for company, Gavaskar guided India to their target on day 4 of the Test and sealed the win with minutes of the day remaining. 'I vividly remember the last partnership with Abid and the winning stroke. Firstly, Abid was one of the fittest members of the team and also a great fielder. We speak of Solkar all the time, but I can tell you that Abid at short fine leg was never far behind. And, as a runner, he was brilliant. He would just drop the ball and run. Abid would actually steal runs from right under your nose, if you know what I mean. Most importantly, he was equally good both when he was on strike and also when he was running for his partner. Because of Abid, we were able to run a number of singles, which may not have been possible with some of the others. With very few runs to defend, it forced the West Indians to concede overthrows because we would just dab and run and put the fielders under pressure,' chuckled Gavaskar.

'Finally, when the leg spinner Arthur Barrett dropped one short, I dispatched it to the mid-wicket fence to finish the game. Scoring the winning runs for India against the West Indies in Trinidad on debut—no cricketer could have asked for more! As we were walking back to the pavilion, Sir Gary came across and congratulated me. It was Sir Gary, the greatest of them all. I had grown up seeing and reading about Sir Gary and Rohan Kanhai. And here I was playing against them and winning a Test match for my country against them for the very first time.' There was elation in Gavaskar's voice, even after fifty years since the victory.

Syed Abid Ali had an interesting aside to add to the story. 'At Port of Spain, I allowed Sunil [Gavaskar] to hit the winning runs,' he disclosed. 'I had ample opportunities to finish the match at Port of Spain but restrained myself from doing so. [Garfield] Sobers had bowled a full toss and I played it for a single, which allowed Sunil to get back on strike to Arthur Barrett. He was a little surprised and asked me, "Why did you do that?" I said, "Sunil, you have batted so well in this Test that you deserve it."'

Several things happened in Trinidad. With Prasanna picking up an injury while trying to take a return catch off Fredricks, Venkataraghavan had stepped up to the task and picked up five wickets in the West Indian second innings to go with the two crucial wickets picked up by Durani. Bedi, as always, was steady and picked up two to go with the three he had in the first innings. In batting, Sardesai, Gavaskar and Solkar had scored vital runs, and Wadekar, despite getting out for a duck—every report stands testimony—had captained the team with skill. At home, the selection committee stood vindicated. Not only had Wadekar's elevation to captaincy proved to be a masterstroke, the captain's support for Sardesai against all odds was turning out to be the most decisive call in the West Indies. Sardesai, both Gavaskar and Viswanath were emphatic in saying, was having his finest hour ever.

The Indians, K.N. Prabhu writes, celebrated in style at a reception organized for them by the Prime Minister of Trinidad and Tobago, Dr Eric Williams, at the Hilton Hotel in Port of Spain. The members of the touring press were also invited to the reception and, to quote Prabhu, 'The presence of the various carnival queens succeeded in pressing a sober and solemn member of the press corps to "jump up" as well.' It was a much-needed evening of relaxation, he went on to say, after what had been an exciting game with the initiative changing hands. Speaking to the press after the victory, skipper Wadekar complimented his teammates for their cooperation on and off the field and said it was when Durani got both Sobers and Lloyd that he first started to believe India had a real chance of winning the game. Back home, M.

Dutta Ray, who was in a way responsible for Wadekar being appointed captain, hailed the team, saying it appeared to be a perfect blend of youth and experience.

Even the normally reticent Vijay Merchant spoke to the press after the victory. He congratulated Wadekar on what he labelled 'an outstanding performance'. He said, 'The selection committee was very happy to have been helpful in a small way. This has been the greatest shot in the arm of our cricket, and nothing can give greater confidence to our cricketers.'

Nari Contractor, who had been extremely critical of Venkataraghavan at the time of selection, publicly owned up to his mistake and complimented the vice-captain for a lion-hearted effort with Prasanna out of action. He rounded off with a word of caution for the boys, saying there were three more Tests to be played and he was hopeful the team would continue to play with the same intensity right through the tour.

The win, undoubtedly, had brought the entire Indian cricket fraternity together. For the moment, all differences seemed buried and everyone involved with Indian cricket had started rallying behind Wadekar and the boys. 'I did not play in the Test match, but the feeling, I can tell you, was like nothing I had ever experienced,' said a normally understated Viswanath. India had beaten the West Indies in the West Indies, and for many, the victory marked the onset of a new renaissance in Indian cricket.

Privately, however, differences remained, evident from our conversation with Bishan Bedi, which is reproduced in full later in the book.

The triumph in Trinidad was the glue which had started to bind everyone together and extraordinary things began to happen. One such outcome was skipper Ajit Wadekar responding to fan questions through the media in the middle of the tour. Not only had Wadekar responded to every question posed to him by journalists, he had also taken the time to thank the fans back home and react to their suggestions following the victory. While such things are unthinkable in this day and age of 24/7 media, in 1971, it helped garner nationwide support for the team. Wadekar went on to say that he was deeply overwhelmed by the countless congratulatory messages he had received from home which, he jokingly mentioned, had 'flooded his hotel room in Georgetown'. In a letter to *Sportsweek*, he said, 'My colleagues and I are deeply moved by the praise showered on us through hundreds of cables sent by enthusiasts as well as institutions.' He stated that the team was especially proud of the win because it had the potential of turning things around in Indian cricket after what had been a forgettable couple of years. And the victory had been made possible because every member 'down to the reserves had played their part exceedingly well'. That Wadekar retained his sense of humour was evident when he spoke about losing the toss. 'I felt relieved when I lost the toss for it was a difficult decision to make, just like the one in the first Test.' Wadekar singled out manager Keki Tarapore for praise, saying, 'He is a strict disciplinarian who admirably mixes pleasure with the serious business of the game.' Tarapore's involvement and elation had earlier found special mention when it was reported that at the end of the Test match, he couldn't hold himself back and had run on to the ground, embracing and lifting Sunil Gavaskar in full view of the packed stadium, much to the embarrassment of the debutant.

That the media's perception of Wadekar as captain had also started to change in the aftermath of the win is evident from the following report by K.N. Prabhu in the *Times of India*. Prabhu, who had earlier written about Pataudi still having his band of loyalists in the team, now praised Wadekar for his ability to string the team together. In what was the strongest endorsement of Wadekar's captaincy, Prabhu wrote:

> Wadekar has always regarded himself as one of the boys. He has not been standoffish and formed his own coterie of friends and sycophants, which some of our former skippers were unwittingly inclined to do. Affable and acceptable to all members of the touring party, including the press, he has set agreeable conventions which have contributed to the success of the tour. All this speaks volumes of the character of the man, for Wadekar the batsman has been passing through a dim phase.

If the Indian story was all about overcoming challenges and channelling self-confidence, the West Indies had started to unravel as a team and looked grossly unprepared to cope with the stigma of defeat. Sobers, the greatest of them all, was challenged at every step, with many asking the board to remove him from captaincy. Losing to a young and unfancied Indian side was proving to be a bitter pill to swallow and there were urgent calls to make sweeping changes ahead of the third Test, which wasn't far away.

Here's how the West Indian media reported the defeat in Trinidad.

'Sobers, Kanhai and Lloyd totalled 115 among them in the two innings. The West Indian supporters have reasons to expect more. Steve Camacho should be dropped and a batsman who can bowl should be included instead,' wrote Tony Cozier in the *Trinidad Express*.

'India were the last of the established cricketing nations to beat the West Indies. Although India fully deserved their win, the West Indies disappointed everyone with their bad batting and atrocious fielding,' argued Brunnell Jones in the *Trinidad Guardian*.

'The West Indian team had always played second fiddle to India, something that has never happened before,' stated Rickford Ferrier in the *Guyana Graphic*.

Jack Anderson, writing in the *Jamaica Evening Star*, called for the retirement of skipper Gary Sobers and 'other fading West Indian stars'. He was particularly scathing and went on to say that 'if the West Indies selectors cannot see the writing on the wall by our inglorious displays, then the public in general and Jamaica in particular must act. I say boycott the remaining Tests if the selectors, apparently afraid of or influenced by Sobers and others, so stubbornly refuse to infuse fresh blood.'

Clearly a statement had been made, but the battle was not yet over. The Indians knew that West Indies under Sobers would come back hard, and there was no scope for complacency. With three Tests still to be played, holding on to the lead was the most important task of their lives and the Indians, it has to be said, were up for it. We now turn to how they did it.

Chapter 5
Winning the Series

In the documentary, *Manchester City: All or Nothing*, which chronicles the journey of the eponymous club to Premier League glory in 2017–18, there is a very poignant moment which sees club manager Pep Guardiola trying his best to stop his players from blaming each other in the changing room. After what had started out as a season of unprecedented success with nineteen straight league wins, City had a horrible week in March 2018, losing twice to Liverpool in the Champions League and once to Manchester United in the all-important Manchester Derby, which would have guaranteed them the premiership title. The loss to United was all the more painful because City was up 2–0 at halftime and appeared to be in control of the game at home in the Etihad Stadium. City supporters had started to celebrate and were not expecting the dramatic turnaround that came in the next forty-five minutes, with City conceding three goals and registering their first defeat of the season at home. In the documentary, shocked and disappointed players are shown ranting in the dressing room about how some of them appeared to have had forgotten the basics of football. Fabian Delph, the midfielder who had a stellar season thus far, vented and fumed over the elementary mistakes the team had made. That's when Guardiola swung into action. He pleaded with the players to stop the blame game and when his pleas fell on deaf ears and the rants continued unchecked for a minute or so, Guardiola, perhaps the best football manager in the world at the time, shouted and told the players to 'shut up'. He asked them to blame the manager if they wished but to stop accusing each other and indulging in a blame game that could potentially destroy team unity. His pep talk had the desired effect, with Delph and the others quietening down soon after and sanity returning to the dressing room.

At multiple points in the documentary, players emphasize the importance of team spirit and how the favourable atmosphere in the dressing room had helped them stay together during times of adversity. Spanish star Bernardo Silva, who had started in only a few games, stated it did not matter who started and who did not. Everyone was united for a bigger purpose under the leadership of Guardiola, and that was to win multiple trophies for the club. From playing paintball to multiple bonding sessions, Manchester City players did everything possible to keep up their spirits, eventually going on to win the Carabao Cup and the Premier League.

As captain, Ajit Wadekar attempted something similar in 1971. At the outset of the tour, the biggest concern for Wadekar was winning the confidence of the players. Many of them were considered close to Tiger Pataudi and had been handpicked by him in his years as captain of India. There was a degree of loyalty to Pataudi that Wadekar could never discount. In fact, Wadekar too looked up to Pataudi to start with. It was under Pataudi that India had won its first away series in New Zealand in 1967–68, where stars like Bedi and Prasanna had played a major part. For them to switch loyalties to Wadekar overnight was difficult. Wadekar's foremost challenge, therefore, was to bind the team together—a difficult ask and something that could well decide India's fate in the West Indies. Wadekar, to his credit, had managed to do this well; an effort he further intensified after the win at Trinidad. In all our conversations with him over the years, he opened up about his relationship with Pataudi and a lot more, making the Wadekar interviews fascinating.

Victory was the glue that helped tide over every difference, and Wadekar, a good man-manager, was not willing to waste the opportunity. All through the tour, there would be regular 'bonding' sessions in his room in the evenings, where people could have a drink and just relax. Team meetings had been converted into informal sessions of trying to unite the group.

'Eknath Solkar and I would be in Ajit's room an hour or so ahead of the team meeting. We would chat, have a cup of tea and unwind. Because the three of us were from Bombay, there was great camaraderie and it was good for each one of us to spend more time together,' said Sunil Gavaskar.

What is of greater interest, however, is what Gavaskar said thereafter. 'We were both Ajit's emissaries in the team. If the meeting was fixed for 6 p.m. and someone had not turned up on time, we would be sent to fetch that person. It could be that someone was waiting for the elevator or that someone had a personal meeting to attend to, but we were under specific instructions to get everyone into the room. Ajit was clear no team meeting would happen without everyone present and had instructed the two of us accordingly. One day, when we were a few minutes late in coming back with the player who hadn't reached on time, he reprimanded the two of us, saying, "Where were you? Don't you know the team meeting is extremely important and integral to team discipline?" Much to our surprise, his ire seemed to be directed against the two of us, when we had in fact been in his room way ahead of time and had acted under his instructions. But knowing him, we kept quiet and only when everyone else left the room did we ask what had happened. Ajit said that with the two of us he could take liberties, tell us anything. With the others he was conscious it could hurt their self-esteem to be ticked off in front of the entire team and, as a result, he made sure the message was sent out to everyone without having to speak to them directly.'

By employing this tactful approach, Wadekar managed individual egos all through the tour, an achievement that stands testimony to his management skills. 'By telling us to come on time for every meeting, the captain was sending a loud and clear message to everyone in the team. However, by not addressing anyone else directly, he made sure no one felt humiliated or upset all through the eleven weeks that we were in the Caribbean,' chortled Gavaskar.

With the all-important win achieved in Port of Spain, it was essential for Ajit Wadekar to refocus on team unity and make sure that there was no let-up in intensity in the three remaining Test matches. While the third Test, played in Georgetown, Guyana, was relatively uneventful and meandered to a draw, India was under the pump for much of the fourth Test at the Kensington Oval in Barbados, which they needed to save to keep their lead intact. In the tour game against Barbados ahead of the fourth Test, they had been subjected to a barrage of bumpers by Wes Hall, who had been asked to come out of retirement and join the team. Hall, the prime architect of the 1962 series win alongside Charlie Griffith, had lost pace but still retained the aura of being one of the best fast bowlers of all time. The Indians were somewhat unprepared for the short ball test and in hindsight, it can be said that the Barbados game prepared them for the Test match which was to follow. 'Losing to Barbados, our first defeat of the tour, was a big reminder of what lay ahead of us. We needed to tighten up and play our best cricket, for it was inevitable that Sir Gary would push us hard,' Gavaskar said when speaking of the fourth Test.

'Yet again, it was Sardesai and Solkar who pulled us out of trouble at the Kensington Oval. Much like in the first Test at Sabina Park, this partnership was key to us saving the game,' said Viswanath. Not only did Sardesai and Solkar play out valuable time in pursuit of the West Indian score of 501, but they also put India in a position where a good second innings effort would help them save the game. And, yet again, it was Gavaskar who saved the day by scoring a hundred, his second for the series. 'It was a very different feeling. To score a hundred and save your team from losing was no less satisfying than scoring a hundred and winning a Test,' said Gavaskar. That it was he who stood between the West Indies and India for much of the series was also mentioned by Wes Hall when we managed to sit him down for a chat at the University of West Indies, Cave Hill Campus in Barbados. 'India was much better prepared in 1971,' Reverend Hall said. 'Gavaskar was a class act and made a big difference to the outcome of the series.' Hall, who has a fantastic sense of humour and is one of the best storytellers in the game, went on to add, 'Calling me back was an indication that we were on the back foot. India had played extremely well and that's why I had been asked to come out of retirement. Such things give a feel to the opposition that we had been forced to change our plans.'

Just like the outbreak of COVID-19 in March 2020, when we as a nation checked the newspaper headlines first thing every morning and prayed that the number of cases stayed under control, in 1971, the first thing that many Indians did in the morning was check the previous day's cricket score. In a country where political violence was escalating because of the developments in East Pakistan, cricket continued to soothe our collective nerves and inject a sense of positivity in us. The board secretary, Professor Chandgadkar, reportedly did not get proper sleep for almost a month because journalists and fans would keep calling him through the night to check on the latest score from the West Indies. Every morning, Professor Chandgadkar would relay the scores to the players' families, as well as to BCCI officials.

Professor Chandgadkar, in fact, did not mind responding to fan queries because it was evidence of the growing popularity of the game in India, and when the news was of the kind coming in from the West Indies, the task was a pleasant one. During the fifth and final Test of the series, played at Port of Spain, it was Professor Chandgadkar who carried the message to the Gavaskar family, informing them that India's newest sensation had scored a hundred in each innings of the drawn Test, ensuring India won the series 1–0.

In an interview published in the *Times of India*, Chandgadkar said that the manner in which Gavaskar was carrying India's hopes at the end of the fifth day (it was a six-day Test since it was the final Test of a yet undecided series) was excitedly discussed in every Bombay mohalla—in trains, buses, schools, colleges, homes and offices. He went on to say that the 'lone exception was Gavaskar's home in Dadar. Here, one could notice the happiness and inward glow among his mother and two sisters. But they said very little. Instead, they were praying hard for Gavaskar and India.'

In the same interview, the BCCI secretary said that no one moved in the Gavaskar household once play started in the West Indies. Though there were no means to follow the match live on the radio or TV in those days, all thoughts were centred on what could be happening in Port of Spain. 'All the family did was pray for Sunil and for the believers, Gavaskar's brilliant run of scores must be another proof of the efficacy of prayer.'

To momentarily digress, the situation was much the same forty years later in Mumbai in the Tendulkar household during the 2011 World Cup final. Anjali, Sachin's wife, would have a dedicated seat in the drawing room from which she hardly moved, refusing to take even a bathroom break when India was batting. Like the Gavaskar household, this was her way of sending good vibes to her husband. This was also incidentally why Anjali refused to attend the World Cup final at the stadium, and only joined in when the game had been won and India became the champions.

While Anjali had the advantage of 24/7 media to keep a tab on her husband's exploits, in 1971, the Gavaskars had to go through what Chandgadkar calls a 'particularly suspenseful night. They lay awake wondering whether Sunil had completed his second century and realized the dream of every batsman.'

Sunil Gavaskar's father, Manohar Gavaskar's reaction upon first hearing of his son's incredible achievement tells us all we need to know about the idea of India that Sunil Gavaskar stands for. 'Sunil's father was left speechless for a while. There was a sense of silent pride. I am sure he fully understood the significance of the feat, though he was unaware his son was still there with 180 at the close when he took an early flight to Calcutta.' Chandgadkar closed the interview by saying, 'The Gavaskars always turn up to watch Sunil play. "But not when he is not out overnight," said Mrs Meenal Gavaskar. Instead, she would wait till she heard that Sunil had got going again.' As it happened, Gavaskar would make his first Test match double century to take India to safety.

Once it was known back home that Ajit Wadekar's men had scripted history and won the series 1–0, cricket was taken to a very different level of consciousness in India. The masses had found new heroes and the stock of the game reached an all-time high. The New Zealand victory in 1967 aside, this was definitely the start of a new era in Indian cricket. In an editorial published on 21 April 1971, the *Times of India* declared that,

> ... such is the public involvement in cricket that given the choice between earning a rupee more and India beating the West Indies in a Test series, most people in Bombay or Delhi or any other big city will opt for a victory. And now that Wadekar's men have actually performed the feat, there will be as much rejoicing as over a major advance in any other national pursuit. The achievement is all the more welcome for being unexpected. It was remarkable enough when the Indian team defeated the West Indies for the first time in Trinidad a month ago. But that it was able to maintain the lead in a five Test series and come

close to another victory in the final Test makes its performance all the more outstanding.

The celebrations weren't limited to India. In Port of Spain on 20 April 1971, the last day of the tour, a large Indian crowd had gathered to witness the action and savour the moment. Soon after the match was over, the crowd had gathered below the players' balcony, and when skipper Wadekar made an appearance in the pavilion balcony, he was greeted with a stirring ovation. It was reported in the local press that members of the East Indian community sang traditional Indian songs.

Back in Bombay, it was initially decided to offer a simple welcome to the team members at the airport for they were due to land in the wee hours of the morning. It was thought that most of them would be tired after a long flight and would prefer to catch up on some much-needed rest before they were felicitated by the BCCI and the BCA. At no point did the BCCI anticipate that 15,000 fans would assemble at the Santacruz airport to catch a glimpse of Ajit Wadekar's warriors, clearly a first in the history of Indian cricket. As reported in the *Times of India*,

> They burst into a mighty roar as Ajit Wadekar and Sunil Gavaskar came out of the customs enclosure and mounted an improvised rostrum on the lounge. Skipper Wadekar was visibly choked with emotion as he waved to the ecstatic fans. Gavaskar too was moved as he held aloft a trophy presented by the Trinidad cricket council for his outstanding performances on the tour.

While some fans had waited all night to celebrate the moment, others, like Union Education Minister Siddhartha Sankar Ray, had flown in from Delhi to receive the victorious team. It should be mentioned here that in the absence of a separate ministerial portfolio dedicated to it, sports came under the jurisdiction of the education ministry at the time, which explains the presence of Siddhartha Sankar Ray, who was also an avid cricket lover.

The scene at the Santacruz airport was such that the *Times of India* described it as 'an oven at 4 a.m.' The report went on to say that,

> ... the police had a trying time keeping the fans behind the barricades. Everyone was sweating profusely ... None, however, cared for the discomfort. They had not only come in force, but also brought with them garlands and placards and drums and crackers. 'Welcome home heroes', 'All Indians applaud your grand victory', 'Sobers sobered' were some of the bold placards that stood out in the crowd.

In this atmosphere of euphoria, two things happened that merit proper analysis. First, Ajit Wadekar was celebrated the country over as captain. Nearly everyone—including Vijay Merchant, who had perhaps the biggest role in appointing Wadekar as skipper with his casting vote—agreed that Wadekar deserved credit for the series victory and for the way he handled the team in the West Indies. There were some, like Bishan Bedi, who held a contrarian view (highlighted in our interview with him), but the overwhelming majority credited Wadekar for the victory. It is important to state that even though Bedi differed with Wadekar in the way he approached the game, he was respectful of his captain and always performed in the team's best interests.

The second and most disturbing thing was the growing chasm between Merchant and Pataudi—a rift that had considerably widened after the series victory. While Pataudi said little at the time and only opened up much later in a detailed interview which we have reproduced, Merchant was dismissive of any question he was asked related to Pataudi in April–May 1971. While it made for great copy, for the sake of Indian cricket it was an unwelcome development.

If Merchant's dislike for Pataudi had been somewhat masked by a veneer of diplomacy when the team had left for the West Indies in February, it became the subject of salacious gossip once the team returned victorious from the Caribbean. Merchant, it can be said, made no effort to hide his dislike and openly spoke about it to the press. Before going into the details of what Merchant said, it is pertinent to state that a series of press reports had come out in April 1971 which suggested that Pataudi was looking to go to England to play county cricket for Sussex. A few reports even speculated about Pataudi wanting to leave India for good. Against this backdrop, Merchant was asked the following by a *Sportsweek* correspondent: 'It is reported Pataudi intends turning out for Sussex in this year's county championship. Will this debar him from consideration from the England tour?'

Under normal circumstances, the chairman of the selection committee could have easily dismissed the question as mere conjecture and refused to answer it. Firstly, there was no truth to the suggestion that Pataudi was going to Sussex. Secondly, there had been no information coming from him that confirmed this development. It was only fair that Merchant dismiss it as speculation without adding any further fuel to the fire. Merchant, however, did the exact opposite. To quote his answer to the question:

> What Pataudi does with his cricketing future is for him to decide. But it is for him to write to the selection committee and make his services available to Indian cricket if selected. No cricketer can convey to the selection committee what he wants to do through articles in magazines and statements to the press. I should know because I have written such letters in 1946, 1948, 1949 and 1951.

For the record, Pataudi did write to Merchant and the BCCI conveying his unavailability for the West Indies tour, something even Merchant had earlier acknowledged. While he may have done it only after he was removed from the captaincy, the fact remains that he did follow protocol and inform the selection committee. Moreover, at no point did he say that he wasn't available for selection for the England tour. It was pure speculation in the media, something Pataudi had kept himself isolated from. Finally, for the chairman of the selection committee to respond to conjecture when there was already a history of disagreement between him and Pataudi is proof of how deep the misunderstanding really was.

In the same interview, Merchant praised Wadekar for the victory and almost made it clear that the appointment of captain for the forthcoming England tour was a mere formality. While this was known and it would be outright foolish to remove someone from captaincy after he led a series win against the West Indies for the very first time, the fact that Merchant chose to say so on record when the captain selection was still a month away was quite revealing.

When asked by *Sportsweek* what the factors behind India's victory in the West Indies were, Merchant was prompt in standing up for Wadekar: 'Astute captaincy on the field, willingness on the part of the captain to take every member into his confidence in the matter of strategy and tactics and total teamwork were primarily responsible for India's victory over the West Indies.'

When the correspondent pushed Merchant further and asked if he had wished Wadekar luck for the England tour in the team's felicitation function, Merchant stated that he had not directed his good wishes for the England tour to Ajit Wadekar alone, but had done so to all those members who would have the privilege of representing India in England. He thereafter went on to add, 'While nothing can ever be taken for granted in our country, surely no one expects me to support someone else after my casting vote for him four months ago!'

This interview was not a one-off, and Merchant had also issued a printed note to every media organization that asked for his reaction after the victory. Inundated with requests for interviews, this was perhaps the only option Merchant was left with for there was no way he could satisfy every journalist who wanted to speak to him. For the record, Sachin Tendulkar had to speak for a continuous ten hours when he completed twenty years in cricket in 2009, trying to meet the demands of every journalist who wanted to interview him. In speaking to each person for five minutes, Tendulkar conducted what was perhaps the longest stint of interviews in cricket history. While the number of journalists in 1971 was not even a third of what Tendulkar faced, for Merchant, it seemed overwhelming at the time for nothing of the like had ever happened before. Enjoying every moment and responding to droves of congratulatory messages, Merchant issued a note to the media that stated,

> Ajit Wadekar must get the credit for wielding the team into a formidable unit. Although he failed to register big scores, he was always guiding the strategy of the team in the manner of an undisputed leader and certainly got more out of the team than anyone has done in previous years ... Our players have done India proud. Never did they dispute the umpire's decisions, although some of them must have created in them grave doubts. I feel that Indian cricket has turned the corner.

Journalists who had earlier questioned Wadekar's appointment were now in agreement with Merchant. Foremost among them was K.N. Prabhu of the *Times of India*. Prabhu suggested that India may have had better teams in the past, but they were never a cohesive unit due to individual egos taking precedence over team solidarity. Team unity and the ability to back each other up was to him the standout feature of the 1971 campaign. Having seen it first-hand, Prabhu wrote, 'It was this spirit that stood them well through many a crisis. It was this that accounted for their victory in the series.' He thereafter singled out Wadekar for effusive praise: 'There were no favourites or sycophants. Everyone was treated on the same level with the same consideration by a captain who had only the other day been one of the crowd. It was a gesture that did Wadekar credit.' Under the sub-heading 'Right Choice', Prabhu went on to state,

> I was among the many doubters when Wadekar was named captain. But I am happy to admit that the men who promoted him to this office were certainly blessed with remarkable intuition and awareness of what was wrong with our cricket. A team with diverse forces can never do justice to itself, whatever be its talents. But here, with proper leadership, it was not difficult to get the best out of the players. Every player was ready to pull his weight for the sake of the cause.

For the entire period of the celebration, and even thereafter, Pataudi chose not to speak a word on Merchant. Knowing full well that whatever he said had the potential of being misconstrued and misinterpreted, the former skipper just decided to lie low and weather the barrage of barbs thrown at him. While he may have been wrong in withdrawing himself from the West Indies tour, and more so in informing the BCCI rather late, the fact that he did not commit himself to a war of words with the chairman will always serve as proof of his integrity and pedigree. While he did put out his side of the story to a select few in the media, in none of these interviews did he speak on his relationship with Vijay Merchant. Restraint on his part was the need of the hour and Pataudi exercised it to the fullest. This could well have been the reason he was able to make it back as captain a few years later during the West Indies tour of India in 1974–75 for what turned out to be his last assignment in international cricket.

Even later in his life, Pataudi mostly preferred to stay aloof and did not open up to many people. With the exception of journalist Rajan Bala, there was hardly anyone else in the Indian media who Pataudi really opened up to. The 1988 interview with him that we have reproduced in full later in the book is an exceptional source into the mindset of the man. Not only did he speak on captaincy, but he also opened up on his rather frosty relationship with Vijay Merchant as the chairman of the selection committee.

When asked if he was in agreement with the view that Vijay Merchant was influenced by zonal preferences, which would explain his choice of Ajit Wadekar, Pataudi did not dismiss the suggestion with any conviction. All he said was, 'I am not sure if Merchant had a zonal bias and if Wadekar's appointment was a reflection of that. However, I can surely say there were extra cricketing considerations that influenced my removal. While some people said to me that Merchant was trying to get even with me because of what my father had done to him in 1946, I am not sure if that's true either. However, what I do know for certain is that the decision was not purely a cricketing one.'

When further probed about why he was so convinced that there were considerations other than cricket behind his ouster, Pataudi said something quite sensational: 'I am convinced because all through my captaincy, Merchant and I had never seen eye to eye. He would always give me substandard teams to play with and, against my wishes, youngsters who weren't ready were pushed into the team. As skipper, my thought process was simple. I have always said that the best fifteen should be chosen to play for India and age or experience should never decide or influence team selection. If you are young and yet you are good enough, you should certainly make the team. The very same thing applies to anyone who is relatively old and more mature. In the 1969 series against Australia, at least 4–5 players were included in the team who weren't ready for international cricket. [Pataudi refused to specify the names.] If you see their records, most of them disappeared from the scene in no time. And when I was removed from captaincy, look at the players who were included in the 1971 team. Sardesai, Jaisimha, Durani were all senior players who were part of Ajit's side that travelled to the West Indies. The plan to include youngsters had been shunned and was perhaps only limited to my captaincy.' While refusing to name any particular player, he concluded by saying that this was a rather unwelcome thing for Indian cricket and something that should have been avoided.

Reading between the lines, this is a serious charge. While both Merchant and Pataudi are no longer alive to comment further, all we can say with certainty is that the two superstars were never able to work together during their lifetime, and in their clash of egos, the real victim was Indian cricket.

While the country was celebrating the West Indian triumph, not every question had been answered. Should Pataudi be brought back for the England tour and should Engineer be included remained key topics of discussion in Indian cricket corridors. Unlike the West Indies, which was a team in transition, England was in peak form, having beaten Australia 4–0. The English media had already started predicting a 3–0 whitewash in the summer. With only a month to go before the team for the England tour was selected, both Wadekar and Merchant were aware that their biggest challenge was just round the corner.

Chapter 6

Tumultuous Build-up for England

India had just won what Sachin Tendulkar called the 'most intense' match of his career. With a TRP of 35.2, not to forget the wraparound programming on news television that stretched for hours and days, the Mohali encounter against Pakistan in the 2011 World Cup had broken all viewership records. Having managed the Indian team superbly, Gary Kirsten deserved a fair share of the credit. But this is Gary Kirsten we are talking about—a perfect backroom man with little desire for the limelight. So when we met him at breakfast the morning after the victory, it wasn't a surprise to see him enjoying his fruits. He was alone, and Paddy Upton soon joined him. In fact, there was an eerie sense of calm in the dining room early in the morning, the stark opposite of what we had witnessed the night before, when all of Mohali and, in fact, all of India had partied and celebrated India's historic win. We hadn't slept in all the excitement and it seemed like Kirsten hadn't either.

'The team is looking great,' we said, trying to make conversation. We knew he wouldn't talk on record, and an interview in the middle of the tournament was out of the question, given that the final was still to be played, but because he knew us well and we had interacted a fair deal in the lead-up to the World Cup, he looked up and smiled. 'The sense of camaraderie and bonding is great to see,' we said, trying to push the agenda. That's when he stopped, put his fork down and said calmly with a smile, 'You think all of the players are friends? To be honest, it doesn't matter to me if they are. All I want is—when the last catch goes up and whoever is under the ball, the rest of the fourteen should pray he takes the catch for India. In their private time, I really don't care what they do and if they dislike each other or criticize each other. There should always be a distinction between the personal and the professional.'

In three profound sentences, Kirsten had unravelled the essence of team sport, of what we understand as team unity. Here were eleven super-achievers with mammoth fan-followings and mountain-sized egos. Each bigger than the other. Each a pan-Indian icon. Some of them were arguably the biggest brands India has ever produced, while others were big brands in the making. How could they all be friends? How could they be expected to like each other's company all the time? Why was it necessary for them to socialize? It wasn't possible, nor was it necessary. Kirsten had redefined the way we spoke and thought about team unity.

More recently, there was much talk about Virat Kohli and Rohit Sharma in the aftermath of the 2019 World Cup.

Questions were asked about whether the two didn't get along, and if things had taken a downturn in the aftermath of the World Cup loss.

Relations between these super-achievers were not always amiable. In fact, they never can be. Anyone who follows high-performance sports will agree that relations between successful high-performance sportsmen are mostly frosty. Do Virat and Rohit have to be best friends to be captain and vice-captain of the Indian team and yield the best results? The answer is an emphatic no. Steve Waugh and Shane Warne, who were not necessarily friendly with each other, presided over the most successful era in Australian cricket. While we in the media are happy debating over and wasting newsprint on a possible rift between Virat and Rohit, I wonder why it is so hard for us to accept that a difference of opinion at this level is the norm and not an aberration? As long as Virat reaches out to Rohit as captain—whenever he feels the need, that is—we should be happy. For the record, he does so multiple times in every game. As long as Rohit is willing to respond to the calls of his captain and do his best, Indian cricket is well served.

On multiple occasions during the 2019 World Cup, Virat Kohli went on record saying that Rohit Sharma is the best white-ball cricketer in the world. By every yardstick, it was praise of the highest order coming from the very best in the world. For the sake of Indian cricket, Virat was man enough to praise his best performer. Whether or not there was an ulterior motive in doing so is the most ridiculous question to ask.

Further speculation was fuelled last year when one of them unfollowed the other on social media. For the sake of argument, let's agree that they don't want to follow each other's posts. The question to ask again is *so what*? When they get on the pitch for India, they do so as the captain and vice-captain of the Indian cricket team. They have one purpose—to win cricket matches for the country. Is it necessary for Virat and Rohit and their respective families to like each other's company socially for them to best serve Indian cricket? Clearly not.

All we care about is how much they like each other's company while batting. The two have batted together enough in their careers and, on multiple occasions, applauded each other's strokes. As proud professionals, they know what they need to do out there in the twenty-two yards. Indian cricket needs both of them, and that's all that matters. That's how it has always been in international sports. A successful campaign like the one against the West Indies in 1971—no questions are asked and all of a sudden team spirit is hailed as the deciding factor. But when there's a loss, our default reaction is to blame the differences within the team.

This is why Kirsten was spot on.

As is evident in the previous chapter, much was said and written about team unity and team spirit in the aftermath of the Caribbean victory. All of a sudden, Ajit Wadekar was hailed as one of the best managers—a man who had brought about a kind of team unity that we had never seen before in Indian cricket. The common strand across the media deluge that followed the victory was the notion that Wadekar was able to conceal the cracks that had always existed in the Indian teams of the past, and it was under him that the cult of 'I' was replaced by a cult of 'we'. Individual interests were sacrificed at the altar of a greater cause, and during times of adversity, the players backed each other up.

Two examples were given to back this hypothesis. In his very first team meeting in the West Indies, Wadekar mentioned that India would play to draw the first Test match in Jamaica. Some of the players, Prasanna and Bedi being foremost among them, were surprised at the comment and felt 'it was proof of a defensive approach from the captain'. Bedi corroborated this by saying, 'Right at the beginning of the tour, you don't expect your captain to say we will draw the Test match. While it was important not to lose, a number of us felt we should have played to win and not simply to draw the game.' However, the difference in mindset among the senior players, it was argued, had no bearing on their performance and each one of them backed the captain in any decision he made. This was yet again evident when Wadekar asked the West Indies to bat first in Barbados, a decision that could have cost India the fourth Test had it not been for Sardesai, Solkar and Gavaskar. 'We should have batted first,' said Bedi. 'It was a defensive call and they took full advantage of it, putting up 500 runs on the board. We were under a lot of pressure in the first innings and had to struggle hard to save this game.' While Bedi and some of the others were not in agreement with Wadekar on sending the West Indians in on a good batting wicket, each one of them rallied behind the captain and contributed to the hard-earned draw, which was pivotal to India retaining the 1–0 lead.

'But 1971,' Bedi argued, 'was no aberration. From the press reports, you would think all Indian teams of the past had always been deeply divided, with personal egos taking precedence over team cause. Was the 1967 team that won against New Zealand any less united, or was the team that ran the West Indies close in 1953–54 any less loyal to the captain?'

A month after the team's return from the West Indies, the media discourse had changed to what Bedi was alluding to. Many had started to feel that the reaction was over the top, and to say that everything started in 1971 was to ignore all the good performances of the past. Without 1967, there could be no 1971, many argued. A number of former players attacked the team unity argument, asking if the Indian team that toured the West Indies in 1953 had lacked team spirit. That was India's first tour of the West Indies, and the opposition the Indians encountered there was a formidable one. With the three Ws—Worrell, Weekes and Walcott—in very good form and the bowling far more potent than in 1971, it was a better side than the one pitted against Wadekar's men. Despite the opposition being much stronger, India only lost the series 0–1, a credible performance in every sense. A year earlier, they had beaten Pakistan at home to win their first Test rubber. Each of these teams, it was argued, was no less united than the one under Wadekar in 1971.

With former players speaking out, fans too started getting into the act. The apprehension stemmed from the fact that India was due to tour England in less than two months, and this trip, almost everyone agreed, was going to be far more difficult and challenging. Not a single expert who was interviewed had given India a chance in England, and the overarching argument was that a crushing defeat, which was a likely possibility, would severely impact the stock of Indian cricket after the high of the West Indies. Most started arguing in favour of bringing Pataudi and Engineer back into the team, for without them, and without Durani and Jaisimha, both woefully out of form, the middle order looked fragile and underprepared. Journalists like K.N. Prabhu and Khalid Ansari, who had sounded cautiously optimistic a month earlier, had started to change their tones as the date of the team selection started nearing. It seemed that the enormity of the English challenge was gradually starting to dawn upon the Indians and had begun to erode the West Indies euphoria. A 0–1 loss in England, it was argued in some quarters, was acceptable. Without quality fast bowlers who could exploit English conditions, expecting Wadekar's boys to repeat the West Indies performance was asking for too much. All of a sudden, people started to credit individual performances for the West Indies victory. The batsmanship of Gavaskar and Sardesai had saved India the blushes, but it was impossible for even Gavaskar to score 700 runs in every series. Many argued that India should be happy if he managed to average 50 in England against the likes of John Snow, arguably the fastest bowler in the world at the time. While it wasn't entirely negative, the mood in the country was ridden with apprehension as debates over team composition and selection gathered momentum.

A Raj Hangover?

Khalid Ansari wrote in *Sportsweek*:

> Delirium seems to have gripped our cricket crazy country. In their ecstasy at our victory over the West Indies, people everywhere appear to be losing their sense of proportion. A first ever series win is sufficient

reason for jubilation. And there is no denying the fact that our victory was well deserved. But let us not forget that the West Indies was hardly a formidable combination this year.

On the notion of a very special kind of team unity under Wadekar, he was scathing. 'For heaven's sake let's put an end to this claptrap about our so-called team spirit. As though team spirit was born to Indian cricket only during the last tour. As though team spirit exists only in victory and not in defeat,' he argued.

In questioning what he called the need 'of parading our cricketers' at all sorts of functions across the country, Ansari advised caution. 'Let us rejoice by all means but with dignity,' he wrote.

Ansari wasn't alone. Every former great called for an immediate stop to the celebrations to get down to the onerous task of preparing for England, which was a much better side in comparison to the West Indies.

Was it a Raj hangover that was pre-empting former cricketers from giving Wadekar's team a chance in England, or were they all guided by pure cricketing logic? Was it still too difficult to think that the Indians could beat England in England and make history? While we will never know the definitive answer to this question, suffice it to say that not one expert had given the team a chance, which was a reflection of the difficulties that lay ahead for Wadekar and his team in England.

'Our chances are 30–70,' said Vinoo Mankad. 'Unless the notorious English weather plays a hand, I do not see how we can even draw the series,' were his rather damning words a week before the team was announced. Mankad, one of the heroes of the 1952 series in England who had serious experience of playing in English conditions, was especially critical of the batting, which, he argued, had more often than not let India down in the past. While in the West Indies, Sunil Gavaskar was an unknown commodity and played with little or no fear and pressure, his incredible debut series meant the whole of India was now looking at him as the 'saviour'. Could Gavaskar, still a young man of twenty-one, adjust to this increased level of expectation and could that impact how he performed in England? Without Gavaskar and Sardesai, the batting wasn't good enough to test England, he argued. Mankad, who had batted for Pataudi ahead of the West Indies tour, yet again argued his case. 'The Nawab of Pataudi must go to England because of his batting, fielding and experience of English wickets,' he wrote.

No nawab himself, Wadekar was now facing his toughest Test against what was considered the world's number one team at the time.

Mankad also called for an immediate ban on all celebrations and said that much had already been made of the victory. 'Winning and losing is part and parcel of the game. Don't other countries win? But do they make such a song and dance about their victories?' he asked. Hailing the side that toured the Caribbean in 1953 (of which he was a part), Mankad said, 'All this fuss over team spirit is overrated. Hasn't our side displayed good team spirit before? Take the 1953 tour of the West Indies, in which good team spirit was largely instrumental in us losing only one and drawing four Tests against a fantastic side.' Not one to stop short, he even questioned the undue importance attached to Wadekar's captaincy and dismissed the suggestion that he had done something exemplary. For him, India had had some really good leaders in the past in cricketers like C.K. Nayudu, Lala Amarnath and Tiger Pataudi; for Wadekar to be ranked in the same league, he'd have to do something special in England.

The pressure on Wadekar was mounting.

Polly Umrigar and Nari Contractor, who had both toured the West Indies in 1962, agreed with Mankad. While Umrigar was somewhat restrained and gave the Indians a 40–60 chance in England, he agreed that the importance attributed to team spirit was overhyped. Contractor, on the other hand, was outright dismissive of India's chances. 'We do not have much of a chance against England. I think we will lose by a clear margin,' he said, before going on to add rather disturbingly, 'The good starts that we've had in the West Indies will not come so easily in English conditions, where the ball moves much more.' Contractor also said that the contributions from the lower order would dry up in England and in the absence of proper technique, a lot of the tailenders would be found wanting; something that had not been the case in the West Indies. Interestingly, Contractor pegged his expectations from Gavaskar rather low and said that everyone should be happy if he managed to average 45 against John Snow and Derek Underwood. He also made a very strong case for Pataudi's inclusion, saying the Nawab most certainly deserved a chance and should convey his availability to the selectors.

Vijay Manjrekar and Rusi Modi, both highly regarded in the fraternity, suggested that the Indians would struggle to cope with the weather in England, which could well turn out to be the deciding factor. While Modi advocated the inclusion of Engineer based on his experience of playing in English conditions, Manjrekar argued that England was the best team in the world and it would 'therefore be too much to expect our team to beat England, especially with the weather being what it is there. If the matches are not curtailed or washed off, we shall have done very well if we can draw one Test and restrict the margin of defeat to two.' He said the overemphasis on team spirit was 'annoying'. 'Are we to understand that a side has team spirit only when it wins? Did the West Indies lack in team spirit just because they lost? If we lose against England, will it be because we will be lacking in team spirit? What nonsense!' he tailed off.

The debate over team spirit did not go away for a while, and was in fact reignited when just three players from the victorious team, Ajit Wadekar, Bishan Bedi and Sunil Gavaskar, were invited by the BCCI to meet Prime Minister Indira Gandhi. While most former players did not want to comment on the controversy and chose to remain silent, Lala Amarnath, always known for his plainspeak, expressed displeasure at just three players being given preference over the rest of the team. What message did the meeting send out to the fraternity of Indian cricket fans? Did it actually mean that captain Wadekar, Bedi and Gavaskar were more important than some of the other members of the team? Why were manager Keki Tarapore and vice-captain Venkataraghavan not invited to the meeting? While it was known that Dilip Sardesai was on a two-week holiday in Europe and had not returned to India with the rest of the squad, it was a glaring omission to leave the vice-captain out of the meeting. Frankly, this meeting with the prime minister went against the grain of everything Wadekar had stood for in the West Indies and was a serious blow to his all-inclusive approach. Lala Amarnath said, 'In the interest of team spirit, it would have been better to have had the entire team up to Delhi to meet the PM instead of just three players.'

Perhaps the only former cricketer who was willing to give the Indians a semblance of a chance was the West Indian legend Conrad Hunte, who was in India at the time to raise funds for charitable work. Hunte decided to stick his neck out and say that India had the team to win at least one of the three Tests in England; he felt the result would be 2–1 in favour of England, with the Indians competing well in the series. He thought Gavaskar, Sardesai, Solkar and Viswanath had the potential to come out with enhanced reputations, and also felt that the world was underestimating the potential of the Indian spinners. Referring to the West Indies series, Hunte praised the efforts of Sardesai and Solkar under pressure and stated that the mental strength exhibited by the Indians in the Caribbean would give them a head start in the tough English conditions. On two occasions, the Indians lost half the side for under 80 and yet did not get bowled out cheaply. On both these occasions, Sardesai and Solkar managed to soak in the pressure and steer the team out of trouble. Hunte was particularly impressed with Gavaskar's temperament. To bat for the amount of time that he did, showed exemplary patience for a debutant, and if he was able to replicate the same in England, there was no reason why India wouldn't mount a strong challenge against a very good England team, Hunte said. In saying that India had the best spin attack in the world, Hunte referred to the success of Derek Underwood on wet English pitches and suggested that if someone from the Indian spin quartet could do an encore, there was no reason why the Indians wouldn't be competitive.

While all this talk was going on in the press, the BCCI was embroiled in trying to sort out its own mess. The Dutta Ray affair, which had brought out the BCCI's internal differences into the public domain ahead of the West Indies tour, was yet again playing out in the backrooms in May 1971. Dutta Ray, for the record, had not resigned, nor had he lost clout within the BCCI. Quick to congratulate Wadekar, Dutta Ray made it clear in every interview he gave that he wanted to be a part of the team selection for England, and that he had no intention of staying away any further. It also seemed that Merchant and Dutta Ray had arrived at a truce, for the chairman had praised 'Dutta babu' on record and said that his contributions in the selection committee meetings were of great value. With president Amar Ghosh on his side, Dutta Ray was actively campaigning to safeguard his place and, when a motion of no confidence was brought against him by eleven BCCI affiliates led by the Tamil Nadu Cricket Association, the Bengal lobby was quick to close ranks, holding its flock together. On being asked by a section of the members to include the Dutta Ray affair as a formal agenda in the board's Special General Meeting (SGM), Ghosh agreed to do so on the condition that the meeting be held in Calcutta. Knowing full well that they could manipulate things better on their home turf, Ghosh and Dutta Ray remained confident of being able to scuttle the move that asked for the latter's removal.

Protecting Dutta Ray

Every election tactic that we have seen being employed in BCCI elections in recent times was employed by the Bengal lobby in May 1971. Positions were offered for votes and invites were sent out to prospective voters to come to Calcutta early to make sure there was no last-minute coup that could catch them unawares. With eleven members against them, all they needed to do was stop the opposition from winning over three more members ahead of the SGM. It was also argued that the resignation, which formed the basis of the opposition's crusade against Dutta Ray, was no longer valid as it had never been placed before the BCCI general body. A private letter written by Dutta Ray to the president could never constitute a formal resignation, as claimed by the opposition. They cited the case of L.P. Jai, who had offered his resignation from the selection committee because of his differences with Lala Amarnath, but had subsequently withdrawn the letter which had not yet been placed before the board's general body. Dutta Ray, Ghosh was quick to remind the members, had been asked by the BCCI to attend Ranji Trophy matches in March–April, at which point not a single member had made a formal complaint. Without the general body's approval, his resignation could never be considered a document of any real significance. Rather, his presence at Ranji Trophy games was considered proof of his acceptance as a member of the selection committee, and to now ask for his removal ahead of the England tour was considered unfair and unethical.

The *Sportsweek* correspondent argued:

There is more than what meets the eye in the cricket board's decision to hold the SGM in Calcutta on May 21. Originally, the meeting was to be held in Poona on 14 May and accordingly a meeting of the selection committee could have been held on 17 May in

Bombay to appoint the captain for the England tour. Now the programme has been postponed by a week. The most important item on the agenda of the SGM is the resignation issue of M. Dutta Ray. A section of the members have sought to replace him with some other candidate before the team for the England tour is selected. The signatories to the requisition are Tamil Nadu, DDCA, Haryana, J&K, Railways, Punjab, Bihar, Andhra, Madhya Pradesh, Gujarat and Baroda. On the other hand Dutta Ray and Amar babu are actively canvassing for the retention of the former on the selection committee. They would be able to do this with ease if the meeting was held in Calcutta, which is their stronghold.

The way Ghosh had structured the SGM was also interesting. In the circular that was sent to members, it was mentioned that the meeting would start at 10.30 a.m., with just the Dutta Ray affair on the agenda. This meeting was to be followed by another at 2.30 p.m., where the manager would be appointed. Clearly, they did not want to take a chance. If they were unable to protect Dutta Ray, the president would have adjourned the manager selection meeting to another day, giving his lobby the necessary time to regroup.

Backchannel talks were also on to arrive at a compromise. Ahead of the West Indies tour, the South lobby had asked for the appointment of Colonel Hemu Adhikari as manager. It was Dutta Ray who had opposed Adhikari and got Keki Tarapore elected in his place. This time around, the South was canvassing for the appointment of C.D. Gopinath, selector and member of the Indian team which had won the first ever Test match against England at the Chepauk in February 1952. Dutta Ray and Ghosh, reports indicated, were willing to support the appointment of Colonel Adhikari as manager if the no-confidence motion against Dutta Ray was withdrawn. Keki Tarapore, who had done a wonderful job in the Caribbean, had office duties and was not in contention. This opened doors for a last-minute compromise.

Just days before the SGM on 21 May, it was yet again decided by President Amar Ghosh and his group that the meeting would be deferred to 1 June in Bombay. The unofficial reason doing the rounds was that the BCCI wanted to put out a united picture and talks were on to solve the impasse. What had further facilitated the last-minute postponement was that M.M. Jagdale, the Central Zone selector, had suffered a heart attack and was unlikely to be present at the manager selection meeting. In his absence, Dutta Ray staying on had become a necessity. He had the experience to make relevant points in what was considered a key selection committee meeting. The deal was straightforward—Ghosh and Dutta Ray would support the appointment of Colonel Adhikari as manager, while the South lobby would withdraw their complaint and allow Dutta Ray to stay on in the selection committee. The agreement was finally reached on the night of 31 May in Bombay and by the time of the meeting on 1 June, everyone was on the same page in finally bringing to an end a crisis that had continued for eight months between October 1970 and June 1971. This was essential, for time was running out and the team selection had turned into a dire necessity with just two weeks left till the team departed for England. At the administrative level, every ego had been placated and the differences finally put to rest.

Chapter 7
Destination England

The functioning of the BCCI has always been subject to scrutiny. While the intensity of the scrutiny has increased in recent times under the watchful eyes of the 24/7 media, in 1971, the BCCI faced stinging criticism for some of its decisions ahead of the crucial England tour. While the Manindra Nath (Bechu) Dutta Ray affair had dragged on for nearly eight months and given the board a bad name, its resolution based on the compromise reached on 1 June was a welcome sign that things would get back on track. Team selection was a pressing concern and, by every count, the BCCI was late. With the departure date fixed for 17 June, it was essential that players were picked with enough time for a preparatory camp before the team headed out for England. Ahead of the selection meeting, the board was confronted with another conundrum. There was considerable debate over whether the team should consist of sixteen or seventeen players. Unlike the present day, the selection of one additional player was a matter of considerable expenditure to the board, and in the absence of adequate foreign exchange, this was one of the key decisions confronting the selection committee.

For the record, the players were paid a daily allowance of GBP 30 in 1971, and even that was considered a struggle for the BCCI. The players had already been paid a bonus of INR 2,500 each for the West Indies series win, and the INR 40,000 spent as unaccounted expenditure had eaten into the board's reserves. While most former players advocated the inclusion of a fast bowler for English conditions as the seventeenth player, the BCCI eventually decided against it and opted to add an extra official to help manager Colonel Hemu Adhikari. Delhi's R.P. Mehra, who had played a key role in the anti-Dutta Ray campaign, was rewarded with the unusual position of treasurer. Mehra, it was announced, would act as a second helping hand to Adhikari and would also perform the role of treasurer, which was considered critical in a two-month-long tour—he would have to ensure the proper disbursement of funds and monitor expenses.

When viewed through an objective lens, this move seems shortsighted. Including an official at the expense of a player for a tour as tough as an England tour typically is could have dealt a serious blow to India's chances. Accounting for injuries and fatigue had considerably reduced captain Ajit Wadekar's options, and it meant that the first-team players would hardly get a break considering several first-class matches were cramped into the first thirty days.

In the month leading up to the first Test at Lord's, the Indians hardly got a break. The tour was due to start on 23 June, with a three-day match against Middlesex at Lord's followed by a match against Essex on 26 June in Colchester.

There was only a gap of one day between the two games, a trend that continued through the series. The Essex game was followed by a match in Eastbourne on 30 June, following which the Indians were to play Kent on 3 July in Canterbury. With four more games against Leicester, Warwickshire, Glamorgan and Hampshire ahead of the Lord's Test starting 22 July, the total number of non-playing days between 23 June and 22 July was a meagre six.

In a first-of-its-kind chat show organized in Bombay on the eve of the team's departure featuring four of India's former greats—Vijay Manjrekar, Nari Contractor, Poly Umrigar and Rusi Modi—all the interviewed players expressed displeasure at the BCCI's decision to choose Mehra ahead of a seventeenth member. Responding to questions, Manjrekar was the most scathing of the lot in saying that the decision was a reflection of misplaced priorities and that the BCCI should have avoided it. If they indeed had to send Mehra, he argued, they should have done so regardless of a cap on personnel strength, and not in place of a seventeenth player. It showed that the BCCI was more concerned about its own band of administrators, and their decision had sent a wrong signal to the country's cricket fraternity. Mehra had done nothing tangible for the sport to earn the junket and his selection was considered a waste of public money.

The BCCI mandarins, on the other hand, had no option but to include Mehra in the touring party. He had been the face of the anti-Dutta Ray campaign and was one of the strongest allies of the South lobby, which included eleven affiliate units of the BCCI. While the South faction had been placated by the appointment of Colonel Adhikari as manager, Mehra had to be doled out a favour to be able to project a united front. What had further complicated the situation was that ahead of the West Indies series, Mehra had been asked to stand down in favour of Keki Tarapore, with the commitment that he would be appointed manager for one of the future tours. With no international fixture in the immediate future after England, he had to be rewarded without any further delay. This was key in projecting to the media that the BCCI was not a divided house. It was never an either/or question for the BCCI top management. All along, their stand had been that Mehra had to travel, and all they needed to do was determine a designation for him. His inclusion was a priority and the seventeenth member was not even a consideration when it came to him.

This, as we've seen, miffed the former greats of Indian cricket. While arguing that undue importance had been placed on the role of the manager in India, each one of them declared that the entire credit for the West Indies victory should be given to the players. Though manager Tarapore was there to ensure the tour went on without a blemish, the greats believed that in no way did he merit credit for the victory. Ensuring the smooth conduct of matters did not mean he had contributed to the win, as a section of the media had argued. Further more, there was unanimity in their opinion that the seventeenth player was a requirement and should never have been sacrificed for the sake of officialdom. One official in the guise of manager was considered enough, with several prominent commentators of the game citing the West Indies tour as a prime example. If Tarapore could do the job in the West Indies for eleven straight weeks without a helping hand, why was it that in England the appointment of Mehra had turned into an urgent necessity?

While the BCCI had bungled the Mehra inclusion debacle, one decision for which they appeared to be getting positive media feedback was the inclusion of Farokh Engineer in the team. Engineer was by far the best wicketkeeper-batsman in India at the time, and to leave him out would have been a grave mistake. Neither Pochiah Krishnamurthy nor Rusi Jeejeebhoy had done well in the West Indies, and Engineer, it was unanimously agreed, would add to the team's balance. He had played a lot of county cricket in England and would prove pivotal to the team's chances of winning under those trying conditions. The board's stated policy—any player who did not play domestic cricket in India was automatically disqualified—came under serious criticism from all quarters. Many believed that choosing the best XI to represent India ought to take precedence, and that the board's argument was inherently flawed. As long as a person made himself available for national duty, he should be eligible for selection, was the argument.

The BCCI, however, was not entirely convinced and was looking for a face-saver. It had unanimously agreed ahead of the West Indies tour that any player who did not play cricket in India was to be left out of the national team. As a result, Engineer and Rusi Surti were not included in the touring side to the West Indies. So what happened in the three months between March and May 1971 that prompted a change in their stance? Could the board justify such a change without having to go back on its own stated guidelines? Knowing that a departure from its stated policy would lead to criticism, the board was urgently looking for a compromise. While it was desperate to pick Engineer, it also wanted to give the impression that it had done so on its own terms. The opportunity presented itself when Engineer confirmed his availability for the Duleep Trophy for the following season. As long as he had committed to playing some form of domestic cricket, there was going to be no problem in picking him for India, even if he wasn't going to be part of the team all through in England. Engineer, who had an existing county contract, would only be with the team during the Test matches, and for the rest of the tour, he would fulfil his county duty. In fact, Mohinder Amarnath and Syed Kirmani were both placed on standby in case Engineer would not be available for the first-class games and could only play the Test matches.

Interestingly, the BCCI did not find this policy discriminatory or preferential. While some of the players argued in close quarters against such a rule, there was very little they could do in the face of the BCCI's support for it. 'This did not go down well with some of the players,' Viswanath said. 'Why should Farokh be allowed to play the Test matches while some of the players would end up playing only the tour games? While no one spoke out against it openly, there was talk within the team that this wasn't a fair policy and should not have been allowed.'

The Engineer debate had gone on for a long time. In sum, the issue with him was never one of ability. The consensus was that Engineer, could walk into any team in the world at the time and had no competition back home in India. However, him opting to play county cricket meant that his name was expectedly missing from the West Indies tour.

What worked for Engineer ahead of the England tour were two things. First, neither of the two wicketkeepers inspired confidence in the West Indies. There had not been a single significant contribution from either of them, and against an English attack, which was more potent than the West Indies, there was little chance that they would be able to do anything of consequence. The second was Engineer's ability to bat with abandon and make a telling impact on the game in a short span of time. Knowing well that runs would be at a premium in England, Engineer was considered the go-to man for Wadekar. Had India not won in the West Indies, chances are the BCCI would have continued to look beyond Engineer. All of a sudden, the stock of Indian cricket had risen and a good performance in England had become a pressing need. A whitewash would mean all the gains made in the West Indies would be lost, and so the BCCI had to do everything possible to ensure Wadekar was given the best team to take England on. Under pressure from the former greats who had all predicted a series loss, the BCCI was left with no choice but to select the best talent available, even if it meant a part revision of its existing policies.

The other important attribute that Engineer brought to the table was experience. With M.L. Jaisimha and Salim Durani left out, the team was short on experience, which was considered essential in giving Wadekar the necessary back-up. Engineer, it was expected, would fill the void and act as a key member of the team's think tank.

Commenting on Engineer's inclusion, the sports correspondent of the *Times of India* wrote:

> The selectors have done well in accepting the Board's clarification regarding Engineer. Rumours that he may be rejected unless he was available for the whole tour turned out to be without any foundation. Engineer's return should not only tone up the wicketkeeping—

he is rated among the best in the business—but should also considerably bolster the batting.

Other sections of the press described the Engineer inclusion as a foregone conclusion and refused to give the board any credit for it. Instead, it was interpreted as an attempt at redemption and reported as an acknowledgement of an earlier mistake. The BCCI may not have accepted it, but it was well known that its earlier policy lacked reason, and it was only a matter of time before it realized its mistake and made amends. Writing in *Sportsweek*, Khalid Ansari stated, 'Engineer's selection was rendered almost automatic by the Board's second thoughts on the policy decision. So it can hardly claim any credit for this very sensible choice.'

Pataudi: The Absent Presence

If the Engineer incident was a tremor, the board's dealing with Mansoor Ali Khan Pataudi was the earthquake that hit the BCCI. It was known that Pataudi and Merchant did not get along, and there was no option available to the BCCI to get the two of them to sit down together and iron out their differences. Unlike the Dutta Ray affair, a compromise formula was not on the anvil. Based on his withdrawal from the West Indies touring team, several questions were doing the rounds about Pataudi, and in the absence of any real clarification coming from his end, rumours were rife in the days leading up to the team selection for England. Pataudi, who enjoyed a cult following in the country, ought to have come out and clarified if his decision to not tour the West Indies was prompted by the desire to save himself the embarrassment of having to play under Wadekar. Was it because he had been removed from captaincy that he had decided to withdraw from the tour? Was his decision to contest the Lok Sabha elections a way to mask the real reasons for refusing to tour? Was he really interested in politics or was it just a cop-out for him to overcome the immediate scrutiny he was being subjected to? Did Pataudi congratulate Wadekar on the series win, and had he spoken to the players following the team's success in the West Indies? Lastly, were the charges of indiscipline and intransigence levelled against him baseless? Did he actually inform the selection committee of his unavailability for the West Indies series in advance, or did he wait for the captaincy announcement to make up his mind?

Pataudi, who had very limited interactions with the press, had not provided answers to any questions. In hindsight, it can be said that his media strategy was not the best and his awkwardness in dealing with the press added to the confusion. As a former captain of India and a player with a huge following in the country, Pataudi could—and should—have handled the situation better and offered an explanation.

With the pressure on him mounting, he decided to hold a press conference on 2 June 1971. While many hoped he would make himself available for the England tour, what transpired was unexpected and shocking. In the press conference, Pataudi announced his decision to never again be part of an overseas tour for India, citing paucity of time. While he would continue to play domestic cricket and turn up for Hyderabad, he said he would not be available to tour England or any other country in the future.

In an interview with *Sportsweek* given two days after this stunning revelation, he explained his side of the story in detail. When asked if 'paucity of time' was indeed the real reason behind his making himself unavailable, he said:

> Business and domestic considerations, as I announced in the press conference the other day, are indeed behind my decision. I'm going into something new and just will not be able to find enough time for cricket abroad ... Would it be enough for your readers if I were to say that I'm going into business in South India with my brother-in-law who is now in the US? Or that I may myself have to proceed to the UK shortly for a brief visit in that connection?

Fifty years on from this press conference, we continue to find his reasoning hard to believe. At the time, Pataudi was still batting and fielding at his best, so his sudden decision to prioritize business over cricket is difficult to come to terms with. It was not as if Pataudi was in desperate need for money. He had more than enough to sustain himself, and his business commitments could have perhaps been put on hold for a few more years until his retirement.

Second, how much time would he have saved anyway if he continued to play domestic cricket, which included turning out for Hyderabad and South Zone in the Ranji and Duleep Trophy tournaments? India did not have a tour of any length in the immediate future, and England was perhaps one of the most important tours in the history of the country's cricket. He could have perhaps taken this call following the England tour; two months, it can be argued, would not have made much of a difference.

When asked if the possibility of him not being selected had influenced his decision, Pataudi treaded with caution: 'On the contrary, from all reports, I thought I had an excellent chance of being included.' He went on to clarify that he did not mind playing under any captain, and that in domestic cricket, he had played under Jaisimha, Venkataraghavan and Rajinder Pal, having given his best in every game. He was even willing to give this statement in writing to the BCCI and the selection committee, but said that he would do so 'at a proper time'.

One of the things Pataudi said that raised doubts over the real reasons behind his withdrawal was his aversion to express in writing his availability to the selection committee in order to be considered. Vijay Merchant had insisted on this, while Pataudi was not at all keen. That he did not approve of Merchant and his ways was evident in his answer. Without once naming Merchant, Pataudi said, 'Yes, the insistence on an expression of intent is unusual. The normal practice, I believe, is for selection committees to first select. To my knowledge, expression of availability is never insisted upon as a condition for consideration for selection. If somebody is not available, too bad, but not the other way round.'

Pataudi was spot on. How and why should a player—without knowing if he is going to be picked—declare his availability? Consider this scenario: say Pataudi declared his availability for the tour and expressed interest, following which the selection committee felt his services weren't required; it could well be that the selection committee did not consider someone good enough despite the player having made himself available. If it was someone of Pataudi's stature, such a situation would have turned him into a laughing stock in front of the public. For Merchant to insist on a written submission was improper and was, in reality, a public playout of the growing differences between the two superstars of Indian cricket.

Pataudi also clarified that he had sent a congratulatory cable to Wadekar at the end of the Trinidad Test match and had wished every player he had met since the team's return from the Caribbean. Becasue he was away in Bhopal for most of the time, he had not met all of them, and this was something he was looking forward to doing sooner than later.

That the situation was taking on a Pataudi-versus-the-BCCI hue was evident when he was asked if he had been disrespectful of some of the BCCI officials as per allegations. To this question, his answer was both aggressive and dismissive. He said:

> I am not in the habit of addressing people, barring a few exceptions, as 'Sir' just because they happen to be in a position of influence. I don't think that should indicate disrespect. Nor should it if I don't jump to attention (as some people do) if I happen to be sitting after a hard knock either at the nets or at a match. It's all a matter of time, place and of how you define 'respect' or rather 'disrespect'. Besides, respect has to be earned, not demanded.

Pataudi was not willing to take things lying down and toe the official line. While he did not spell out names, that he was upset with Merchant was evident from his answers. He was unhappy with the way the BCCI had allowed Merchant to attack him and not said a word to the chairman of the selection committee. His decision to never again be a part of an Indian team overseas was clearly influenced by each of these factors and wasn't simply a business consideration, as he wanted everyone to believe.

The Pataudi press conference—although it deprived India of the services of one of its best players—did solve a major headache for the BCCI and Merchant. Pataudi's withdrawal meant Merchant and his committee would not have to consider Pataudi's name when they met to pick the Indian squad for England. In fact, had he not clarified his position, and had Merchant and Co. not picked him on the team, there could have been a wave of criticism directed against the committee on charges of partisanship and discrimination.

As Pataudi mentioned, the argument would be straightforward. Not many would have agreed with Merchant on Pataudi needing to make himself available. Questions would have been asked about whether or not every other player who had been picked had formally notified the BCCI of their availability. It is also pertinent to ask how a player would have known for certain if he was being considered by the selection committee for inclusion in the squad so that he would declare himself available. Going by his calibre, Pataudi's inclusion was a no-brainer. The middle order had not done much in the West Indies, with the exception of Dilip Sardesai and Eknath Solkar. Pataudi, there was consensus, would have made a significant difference to the Indian cause in England. His fielding, which had always been a big plus, would have helped plug a lot of holes and reduce the number of dropped catches, which had hurt the team in the Caribbean. Had he been available for selection, Merchant, whether he liked it or not, would have had to pick him.

This was no longer the case following the press conference. At no point did Merchant or any of the committee members mull over requesting Pataudi to reconsider, yet again drawing attention to the growing divide between Pataudi and the members of the selection committee. Dutta Ray, who had openly canvassed for Pataudi ahead of the West Indies tour and would have voted for his retention had he not been forced to stay away from the meeting, was also silent, indicating the shift within the BCCI. Dutta Ray and Merchant had closed ranks, and Pataudi, it was clear, was cornered. In the absence of any form of assurance from the BCCI, Pataudi had been forced to work out a way to avoid further embarrassment and complications.

What is disturbing to note, even after all these years, is the scant reportage on the Pataudi press conference. The *Times of India*, for example, published just one report on the issue in the first week of June, in the lead-up to the selection committee meeting. Most other newspapers carried a solitary report of the press conference, and nothing more. No one questioned why Pataudi was not asked to reconsider his decision and not one journalist argued that he might have been pushed into a corner by the goings-on in the board. While it is difficult to understand the real reason behind the lack of coverage, it can be surmised that Pataudi's lack of media engagement may have contributed to his loss of favour among the media. Yet again, the ultimate loser in this whole saga was Indian cricket.

The Return of Chandra

Pataudi may have announced his decision not to tour, but there was one key inclusion in the squad: Bhagwat Chandrasekhar. Coming off strong performances in domestic cricket, Chandrasekhar had been the star performer for the Indian team in England in 1966–67, though he had started to lose form towards the end because of excessive bowling. He had been forced to come back from Australia in 1967 and had been left out of the team ever since. A man of prodigious ability, he gradually got himself back into the reckoning based on an impressive Ranji and Duleep Trophy season. England's weakness against leg-spin also worked in his favour, and many argued that if Derek Underwood was able to exploit the wet pitches on offer with his fast-ish spin, there was no reason why Chandrasekhar, who had more ability and variety than Underwood, wouldn't be able to do so.

His inclusion was not without controversy, though, and in the end, it may well have worked to his advantage. In the team briefing ahead of the side's departure for England, Merchant, as discussed earlier in the book, picked Chandrasekhar out and told him in front of everyone that it could well be his last tour if he did not perform to potential. It could have been Merchant's way to tickle his ego, but Chandrasekhar, as Viswanath argued, wasn't amused. He was upset and angry, and even considered withdrawing from the touring party. He found the barb insulting and felt that Merchant could have spoken to him in private.

The press, however, was overwhelmingly positive in favour of Chandrasekhar and suggested that he could be the X factor for India in England. The *Times of India* reported:

Chandrasekhar's return is also to be welcomed. Properly nursed, he should provide the surprise element to our spin attack. All his woes began when he was overbowled on the last trip in 1967, when he was highly successful with 16 wickets in the three Tests and 57 wickets on the tour. Thereafter, he faded from the scene under somewhat strange circumstances. Chandrasekhar rested for a season and appeared to have recaptured near-peak form in the Ranji semi-final against Maharashtra towards the end of last season. His comeback marks another triumph over odds for this polio victim. At twenty-six, he still has much cricket left in him.

With the media talking up India's spin quartet ahead of the tour, England captain Ray Illingworth decided to get into the act and sound out a warning to the Indians. Illingworth, who had led England to a terrific away-from-home Ashes win and just managed to beat Pakistan at home in a closely fought series, wrote in one of his columns: 'India's quartet of spinners are getting good write-ups in every paper I turn to, but while I love watching quality slow bowlers in action and I'm glad they're here, I doubt whether they'll shake the English batsmen over much.'

Illingworth went on to say that England had successfully negotiated Lance Gibbs, Mushtaq Mohammad, Garfield Sobers and Intikhab Alam when they had turned up for the Rest of the World side and easily played out the Australian spinners during the Ashes. Against Pakistan, in the recently concluded series, they had to face Mohammad and Alam yet again and did not have any major issues in doing so. 'None of these got the better of us. The Indians shouldn't either, even though they will play all four in the Tests,' wrote Illingworth.

In a bid to give his players confidence, he went on to write that Bedi was in England in 1967 as part of Pataudi's side and coul not spin the ball much in English conditions. Venkataraghavan, too, was in the same category, and wasn't expected to pose much of a threat to the English batsmen. Prasanna, who was a bigger spinner of the ball, had struggled in English conditions. Illingworth went on to pick Chandrasekhar as the one to watch out for. 'All four of them bowl fast, but Chandra pushes them through so quickly that sometimes he must reach medium pace. I remember playing against him at Lord's on the last tour and there was bounce in the wicket. Chandra was bowling so fast that the ball was going over my shoulder!'

While praising the Indian spinners for the ability they possessed, Illingworth concluded the column with a few words of caution for them: 'These four might find themselves up against one major problem ... they might not have enough runs to bowl at.'

The English captain had clearly sounded the bugle. He had rather politely challenged the Indian batting against his bowling attack, led by John Snow. On wickets that were expected to help swing bowling, there was no doubt that the Indians would have to be at their best, and Illingworth's words had helped up the ante.

It was only at the team's pre-departure press conference that Wadekar would talk up his team's chances and sound out the war cry. 'The way we played in the West Indies is enough to give us confidence on the tour of England,' he said. 'With the addition of Chandrasekhar, our spin attack is the best in the world. Chandrasekhar has done well in England and this time round he should do better.'

The upcoming England tour was the biggest challenge that Wadekar had faced in his career, and also an opportunity for him to prove his critics wrong.

Chapter 8
Firing the First Salvo

During the felicitation function at the Cricket Club of India, BCCI secretary Prof. M.V. Chandgadkar declared that the board would organize a red-carpet welcome—stretching from the Santacruz airport to the Brabourne Stadium—for the team if they were able to beat England in the latter's own backyard. While the comment had been made in passing, it had a telling effect on the players, a fact corroborated by Gundappa Viswanath. While no player said it openly, every member of the team believed that beating hosts England would be Indian cricket's greatest achievement ever.

No one knew this better than Ajit Wadekar. He had seen potshots taken at him followed by a period of unprecedented praise. The same former greats who had labelled his appointment 'disgraceful' ahead of the West Indies tour congratulated him after the series win and described the victory as a watershed moment in Indian cricket. Wadekar was praised for his handling of the team in difficult

113

circumstances and hailed as a leader who had brought in a new meritocracy in Indian cricket.

He hardly had any time to dwell on the praise that came his way when the discourse changed dramatically. Most people who had commended him for the West Indies win were now of the opinion that things had been overdone in the euphoria of victory. A full-strength England team at home was a very different prospect from what the Indians had encountered in the West Indies, and this series, it was argued, was the true test of Wadekar. It was as if he had it easy in the West Indies and now had to deliver in England to be recognized as a good captain. Stung by growing scepticism, Wadekar had withdrawn into a cocoon. From his limited interactions with the media, it was evident that he was under pressure and had started to feel that the press was turning against him. He had at no point asked the press to talk up team spirit the way they had. And now it was being written that unity within the team had been a feature of most Indian sides of the past and there was nothing special that Wadekar had achieved. With no role in shaping the discourse, he was at the receiving end for no fault of his own.

Over-the-top reactions have long been a feature of Indians' attitude towards cricket. The series triumph in the West Indies was first regarded as the best thing ever to happen to cricket in India. The players were worshipped as superheroes and community funds were started in Bombay to reward them for their feat. But as the ecstasy of the victory started to wear off, people grew sceptical and began looking at the England tour with a degree of apprehension. They had all moved on from the West Indies triumph and all that mattered now, it seemed, was beating England on their own turf. The fact was that there was no denying that a series win in the West Indies was a massive achievement and, as Viswanath said, the win in the Caribbean had injected in the team the confidence that made them believe they were capable of doing something special in England.

In a rare interview ahead of the team's departure for England, Wadekar sounded cautiously optimistic. For one, the team had overcome the fear of playing fast bowling. While none of the West Indian quicks bowled express pace, they weren't exactly medium pace either, and the Indian batsmen, led by Dilip Sardesai and Sunil Gavaskar, had demonstrated that they were no longer uncomfortable against quick bowling. While Gavaskar says that he hadn't really thought about it this way and all he had wanted to do as a twenty-one-year-old at the time was play for India, there was no doubt in Wadekar's mind that Gavaskar had led the way in overcoming the stigma that the Indians were incapable of playing against fast bowling. Drawing inspiration from Pakistan's showing in England in June 1971, he felt that India's ability to put up good scores could make a key difference in the forthcoming series.

Then there was the matter of team bonding, which Wadekar considered extremely important. Most of the players had been together for three months in the West Indies and had developed a sense of camaraderie that had been lacking at the start of the tour. They knew each other's strengths and weaknesses well. Playing as a team for a substantial length of time has always been a feature of good sides, and Wadekar was relying on this heavily while getting ready for England. Barring the three new additions in Farokh Engineer, Bhagwat Chandrasekhar and Abbas Ali Baig, all the other players in the touring party for England had been part of the West Indies series and had an equal share in the team's successes and failures.

A divide between the team and the press has been a feature of Indian cricket for the last five decades. If anything, the divide has grown, with brief interludes of camaraderie in between. One such interlude was in Pakistan in 1989, when the players and the touring media spent social time on the weekends in an attempt to develop a closer bond. Sachin Tendulkar's much-talked-about moustache photograph was taken in one of these player–media bonding sessions. Sunil Gavaskar, who has been on both sides in the course of his long career in cricket, has been immensely vocal about the need for this player–media synergy with reference to the 1971 series.

'Whenever the English or the Australians came to India, the travelling media, which is an extension of their team, started putting pressure on Indian umpires before the tour started,' Gavaskar said. 'They would invariably target a few umpires and pick on a set few, putting pressure on the board to appoint umpires of their choice. This would have a two-pronged effect: umpires would always be weary of criticism and veered on the cautious side when giving a decision against the visiting team. Nothing like this happened when we toured abroad. As I have written in *Sunny Days*, the only constant about umpire David Constant in England was the string of wrong decisions he had given against us, which benefited Ray Illingworth and the English team. None of our correspondents who covered international cricket highlighted the poor umpiring we were subjected to series after series,' Gavaskar said.

While most of the others we interviewed did not say so openly, there is no doubt that Wadekar and his team rued the absence of support from the Indian media. Despite the occasional article which sought to address the growing lack of trust, the media did little to get things back on track.

In an article titled 'The Press Is Not Against You, Ajit' in *Sportsweek,* Khalid Ansari stated that Wadekar had developed a misconception about the local press and had misconstrued some of the comments that had been made.

> There has been, we most certainly agree, widespread and strong criticism of the selection committee for not electing Pataudi skipper in the West Indies and of the unfortunate circumstances in which your appointment came about. We are referring to the wranglings in the Board which the press in this country generally believed to have been responsible for the fact that only four selectors were present at the crucial selection committee meeting.

He went on to request Wadekar to 'banish the thought' from his mind. 'The press is not anti-you. It is anti-sports politics. You just happen to be in the thick of it for no fault of your own,' he argued.

The strongest support for Wadekar came from the *Times of India*'s K.N. Prabhu, who took a dig at the cynics and argued:

> There has been much speculation as to what awaits our players in England. On the eve of the departure

of the team, the coffee house commentators, having failed to belittle the performance of the team in the West Indies, are now busy in an attempt to raise a scare. Fast bowlers, wet wickets and cold and unfamiliar conditions are among the bogeys raised by them, so that they can claim to have foreseen it all in case of any failure.

Singling out Wadekar, he wrote:

As I see it, there are other challenges and more potent factors that will face Wadekar. His powers of leadership will be subjected to a long and harsh Test ... He will face captains who play the game hard with no holds barred. The spotlight of press and television will fall harshly on Wadekar. He will have to contend with critics grudging in their praise and [be] ready to cavil at any tactic that does not meet their approval.

In the same piece, Prabhu mentioned that it would take a lot on Wadekar's part to defy the British press, for they would come at him hard at every opportunity. One of the first decisions that Wadekar had to take was on how to approach the county games. Should he aim to play entertaining cricket to woo the crowds or should he just play with the purposeful aim of getting ready for the three Test matches? Reminding Wadekar of the criticism he had received in the West Indies, Prabhu said that copping the criticism was worth it, with the final scoreline in mind.

The press–player relationship is a rather delicate one. While the independent press is expected to be constructively critical, it is also important for the press to support the players on key issues like the one referred to by Gavaskar. To let international teams get away with putting pressure on Indian umpires was not fair and the Indian media could certainly have played a corrective role in the matter. Recent Indian captains like Sourav Ganguly, M.S. Dhoni, Anil Kumble and Virat Kohli have all had their good and bad moments with the media. While the media backed Ganguly in his comeback trail and was the voice of reason against steps taken by Greg Chappell as coach, it was supportive of Kumble and the team during the 'Monkeygate' controversy in Australia. Frankly, Gavaskar's criticism of the Indian media not standing up for the team doesn't hold good as far as the Australia series in 2007–08 is concerned. From backing Harbhajan Singh in the 'Monkeygate' episode to giving Kumble a standing ovation in the post-match press conference in Sydney, the Indian press did more than what was expected of it Down Under. Having been a part of the touring Indian media for over two decades, we can say with certainty that not one of us held back in criticizing the umpires for the string of wrong decisions they made in the Sydney Test in January 2008, and we also labelled the Australians 'unsporting' for claiming catches when the balls had been grassed. The fact that the 'Monkeygate' controversy became the biggest of our time was largely because of the campaign in the Indian press.

Media and player relations in India reached their nadir when the team was led by Dhoni, with the media not being allowed to ask perfectly legitimate questions at press conferences. One such press interaction was addressed by Dhoni on the eve of the Champions Trophy in May 2013. The media manager, R.N. Baba, actually stopped journalists from asking a single question on the contentious issue of spot fixing that had taken the country by storm a week earlier. Dhoni, who was at the forefront of this controversy, should have cleared the air rather than sitting in silence amid considerable pandemonium. The media wasn't against Dhoni, as it was made out to be. He was the Indian captain, and it was imperative he offered answers on what was going on. It was the duty of the press to ask questions, considering India is a country that prides itself on having a free media. And we felt it was morally necessary for a person leading India to take a stand on a controversy that ended up dividing our cricket.

The Challenge Begins for Wadekar

In the midst of a tense build-up and a rather fraught relationship with the media, Wadekar's team needed to start well in England. A string of good performances in the first-class matches ahead of the Lord's Test eased the tension to some degree and helped rally the fans around the team. Feeling confident of the team's form, fans started writing letters to the editor, taking on England captain Illingworth for saying that the English batsmen would easily negotiate the Indian spinners. One of the many letters that were published noted that at the end of the six-tour games, each of the three frontline spinners—Bishan Singh Bedi, Bhagwat Chandrasekhar and Srinivas Venkataraghavan—had picked 20 wickets or more, which was proof of the impact they were starting to have. A second letter commended Pakistan for putting up a 600-plus total in the first Test against England and said that none in the cricket world had expected Pakistan to enforce a follow-on against England, and it was a telling comment on how the series had progressed. Pakistan, the writer said, had been robbed of a victory in the Test because of rain and should have been a little more careful in the third and final Test. A third letter hailed the Indian team for winning four of the seven tour games and said these were worrying signs for England. 'The performance of the touring team is excellent and record-breaking,' the letter read. 'Out of the seven matches played to date, they have won four matches, and that too by huge margins. The Pakistan team has not won four matches in their whole tour, nor have any previous Indian or Pakistani teams won so many matches at such an early stage of the tour. Kudos to the Indian team.'

The nature of media coverage had also changed, with every dispatch from England talking up the team's performance. And when the Indians thumped county champions Warwickshire by an innings and three runs, most felt that India, contrary to what had been said in the press, was ready to challenge England in every department of the game. Not only had the top order scored runs, but each of India's key batsmen—Gavaskar, Wadekar, Viswanath and Sardesai—had notched up hundreds. In the first five matches of the tour, Gavaskar had led the way with nearly 400 runs at an average of 55, and Viswanath was a close second with 379 runs in eight innings.

'I was batting well. From the very start of the tour, I felt confident of my form, and it was not only me but the entire team that was doing well,' said Viswanath. 'While Ajit and Sunil had both scored important runs, our spinners were among wickets, which made us feel we were ready for Lord's and had a real chance to make history.' What had come as a welcome relief for the Indians was Wadekar's return to scoring big runs. He had a relatively quiet series with the bat in the West Indies, which fuelled speculation regarding whether captaincy was taking a toll on his batting. Ahead of the England tour, Wadekar had mentioned in his private circles that he was batting well and at no point felt any pressure because of the captaincy. He had captained at the school, college and university levels, and had also led Bombay to a Ranji Trophy triumph as skipper. His scoring a hundred against Leicestershire early on in the tour helped set the tone, much like the impact Ganguly's 144 runs had in Brisbane against Australia in 2003–04. A captain scoring runs always works well for the team and adds to the confidence of the man in charge while making key decisions. It was no different for Wadekar, which became evident from some of the decisions he took in the first Test at Lord's.

Speaking on the issue, Sourav Ganguly has had some very interesting things to say. 'I don't know about Wadekar, but the 144 in Brisbane added a great deal to my confidence. I had proved to myself that we could compete in Australia, and as captain, there is no better feeling,' he said. 'You feel empowered and the confidence helps in the decision-making. With runs behind you, leadership becomes easier. You feel much more confident that the team looks up to you. They know you are capable of leading from the front, and that makes a massive difference. I am sure Wadekar must have felt the same.'

In bowling, a healthy competition was on between Bedi, Chandrasekhar and Venkataraghavan, with the three sharing 66 wickets between them in the first five games. While Chandrasekhar had picked up 23 scalps, Venkataraghavan had taken 22 and Bedi 21. Erapalli Prasanna had also picked up 12 wickets, giving the Indian spin quartet a fearsome look.

Buoyed by the performances, Prabhu began his dispatch from Bournemouth less than a week ahead of the Lord's Test with the following words: 'Five victories, including four in a row. That is the Indians' record before the first Test at Lord's which begins on Thursday. Today, the gallant side beat Hampshire by five wickets and the Man of the Match was vice-captain S. Venkataraghavan.'

He was effusive in his praise for Venkataraghavan. 'For some time to come, people here will talk of Venkataraghvan,' Prabhu wrote. 'The off-spinner not only touched his career best, but also came out with the best performance of the English season.'

English writers had also started to talk the Indians up. A headline in the *Guardian* declared that the Indians were after their best-ever record in England. The widely respected John Arlott singled out Viswanath and said it was rare to see someone of such slight build play with enviable power and elegance.

One other important development ahead of the Lord's Test was Vijay Merchant announcing his decision not to file his candidature seeking re-election as the chairman of the selection committee in the Board's Annual General Meeting in September. Merchant, who had been pivotal in the appointment of Wadekar as captain, had overseen the transition of Indian cricket from the control of the British Raj to the middle class. Merchant, a successful businessman and one of India's finest batsmen of all time, had meshed his corporate philosophy and batting discipline in picking Indian teams of the future. Having suffered at the hands of royalty in the course of his own playing career, he was always conscious of rewarding talent irrespective of their background or where the player came from. While he was keen on experimenting with youngsters for a period, in 1971, he had gone back to the time-tested formula of blending youth with experience. Rusi Modi, who had played with Merchant for years in the Ranji Trophy, mentioned in one of his columns that Merchant had already picked Gavaskar in 1968 as the star who would eventually break all batting records in cricket. He, in fact, labelled Gavaskar as Merchant's 'protégé' and credited the latter for having an eye for talent. Modi, who was critical of Merchant for selecting as many as eight youngsters for the Australia series of 1969, added a caveat, saying Merchant 'had always acted in the best interest of the game'.

While not much was published on Merchant's decision to step down, one can speculate that the decision was prompted by two key developments. The first, as we've seen, was that the Merchant versus Pataudi duel, which had been a key feature of Indian cricket between 1965 and 1971, had finally come to an end with Pataudi announcing his decision not to be a part of an Indian touring team in the future. With his main adversary gone, Wadekar's position as captain was secure and Merchant, it can be argued, had started to look beyond the job of the chairman. Second, with Gavaskar, Viswanath, Sardesai and Wadekar in the batting department and the spin quartet in the bowling department, the team had a settled look to it, which Merchant had been instrumental in achieving. With the core in place, it was time for him to focus more on his business activities, moving on after a job well done. In hindsight, the move was an extraordinary one. Merchant had already picked the team that had beaten the West Indies, and as it turned out, the other team he picked went on to beat England on their home soil, capping an extraordinary career for Merchant as the chairman of the selection committee.

While the Indians would go on to beat England at The Oval—a game dealt with in detail later in the book—it was in the first Test at Lord's that Wadekar and his boys showed what they were capable of. 'We won the first session convincingly and that's always an important thing at the start of an away series. England had been reduced to 71 for 5 and each of us felt we could get them out for 150. While that did not happen and they managed to reach 304, we had done enough to believe that we had the bowling to trouble them,' said Viswanath.

Though the Indians had let the English off the hook and allowed the tail to wag, a relative shortcoming of Indian bowling attacks over the years that continues to be written about, they batted extremely well and secured a first-innings lead for the first time against England since 1936. Former players and journalists had questioned the ability of India's batting contingent, and the first innings at Lord's was a befitting reply.

Yet again, the similarities with the Brisbane Test of 2003–04 becomes relevant. 'While the lead wasn't anything substantial, the fact that we had scored 400 runs in the first innings of the first Test of the series, chasing 323 was a massive statement,' said Sourav Ganguly, remembering the Brisbane Test. 'Internally, within the team, it had given us a big boost. We may not have won the Test, but that one innings was the kind of perfect start that we needed.'

Uncannily, this is what Viswanath had to say about the first innings at Lord's in 1971, too: 'We did not lead England by many, but I have to tell you that too few or too many wasn't of much relevance. That we had scored more than their first innings score of 304 was good enough, and it made us believe that the series was going to be different.'

With an excellent bowling effort in the English second innings, the Indians had given themselves a chance to win the Test on the last day. 'We planned based on what Farokh [Engineer] had told us. As a local, he knew about the conditions and said that if the weathermen predicted rain, it would surely rain. The time could vary a little, but there was reason to plan around the forecast,' Viswanath recalled. It was this calculation that prompted Wadekar to promote Engineer in the batting order to see if he could get India some quick runs in pursuit of 183. At one point, it seemed that Engineer and Gavaskar had set India on course for a historic victory in the first Test of the series. While that did not happen, and the Indians lost a cluster of wickets to end up on 145 for 8 when the rains came down to signal the end of play, it must be said that they had more than made a match of it. 'You can possibly say that England had the upper hand in the end, but only just. We could still have won the game with Solkar batting,' said Viswanath. Gavaskar, too, states the same in *Sunny Days*, though by every rational analysis, it can be argued that England had their noses firmly in front when weather played spoilsport.

At Lord's, the Indians had clearly punched above their weight. The team had exceeded expectations and had validated what they had achieved in the West Indies. The victory in the Caribbean was no fluke and the team looked set to challenge England in the remaining two Test matches. It is perhaps fair to argue that even before The Oval victory, India had made a statement to the world cricket fraternity and had started what many see as the reorganization of the global cricket hierarchy. India, as the performance at Lord's had conclusively proved, were no pushovers. They had the bowling and the batting to take on the world's best, and, with a little bit of luck, could beat England in their own backyard.

This assessment was not limited to the Indian media. The usually partisan English press hailed the Indian performance too, and published glowing headlines like 'India's Spin Emphasises Shift in World Power' (*Guardian*) and 'England Scarcely Deserved to Win nor India to be Beaten' (*Daily Telegraph*). Summing up the game for the *Guardian*, John Arlott lavished praise on the Indian spin trio of Bedi, Chandrasekhar and Venkataraghavan, saying they were the best in the world by a distance, and the fact that India could have someone like Prasanna, who could have walked into any team in the world, on the bench spoke volumes about India's spin resources. He labelled the Indian spin attack the most dangerous combination in the world and warned England to be at their best for the rest of the series. E.W. (Jim) Swanton in the *Daily Telegraph* argued that justice was done in the end with the rains stopping an English victory bid. According to him, India did not deserve to lose and a draw was a fair result under those circumstances.

Ecstatic at the way India had performed at Lord's, K.N. Prabhu had turned into a cheerleader. In a piece published under the headline 'Indians Have Forced Revaluation in World of Cricket', Prabhu argued that 'the cynics who used to refer in contemptuous terms to the "dull dogs of cricket" have been exposed. So, too, have the philistines who used to draw up a league table of the position of various countries in the world of cricket.'

An ardent Wadekar supporter, it was no surprise to see Prabhu write that at the forefront of the achievement at Lord's was astute leadership:

The Indians have won this esteem by good all-round cricket, astute leadership and a methodical, practical approach ... If India ever rose to the challenge it was on this grey and tension-ridden Tuesday when a mastermind promoted Engineer in the order and an effort was made to strike out for victory. If Chandrasekhar's powers have been conserved, if Venkat is now a match winner, it is all on account of the wise logical mind that now directs and controls our cricket on the field of play.

With moral victory achieved and with a new-found self-belief, the series was off to an exhilarating start for India. The pressure, which was squarely on Wadekar and his team at the start of the tour, had shifted to England with cricket writers questioning the depth of the English team and their ability to deal with the quality of Indian spin bowling. What was also important was that unlike Pakistan, who were unlucky, the Indians had all the luck in the summer of 1971. In the second Test, for example, it was luck that would save Wadekar from certain defeat. Had it not been for the rain, Pakistan could have won the series. In contrast, had it not been for the rain, the Indians could have been down 0–2 by the time they reached The Oval to play the third Test. Under the pump in the second Test, rain saved India on the last day, with the entire day washed out when India was already 3 down for 65, chasing 420. Ability, form and luck—it was all working out for Wadekar, and all he needed was one final spark.

Chapter 9
The Oval Challenge

While it is now common knowledge that India won the third Test match at The Oval in 1971 and created history, the story we deal with in the course of this chapter—the build-up to the third and final Test and how it was anything but smooth for Wadekar and his team—is lesser known. After what was considered a stellar performance at Lord's, which many considered was a wake-up call for England, India was outplayed in the second Test at Old Trafford. Had it not been for the rain on the final day, England would have travelled to The Oval 1–0 up in the series. Even Viswanath acknowledged this, saying, 'We were in a difficult position at the end of the fourth day, having lost 3 wickets for 65, chasing 400 plus. Dilip and I were at the crease and it would have been extremely difficult to save the game against a good English attack.'

Something that Viswanath refers to as 'difficult' was for all practical purposes impossible. Even in the absence of John Snow (penalized for pushing Gavaskar at Lord's), England had complete control of the game, and India, the British press was unanimous, were lucky to have staved off defeat because of the weather. While the series scoreline read 0–0, the gains made at Lord's were lost and England was going into The Oval Test with its tail up. This was evident from the press interactions of captain Ray Illingworth, who said that India was 'lucky' it was not going into the final Test match two down in the series. When pushed further, he added rather sarcastically that Bedi and Chandra were hardly the batsmen the world feared, and with the amount of time left in the Lord's Test, England would have wrapped up the Indian innings had it not been for the rain. While agreeing that the Indians had exceeded expectations and made a match of it, at no point was Illingworth willing to concede that the first Test match could have gone either way.

In talking up India's luck at Old Trafford, Illingworth also suggested that Lord's was closer than expected because of two things—poor English batting and a substandard wicket, something he had alluded to in his post-match report to the England Cricket Board as well. More than the Indian spinners, he attributed India's success to the conditions and said the second Test match was proof that the spinners weren't unplayable as was being touted in the press. They were good, said Illingworth, but certainly not unplayable. On a good wicket like the one at Old Trafford, England was a much superior side, according to the skipper, who had not lost a single Test in his twenty-six months at the helm of English cricket. All he wanted was a good wicket at The Oval, which was considered essential for England to close out the match and register yet another series win.

The Nadkarni Affair

While Illingworth was sounding the bugle, India had a series of problems of their own. All of a sudden, there was bad blood between the manager and the players, which could have impacted performance. It started with the Bapu Nadkarni incident, which was barely reported in the Indian press. One reason for this may be the victory at The Oval, which helped mask differences and made sure the controversies were glossed over at the end of the series. Needless to say, if an incident like this happened in 2021, the media would have a field day decoding the incident, passing a verdict and taking sides. Careers would be put on the line and reputations trashed. Not so in 1971, when the incident was conveniently hushed up and swept under the rug. In fact, most of the players we spoke to have no recollection of the incident and expressed surprise that such a thing had taken place. For almost all of them, England in 1971 remains the perfect memory, and any rupture in the perfect narrative is rejected outright.

Nadkarni, one of the most respected Indian cricketers, was playing club cricket for Ramsbottom in the Lancashire League at the time. For cricketers past their prime, or for those whose skill set was a rung lower than the national team, club cricket in England was a viable option to make a living. It was a substitute for something like the Indian Premiere League (IPL) at the time, and was looked upon as employment for an entire generation of Test and first-class cricketers. This practice continued till the early 2000s, with many Indian cricketers playing in English clubs right through the summer. 'I made significant money playing club cricket in the 90s,' said Saradindu Mukherjee, one of Bengal's premier spinners who had a relatively short India career in the early 90s. 'In those days, GBP 20,000 was a significant amount of money and was something that made a real difference to me and the family,' he said.

In Bapu Nadkarni's case, the club, in recognition of his services, decided to support him by organizing a benefit match during the Indian team's visit to Old Trafford for the second Test. The match was to be played on the Sunday in the middle of the Test, which was the rest day, and in consultation with manager Hemu Adhikari, it was decided that the Indian players who weren't playing the Test match would make a guest appearance for Ramsbottom. Adhikari, reports suggested, had spoken to the club officials and confirmed the arrangement. It was only after receiving formal confirmation from the Indian manager that Ramsbottom went ahead in publicizing the game and selling tickets for the fixture. On Sunday, the club was packed to capacity with a large section of the local community having come to see the touring Indian players. Nadkarni was there to receive the Indian players and soak in the moment.

However, while Adhikari had confirmed the arrangement to Ramsbottom, he had done so without speaking to the players or to the BCCI. No formal permission had been sought and it was highly unlikely that the BCCI would have agreed to such an arrangement in the middle of a Test match. All Adhikari did was inform the players, after which he left it to their discretion to decide whether they wanted to attend the event or not. Fearing censure from the BCCI for playing the game, the players decided not to turn up for the fixture. Yet again, Adhikari did not communicate this to either Nadkarni or to the club. With the Indian players staying away, it was natural that the crowd, which had paid to watch the stars, turned restless and started hurling abuses at Nadkarni. For no fault of his, Nadkarni was in the firing line and the incident caused him much embarrassment in front of the club and the thousands who had gathered to watch the game. With the situation getting out of control, Nadkarni had to be rescued by club security and taken away from the ground. For someone who had served Indian cricket with distinction, this was an uncalled-for moment of embarrassment and humiliation.

Subsequent reports on the incident mentioned that Adhikari should have been transparent with the club and cleared the air regarding the players' participation. Moreover, he should have spoken to the BCCI in advance and sought permission to release the players for the match. For someone as respected as Nadkarni, the BCCI may have agreed to make an exception and allowed players to attend the game. Either way, this was a classic case of misunderstanding and miscommunication. Nadkarni was the big loser and had to suffer the public, wrath while also missing out on much-needed financial support.

The players, on their part, were clear. Without formal permission from the BCCI, it wasn't feasible to go and play for a fundraiser in the middle of a Test match. Not only was this unheard of, but it could've also been construed as an act of indiscipline and invited sanctions from the board. More importantly, it was a distraction they wanted to avoid in the middle of a series that was considered the most important of their lives. Some of them were worried about possible injuries that could derail team plans ahead of the third and final Test match. Their concerns were all reasonable, but why they did not communicate them to Nadkarni, sparing him the ignominy on a day he was much looking forward to, is unclear.

Either way, the incident created a misunderstanding between the players and the team manager, Hemu Adhikari. Most players privately blamed Adhikari for the fiasco and felt he should have been more forthcoming on the matter, specially since it involved a former India player of the stature of Nadkarni. While on the one hand, the result at Old Trafford did not go in India's favour, on the other, the Nadkarni incident had driven a wedge between members of the team management. The unity that they'd forged from the start of the tour was now being questioned, and so it was essential that Wadekar step up as leader to mask the cracks ahead of the most important game of the series.

The Nadkarni incident was an unnecessary distraction. Midway into the tour, and especially when India had managed to keep the scoreline at 0–0, it was essential that the team was fully focused on the enormity of the challenge that confronted them. In the forty years between 1932 and 1971 that India had been touring England, no Indian team had managed to draw a series, let alone win one. This was a great opportunity considering what the team had managed to do at Lord's, and incidents like the Nadkarni fiasco could take away the players' attention from the immediate task at hand. Adhikari, who had till then performed the manager's role to perfection, was all of a sudden under the scanner, and comparisons to Keki Tarapore, who had done an excellent job in the West Indies a few months earlier, were inevitable. Adhikari had to win back the players' trust, and in the middle of a tour with the pressure building, it was not an easy task to accomplish.

This was also a test of Wadekar's leadership skills. With Adhikari by his side, it was an easier challenge to keep the flock intact. Now, he was having to do two things all by himself—not only did he have to keep the team together and ensure there was no revolt brewing against the manager, but he also needed to reignite the players' support for Adhikari and move past the incident as soon as possible. Added to these was the challenge to keep the incident below the radar so that the hostile English media did not catch wind of it and add to the pressure on the Indians ahead of The Oval Test. Going by contemporary reports, Wadekar was successful in achieving these objectives and there was not a single report in the English press on the Nadkarni incident leading into The Oval Test.

Even years later, Wadekar was conspicuously silent on the issue in his memoir, *My Cricketing Years*, which he co-wrote with K.N. Prabhu. This may have been a deliberate decision to ensure the controversy remained buried and did not fracture the narrative of success associated with the 1971 tour of England.

The BBC Bombshell

Interestingly, the Nadkarni mess was not an aberration. There was also the incident involving the BBC, which caused much heartburn within the team. Unlike now, when the size of the Indian cricket media is enormous and it is nearly impossible for players to speak to individual journalists, in 1971, things were radically different. Speaking on this issue, Mahendra Singh Dhoni said in December 2019 that the reason he does not give one-on-one interviews is because he does not want to be accused of favouritism. 'It is not that I don't want to speak to journalists or that I don't have friends within the media fraternity. But unlike 2004–05, when I started playing, the number of journalists covering the sport has grown exponentially and it is now impossible to speak to everyone at the same time. As a result, it is best if I don't do exclusive interviews, for I don't want to cause any heartburn within the fraternity,' Dhoni said. To a degree, he was right. In age of 24/7 media, an exclusive interview with Virat, Rohit or Dhoni can make or break careers. While this has prompted the BCCI to set up a media cell of its own, which now produces content on every single day of a series, in 1971, media exposure was necessary for Indian cricket to add to its growing stock. With very limited money in the game, exposure was a necessity to reach out to the masses and transform cricketers into larger-than-life figures who could then endorse products to supplement their income from the game. Cricket needed brands, and the media could help in brand building. The public needed to consume content on cricketers every single day, and with television still not widely available in households, radio and print were the best options available. This was more so in England, where the presence of a growing Indian diaspora with a serious affinity for the sport meant that a strong media policy was an urgent necessity. As a result, when BBC Hindi approached the Indian team for a special programme, the proposal was met with a serious degree of excitement. BBC Hindi had a substantial reach among sections of the Indian diaspora and it was hoped that the programme would go a long way to further popularize the tour. The Pakistani players had done a similar outreach programme in June, and its success meant that there was huge interest in the show involving the Indians.

BBC Hindi journalists had formally approached Colonel Adhikari ahead of the Old Trafford Test and it was decided that the Indian players would make a special appearance on the show, which was to be broadcast nationally and would reach the entire South Asian diaspora in the UK. Mahendra Kaul, the host of the show, went ahead and obtained special permission from the head office in London, following which he made extensive arrangements to ensure a high-quality broadcast. Once things were in place, the BBC publicized the presence of the entire Indian touring team on the show and built it up as one that could not be missed. However, for reasons unknown, not a single Indian player turned up for the event, leaving Kaul and the entire BBC team red-faced. Not only did the Indians not turn up, but no reason was given as to why they decided to cancel at the last minute, leaving the organizers embarrassed and angry. The incident was widely reported and ended up giving the Indians a very bad name. It also showed manager Adhikari in a bad light. One of the reports published on the incident read:

> Our efficient officials, in what appeared to be a rare instance [of] good public relations, agreed to let the Indian cricketers appear on the BBC Hindi service which caters essentially to Indian immigrants here. Mahendra Kaul, the interviewer, had made special circuit arrangements with London. The crew stood by but no Indian player or official turned up. One cannot blame Kaul for being livid or embarrassed. Perhaps our officials would care to explain why false promises

were made and why the Indian population in England
was deprived of seeing our players on television,
whereas the Pakistanis had only too anxiously agreed
to a similar request from the BBC in the process
creating goodwill for themselves and for their country.
As it turned out, Kaul was constrained to inform
viewers that the Indian team could not appear because
of problems best known to the Indian officials.

While the report did not name the official in question, it
was clear that the target of the attack was Colonel Hemu
Adhikari. As the administrative head of the touring team, it
was Colonel Adhikari and R.K. Mehra who had the final say
in these matters. It was their job to shield captain Wadekar
and the players from any serious off-the-field distraction
and insulate them from any brewing controversies. Clearly,
they had failed in their objective. Adhikari let his guard
down not once, but twice in two weeks. It is not known if
Colonel Adhikari had spoken to the BCCI on the matter,
nor is it known if he had taken the players into confidence
at the planning stage. What is evidently clear, however, is
that there was a serious miscommunication between the
team management and the BBC that ended up creating a
lot of bad blood. Seeing that the BBC crew had made all
the arrangements, which wasn't easy in those days, it can be
conjectured that they did so only after being given a formal
go-ahead by the manager. What happened thereafter and why
the Indians did not turn up for the event remains a mystery.
What this did was make the Indians unpopular in front of
their own diaspora and dented the image of the touring unit
ahead of the crucial third Test.

In the midst of all this, the BCCI announced that the English team's tour of India later that year would take place as planned. This was in contrast to the stand of the English board, which had declared that the tour would be pushed back by a year because of the growing political uncertainty in India over the conflict in East Pakistan. Skirmishes in Calcutta and other parts of eastern India had already started by the end of March and things were intensifying with every passing day. It was only on 16 December 1971 that the ceasefire with Pakistan was announced—a day the Indian Army continues to celebrate as Vijay Diwas. It was in December 1971 that East Pakistan was finally liberated and Bangladesh was officially born, ending months of bloodshed and violence in eastern India.

Amar Ghosh, the BCCI president and a native of Calcutta, had met the English officials during his visit to London in early May and had discussed the issue in detail. With a clear roadmap in place, there was no scope for any further confusion. However, for reasons best known to Ghosh, he announced in the press that every arrangement was being made for the English tour, which was expected to go on as planned. Not only did this announcement spook the English authorities, but it also resulted in a sharp backlash and was perceived by the England board as an act of deliberate non-cooperation. The players also got involved, with opinions flying thick and fast. The last thing Wadekar and his boys wanted was a distraction of this sort. In fact, the touring team was in a fix—they could neither contradict the stance of the BCCI in public, nor could they criticize their own board president for his comments. When prodded by English journalists, all Wadekar could do was deflect questions, saying such things were best left to administrators and the team had little or no say on the matter. And he had to field such questions just days before The Oval Test began, highlighting the team's unfortunate predicament.

The Role of Luck

Much has been written about Wadekar being a lucky captain. Ray Illingworth, the English captain, saying the Indians were lucky to be saved by the weather at Lord's and Old Trafford added to this narrative. Of the hundreds of news reports we researched for the days between the Old Trafford and Oval Tests, 60 per cent mentioned how lucky the Indians were to escape defeat in the second Test. Such reportage had the effect of taking the sheen away from India's performance at Lord's, while also shaping people's perception of the role of 'luck'. While it is true that the rain did come to the rescue of the Indians, questions need to be asked about the standard of umpiring and if it was something that could also be put down to luck. In fact, based on conversations with Gavaskar, Viswanath and the others, it is clear that all through the series, England benefited from biased umpiring. Similar to how East Germany's Olympic gold medals are looked upon with scepticism in Olympic circles, a team's performances at home in the era before neutral umpires should also be looked upon with a degree of circumspection. In other words, England winning at home with contentious umpiring decisions going their way can also be ascribed to an element of luck. Sunil Gavaskar, in his memoir *Sunny Days*, makes this point very strongly. On the subject of the Lord's Test, Gavaskar writes, 'At 71–5, England was in a virtually hopeless position. At this stage, Illingworth played back to a flipper from Chandrasekhar, which skidded low and benefited from umpire David Constant negativing [sic] an appeal for leg before wicket. Incidentally, Umpire Constant was constant in his support for England that year.'

England went on to score 304, with Illingworth playing a very important hand.

This wasn't the only time Illingworth was saved by the generosity of English umpires. Even at Old Trafford, in a match that England dominated, things did not start well for the home team and at one stage, they were reduced to 41 for 4 on the first day. Yet again, it was the English captain who came to the team's rescue, scoring a gallant hundred and sharing a record eighth-wicket partnership with Peter Laver, who scored 88 on debut. What is rarely mentioned, however, is how Illingworth was 'lucky' each time he went in to bat. To go back to what Sunil Gavaskar wrote in *Sunny Days*, 'As far as we were concerned, however, the turning point of the game came when Illingworth was given not out to a straightforward bat and pad catch by Solkar off Chandrasekhar. This was the third time in three innings that Illingworth had been given a second life by the umpires. I guess there are advantages of being an England captain in England.'

In almost every conversation we had in the course of writing this book, Sunil Gavaskar made a reference to the standard of umpiring in England. Reproducing a few of the WhatsApp messages sent by Sunny bhai (with his permission) helps put the issue in perspective. 'The umpiring in England and many other overseas series was abysmal bordering on chicanery, but none of our media present there ever wrote about it,' Gavaskar wrote. He continued, 'In

1971, we had David Constant and Tom Spencer. Each was worse than the other. If you see the scenes after The Oval win where the umpire fights with Abid [Ali], trying to get the souvenir stump ...'

Kapil Dev, while speaking of 1971 and its significance, also touched upon the importance of umpiring. While we have reproduced the entire interview with Kapil later on in the book, it is pertinent to mention this one comment here: 'Just think about it: a team winning abroad, in front of foreign umpires, where 50–50 decisions always went in favour of the home team ... to counter that and win made the effort timeless. These days, it has become 100 per cent easier with neutral umpires.'

Wadekar and Viswanath were less vocal. While Wadekar has written in his book that it all evened out in the end, both he and Viswanath felt Charlie Eliot, who officiated at The Oval, was a good umpire and less partisan. Wadekar went on to praise umpire Eliot for picking up a nick off John Edrich caught brilliantly by Engineer, a decision considered to be a turning point under the circumstances. However, it remains debatable if Wadekar would have been so generous if India had lost the series, and if a good decision can mask a wrong one.

Each of these conversations bring the focus back to what we can label as 'luck'. If a team that benefited from the fickleness of the weather can be called lucky, can we also say that England, which benefited from biased umpiring in each of the three Tests, was any less lucky? Can home teams, which benefited from the munificence of home umpires in the absence of television referrals, be considered fortunate,

The 1971 Indian team to the West Indies. Top row (*left to right*): Kenia Jayantilal, Syed Abid Ali, Ashok Mankad, D. Govindraj, Rusi Jeejeebhoy, P. Krishnamurthy, Eknath Solkar, Sunil Gavaskar, Gundappa Viswanath. Bottom row (*left to right*): Salim Durani, Erapalli Prasanna, M.L. Jaisimha, Ajit Wadekar, Srinivas Venkataraghavan, Dilip Sardesai, Bishan Singh Bedi.

Mansoor Ali
Khan Pataudi.

Pataudi and Wadekar
fishing together —
once upon a time.

Indira Gandhi congratulates
Wadekar after the Indian team's
return from the Caribbean.

Dilip Sardesai, one of the architects of India's triumph in the Caribbean.

Srinivas Venkataraghavan, a mainstay of India's famed spin attack.

jit Wadekar, a stylish, elegant left-hand batsman.

Sunil Gavaskar in action in the Caribbean; a twenty-one-year-old Gavaskar made his spectacular debut in the series, scoring an incredible 774 runs in four Tests.

A young Sunil Gavaskar ready to take on the opposition.

Sir Garfield Sobers congratulates Syed Abid Ali and Gavaskar, who hit the winning runs, after the triumph at Port of Spain.

Gavaskar hooks a rising delivery.

Ajit Wadekar, Bishan Singh Bedi and Sunil Gavaskar with Prime Minister Indira Gandhi after the West Indies tour.

Sunil Gavaskar in
England, 1971.

Gavaskar pushes
John Price to leg
in Manchester.

Eknath Solkar, a brilliant
close-in fielder, misses this
one, and Ray Illingworth
survives at Lord's.

Captain Wadekar introduces his teammates to the Duke of Edinburgh: *(from left to right)* D. Govindraj, Syed Kirmani, Sunil Gavaskar and Gundappa Viswanath. At extreme right is team manager Hemu Adhikari.

The Indian team meets Queen Elizabeth II: *(from left to right)* Ajit Wadekar, Dilip Sardesai, Abbas Ali Baig, Erapalli Prasanna, Bishan Singh Bedi.

Bishan Singh Bedi in
England; with Alan Knott.

Gundappa Viswanath, Bishan Singh
Bedi and Bhagwat Chandrasekhar at
a dinner.

An elephant was part of India's
celebrations at The Oval.

Bhagwat Chandrasekhar's devastating spell at The Oval.

Syed Abid Ali hits the winning runs at The Oval.

The Indian team returns to the pavilion, led by Chandrasekhar, followed by Bedi and Farokh Engineer.

Abid Ali lifted by spectators after scoring the
winning runs.

Captain Wadekar receives the winner's cheque after
the match.

Ajit Wadekar waves to the crowds after the victory at The Oval.

The triumphant Indian team arrives at Delhi airport.

The victorious Indian team with Prime Minister Indira Gandhi.

Captain Ajit Wadekar greeted with a victory tilak at Bombay airport.

The entire team
was garlanded.

The felicitation at the Cricket Club of India in Bombay.

Large crowds gathered in Bombay to greet the Indian team, a sight seldom seen in those times.

The 1971 Indian team that created history in England.

or should such decisions be dismissed as something that was always a part of the game? Going by the same logic, weather has forever been a part of cricket and should not be used as an element to decry a team's performance as 'lucky'.

This argument gathers steam when we consider that cricket is all about winning key moments. One critical decision at a crucial moment in the game can make all the difference in a closely contested match. Sachin Tendulkar getting out for 136 to Saqlain Mushtaq in the Chennai Test match in 1999, with India within striking distance of the total, made the difference between victory and defeat. Mahendra Singh Dhoni's run out in the 2019 World Cup semi-final sealed India's fate in the tournament. If we indulge in counter-history, it can be argued that Dhoni's dismissal was too close-to call, and in the absence of television replays, he could have been declared not out. In fact, none of us in the commentary box were sure and it was the television replays, that confirmed Dhoni was an inch short of his crease. To the naked eye, it was a decision which was impossible to call. And with the pressure the umpires were under, such decisions, more often than not, go in favour of the batsman. In a scenario where Dhoni was declared not out, it could have been India, and not New Zealand, that played the 2019 World Cup final against England at Lord's.

The point is simple—had Illingworth been given out to Chandrasekhar at Lord's when the score was less than a hundred with five wickets down, the fate of the game could have been sealed, giving India a decisive advantage. England, it is likely, would not have crossed 200, let alone get to 304, which they eventually did. At Old Trafford, it was Illingworth who yet again made the difference with a century. Had his bat-pad catch been given, England may well have scored half of what they did in the first innings.

These 'what ifs' will never have consistent answers in cricket. While they throw up probabilities, there can never be definitive answers to any of these questions. As a result, it is unfair to label a team's performance as 'lucky'. If Wadekar was a lucky captain and his team was lucky in England, it is true in equal measure that Illingworth was lucky at Lord's and Old Trafford and his team benefited hugely as a result. India's 145 for 8 at Lord's in the second innings may have been enough had the Illingworth decision in the first innings gone in favour of the visiting team. Or for that matter, India may have had half their target to chase down at Old Trafford if Illingworth had not scored the hundred and partnered with Peter Laver for the crucial eighth wicket partnership.

The other thing that will never be known is whether the 'lucky' argument was consciously used by the England captain in an attempt to derail his opposing number ahead of The Oval Test. A slight loss of focus could turn into a massive advantage for the opposition, and such plans have forever been a part of international sports. What is also worth questioning is why the touring Indian journalists did not refer to poor umpiring in their reports. While they celebrated the Indian team's performance in glowing terms, not one among them, be it K.N. Prabhu, Dicky Rutnagur or Khalid Ansari, referred to the appalling standards of umpiring. Was it because there was still a kind of colonial hangover, and because the touring Indian media had not yet broken free from the shackles? Was criticizing English umpires still not something the Indians were confident of doing?

Frankly, this wasn't limited to the scribes. Many Indian players we have spoken to said that till the early 1990s, there was a sense of inferiority the Indians suffered from when touring the UK. English remained an instrument of discrimination in India, and the inability to speak the language bred a negative mindset and a sense of inferiority. Things changed decisively with Sourav taking off his shirt on the Lord's balcony in 2002, something Boria has documented in his book, *Eleven Gods and a Billion Indians*. A traditionalist of sorts who belonged to a conservative upper-class Kolkata family, it was unthinkable to see Ganguly take off his shirt and wave it from the Lord's balcony. Yes, it was done in response to what Andrew Flintoff had done in Mumbai a year earlier, but that Ganguly, a soft-spoken Bengali, could do what he did was in itself a statement on what his team was capable of. This was a team that wasn't going to be constrained by traditional values and ideas, and was willing to express itself anywhere in the world.

However, there was no Ganguly in the Indian team in 1971, and, of course, the context wasn't the same as 2002. While Sunil Gavaskar did raise a voice, he was a youngster playing only his second series and not someone who could rally the team behind him. The media, too, was gradually gaining its footing and had not entirely shed its sense of awe in covering cricket in England. Each of these things helped Illingworth and the English team get away with the 'lucky' narrative, something that could be turned on its head if the number of umpiring howlers made in the series were debated in the press.

Each of these things conclusively draws attention to one simple truth—the Indians were under intense pressure going into The Oval Test. This was a match that could change the trajectory of Indian cricket forever.

And it did.

Chapter 10
Victory

India's win at The Oval was a miracle. Much like the 2001 victory against Australia at Eden Gardens where India won after following on, in 1971, India came back from behind at The Oval to hand England their first series loss in years. The victory was proof of a concept that had started in the West Indies, giving a serious shot in the arm to the Ajit Wadekar–Vijay Merchant pair. While Wadekar was now the undisputed leader, Merchant could hang up his boots as chairman of the selection committee later in the year, leaving behind a legacy that became difficult to replicate. While the victory has been much talked about and analysed, there are stories subsumed within the bigger story of success that helps liven up The Oval win as one of the greatest moments in the history of Indian cricket.

With just three runs to get for the win, Farokh Engineer, who was batting with Gundappa Viswanath, walked up to the little master to caution him against playing a rash shot. He

147

said that with just three runs remaining, all they needed to do was take singles and not try anything adventurous—a rather innocuous statement that triggered a very strange reaction in Viswanath. A calm and composed man, Viswanath had a horrible rush of blood and played what he calls the worst shot of his cricketing life. 'I have got out to poor shots, but this was something different. It was a horrible shot and I still regret it. It was perhaps the worst shot I have played in my entire cricketing career. I still don't know why I played that shot with victory round the corner,' said Viswanath. We were all ears as he went on. 'It was when Abid Ali passed me on my way back to the pavilion that I realized what I had done.'

It was natural for us to ask—why? Why would someone who had not played a single aggressive shot in an innings of 33 all of a sudden attempt to hit the ball big, and get out? With just three runs left to make history, what was it that induced a rush of blood and prompted Viswanath to do what he did? His answer, candid and straight from the heart, was the most incredible moment of introspection in the course of researching and writing this book. It showed the multiple layers of the human mind and helped us gauge the mindset of performers. It also showed us what Viswanath is like as a person. It wouldn't be wrong to say that most others wouldn't have wanted to tell us this backstory. It is a human tendency to try and block the unpleasant and move past it with time. Why reveal human frailty and insecurity? Why give away an anxiety that doesn't really project you as a hero? But that was the best part about speaking with Viswanath; the best part about gaining his confidence and bringing to light stories that have always remained buried under the bigger story—the series win.

333

'The moment Farokh said to me, "Vishy, there is no need to do anything rash, and all we need to do is take three singles," I thought to myself that this was his way to ensure he hit the winning runs. We were on the cusp of history and Farokh was eyeing his moment of glory and wanted me to give him the strike at the start of the over. I thought to myself—why not seize the opportunity and be the one to score the winning runs? This was history being made. We were about to beat England in England, and I was fortunate to be out there and script the miracle for my country. It was a strange feeling. While I wanted to win the game for India, I also wanted to do it myself and not leave it to anyone else. I wanted to be the hero, if you know what I mean. No question, it was wrong of me, or rather foolish of me to do so, but that's what I did. I wanted to finish the match and score the winning runs, and that's what resulted in me playing that awful shot, which I still regret,' said Viswanath.

It was when he passed Abid Ali on the way back to the pavilion that he thought to himself why it was important to listen to an experienced partner. Farokh Engineer's advice was not motivated by wanting to hit the winning runs himself, but rather by a wish that Viswanath should remain out there and close the match for India.

Was Viswanath wrong in trying to do what he did? Was the act of trying to finish the game inherently opposed to the spirit of team sports, or is it fair to expect an elite performer to do so when he is sure of his team winning the contest? Can anyone fault Viswanath for trying to close out the game?

While the easiest thing in the world would have been to take the three singles and close out the match, such a thing is easier said in hindsight. For a change, we need to understand the context in which Viswanath was batting. He had not played a lead hand in India's win against the West Indies. Questions had been asked about how he could travel to the Caribbean while nursing a serious injury, which had ruled him out of the first half of the tour. Even after he was declared fit, he had not performed to his full potential, and there were a few murmurs ahead of the England tour if Viswanath should be persisted with. In England, he started the tour well and was a leading run-scorer ahead of the Lord's Test, with only Sunil Gavaskar having scored more than him. (Viswanath, however, had the better average of the two.) When it came to the Test matches, he could have done better. By his own high standards, it was a modest tour at best. But at The Oval, he had the opportunity to change it all. Having played an uncharacteristically dour innings, he had anchored the Indian run chase and was literally within striking distance of the victory. English journalists such as Jim Swanton and John Woodcock, to name a couple, singled out Viswanath for praise and said it was his ability to drop shutter and not get out that helped win the match for India. To be able to do something against the grain of your character is always a difficult task, and that's what Viswanath was able to accomplish.

To try and get into Viswanath's head and understand what he was going through at that exact moment is an impossible task; more so fifty years later. Suffice it to say, though, that for a twenty-four-year-old man, it was a moment of reckoning. He was on the cusp of making history for his country and it was understandable that he would want to do it himself. Had India still been 50 runs shy, Viswanath would probably never have played the shot that he did. But with just three runs to get, it was a different call. In his mind, he knew that India had won the game and he wanted to be the hero by striking the winning runs. That's what makes cricket one of the most individual of all team sports. While it is the team that wins, it is the individual who is put on a pedestal. Each player wants to contribute to the team cause, and that's why there is a Man of the Match award at the end of the game. To say that Viswanath was wrong is like saying there should be no individual award associated with a team sport, for it can create a sense of disharmony within the group.

To illustrate the point with a more contemporary example, Gautam Gambhir, it can be argued, nurtured an ambition to captain India at the end of the disastrous Australia tour of 2011–12. In fact, anything to the contrary would be unnatural. Having played a stellar hand in the 2007 and 2011 World Cup finals, Gambhir was right in wanting to lead his country. It is human to do so. Cricket is about aspiration, and leading the country is one of the highest achievements a performer can aspire to. That he wasn't appointed captain of India may have made him bitter. Yet again, it was natural, for he had every reason to feel let down. That Dhoni's 2011 World Cup final innings is celebrated more than Gambhir's match-winning 97 may remain a sore point with him. Or so we think. But to say that Gambhir might be wrong to think this way is rather myopic. Each one of us wants to be praised for the work we do; it is and will always remain a natural human instinct.

Viswanath's situation was similar. Having brought India to the finish line, he did not want to share the moment with Farokh Engineer. And in doing so, he paid the price. Though he was out with three runs still remaining, the fact remains that Viswanath had done the job for his team. In showing extraordinary patience and determination, he had steered the team to safety after India lost Ajit Wadekar to a run out at the start of the final day. With 75 runs still to get, the game was in the balance, and it was essential that Viswanath stayed firm and did not get out. In fact, it was apparently the only time in his career that captain Wadekar spoke to Viswanath and asked him to curb his natural stroke-play to make sure he stayed put till the end of the game. 'Ajit called me "Vishy Ba", and this was the only time in my career that he said to me what he did at The Oval,' Viswanath recalled. 'At lunch, when we were within striking distance, Ajit came up to me and said he did not want me to get out. There was something in his voice that had a rather strange effect. I thought to myself, if my captain is saying something to me that he never has, it was important I stood up and did what he was asking of me. I scored all my runs in singles and took very few twos in the innings of 33. I did not play a single risky shot in the entire innings,' he concluded.

For Viswanath, this was a massive opportunity. Out for a duck in the first innings at The Oval, he needed to stand up in the second for it could be the difference between victory and defeat. 'You may have scored hundreds in games that you lost. Such hundreds hold little significance for a player. While it might give you a sense of personal satisfaction, when you are playing a team sport, it is how the team fares that eventually makes a difference. I may not have scored too many, but the 33 at The Oval was one of the most important knocks of my career. It played a part in India winning the series and I wouldn't be wrong in saying it changed Indian cricket forever,' Viswanath said.

Speaking of putting the individual before the team, it is also said that Engineer was upset with Abid Ali for scoring the winning runs, and this led to a serious misunderstanding between the two. When interviewed for this book, Abid Ali recounted: 'Farokh Engineer came running to me from the non-striker's end to tell me to take a single. He wanted to hit the winning stroke. I felt it was strange and saw no need to listen to him. I thought it was important that an Indian was hitting the winning stroke. It did not matter whether his name was Abid or Farokh.' While it is impossible to corroborate the story, it is natural that Engineer would have wanted to finish things off, having played a stellar hand for his team. It is also possible that just after Viswanath's dismissal, he was being extra careful.

As it happened, it was Abid Ali who cut Brian Luckhurst to the boundary to score the winning runs.

If Viswanath's was not the perfect ending, Engineer's was to a degree. Not picked for the West Indies tour, Engineer wasn't sure of a place in the English touring team till the very last moment. While the quality of his game was never in doubt, the BCCI's archaic policies meant merit wasn't the only consideration in team selection. When he finally got the opportunity, there was always that extra incentive to showcase his potential. Promoted up the order at Lord's, Engineer almost made history for India before throwing it away. The Oval had offered him a second chance. Not only did he counterattack, but he made sure that he guided the young Viswanath, who was batting at the other end. In fact, even before he came out to bat, Engineer had done something dramatic that ended up having a telling impact on the outcome of the game.

Plotting the Alan Knott Dismissal

Right through the series, wicketkeeper Alan Knott had been a thorn in India's flesh. With consistent scores each time he stepped out to bat, Knott played a key role in making sure England was able to script a turnaround after being reduced to 71 for 5 at Lord's. His 67 in the first innings and 24 in the second were vital in giving England an upper hand in a closely contested game. At The Oval, he played an even more important knock. His score of 90 in the English first innings was crucial in giving the home team a handy 71-run first-innings lead, which was expected to play a pivotal role in the eventual outcome of the game. As a result, when Knott came out to bat in the second innings with England reeling under the magic of Chandrasekhar and Venkataraghavan, the Indians were aware of the threat he posed to their chances of scripting a miracle.

Enter Engineer.

As Viswanath says, 'The moment Knott came out to bat, Farokh called all of us to say he had noticed something interesting each time the English wicketkeeper reached the crease. Knott, he said, would inevitably touch the bails before he played the first ball; it appeared to be some sort of a superstition with him. He had observed Knott closely and had come to the conclusion that the action of touching the bails was a habit he could not do without.'

Engineer, Viswanath said with a chuckle, was not willing to let him perform what was a ritual with him. First, he decided to stand in between the stumps and the batting crease, posing as if he was making some changes to the field. He would stay there till the time Knott marked his guard and was ready to play the first ball. For Knott, it would be awkward. He could neither push Engineer away nor could he go around him to touch the bails, for that would make the whole thing obvious. No one wants the world to know about a superstition, and it was the same for Knott. He was left with no option but to take guard and face the first ball without doing what he was accustomed to. Even after Engineer went back to his position behind the stumps, he was determined to stop Knott from touching the bails. The plan was to cover the bails with his wicketkeeping gloves while not making the English wicketkeeper conscious of the plan. It would all seem very natural. 'Farokh would go stand behind the stumps and keep looking at the fielders and giving instructions while his hands with the gloves on were directly above the bails as a protective cover. There was no way Knott could have touched them,' explained Viswanath. The plan, he states, was executed to perfection.

While there is no way of confirming if this irked Knott, the fact remains he went out to a stunning catch taken by Eknath Solkar off Venkataraghavan for 1. A key threat had been neutralized and the Indians were cock-a-hoop. Did Knott get distracted by what Engineer had orchestrated? Did it play on his mind as he took strike at The Oval? Do such things matter? Can we take such actions seriously and talk about them with any degree of certainty?

Ultimately, as Viswanath said, the Indians had worked out a strategy and would like to believe it had paid dividends.

This wasn't the only time that out-of-the-box plans have been tried out in cricket. Superstitions are integral to sports, and most players have some quirk or the other. Sachin Tendulkar, for example, hated it if someone wished him luck ahead of a crucial run chase when he was getting ready to go out to bat. 'I just loathed it if someone walked up to me to wish me well. I did not need it. I knew they wanted me to do well, but this was not the time,' he said. The list of people who would do this included his teammates and the coach. Ahead of the hugely important run chase at Centurion against Pakistan in the 2003 World Cup, Tendulkar deliberately put his headphones on during the dinner break while having a huge bowl of ice cream. Two bananas and some ice cream was all he had on that particular day. Focusing on the task at hand, Sachin tried to insulate himself from any possible distraction. In fact, he had no idea that Harbhajan Singh and Mohammed Younis had had a war of words, and that there were frayed tempers in the dressing room. 'I was in my zone. I was listening to music and wasn't concerned with what was going on around me. In fact, I did not even want John Wright to come and wish me as I was getting ready to walk out,' he said to Boria while working on his autobiography, *Playing It My Way*.

What Tendulkar did in Sydney in January 2004 was even more startling.

'When I think about this Test, I can't help remembering that for some reason, I turned unusually superstitious. Anjali, her parents, Sara and Arjun were with me on the eve of the match, and we decided to go to a Malaysian restaurant for dinner. The food was excellent and we ended up ordering noodles, chicken and a host of other dishes. My family then left for India the next morning, but I had a very good first day and was unbeaten on 73. In the evening, I decided to stick to the routine of the previous night and went to the same Malaysian restaurant, this time with Ajit Agarkar and a couple of other players. Not only did we sit at the same table, but I had exactly the same food. The next day went even better and I was not out on 220. That night, I again went to the same restaurant and occupied the same table and ate the same food. On the third day of the match, with the Test match going really well for us, we went to the same restaurant one final time. The restaurant manager must have thought we were mad. At the same time, he must have been elated at the thought that we had returned because of the food. Little did he know the real reason for our fourth consecutive visit!' recounted Sachin.

To return to 1971 and The Oval. With Alan Knott out of the way, based on the combination of Engineer's strategy and some fine bowling and catching from Venkat and Solkar, Chandrasekhar ran through the English innings in just two and a half hours, setting up what was one of the most important chases ever in Indian cricketing history. And in doing so, Chandrasekhar had successfully proven a point. Dropped for the West Indies tour and picked on by the chairman of selectors ahead of the England series, the team witnessed a special effort from one of India's greatest leg-spinners. This effort, to many of his colleagues like Gavaskar, Viswanath and, of course, skipper Wadekar, was the best Chandrasekar had ever bowled. It was fitting that he would do so in what was perhaps the most important Test match of his career. While he did not say much about Merchant's jibe ahead of the team's departure for England, except that the chairman should not have picked him if he did not have faith in his abilities, there is little doubt that it was playing on his mind, something repeatedly attested to by Viswanath in the course of our conversations. While Chandra was less vocal on the issue, that he had a point to prove after being overlooked for close to two years is beyond doubt. He had fought his way back into the team with strong domestic performances and was a top performer in England all through the series. What was missing was that one miracle effort. There could be no better stage than The Oval, with England in the driver's seat and seeking to take control of the game. They had scored 24 for the loss of Jamieson, a close run out call which went India's way, by the time Chandra was asked to bowl a few minutes before lunch. England, at that point, had an overall lead of 94 runs, which was substantial in the context of a low-scoring game. India, by every estimate, was praying for a miracle. And, by every estimate, India got one.

Chandrasekhar at The Oval

Chandrasekhar, as many of his colleagues suggested, needed a little time to settle into his rhythm. He took 3 or 4 overs to get into the groove, after which he started to have a telling impact on the game. India did not have time on their hands at The Oval, with England starting to dictate terms and each run being added to the score, making the subsequent run chase that much more difficult. With lunch round the corner, it was a critical moment in the game. Had England played out the last few minutes before the interval without losing a wicket, it could've meant that the game would go beyond India. England would have time to recalibrate and, with a lead of close to 100 in the bank, they could easily start to control the game going forward.

Did any of this play on Chandra's mind as he stepped up to bowl to John Edrich? Did he think he had to pick a wicket in his very first over to dent England? Do performers think like this? Did he dream of pulling a Durani at The Oval and changing the complexion of the game in a matter of minutes?

In the absence of great television coverage, all we have is Edrich facing up to Chandra with his back to the camera. And while it is not a close shot, what we do see is Chandra running in from over the wicket and, in a flash, Edrich's stumps being shattered. It seems very sudden. Edrich turning back, not really knowing what had happened, Chandra trying to come to terms with what he had done and the close in-fielders waking up to something unexpected. The celebrations at the fall of the wicket remained muted, for the Indians could not gauge what was to follow. Chandra, too, went about his celebrations in a rather routine manner. No hugs or high fives—all he did was walk up to the wicketkeeper, Engineer, with Bedi running in to congratulate him.

Things were dramatically different at the fall of the next wicket, off the very next ball. With lunch round the corner, Wadekar had Fletcher surrounded by five fielders close to the bat, and India was on the prowl. And just as Fletcher edged to Solkar, who was brilliant at forward short leg, Chandra jumped in with an unexpected burst of energy. Chandrasekhar was in business, and so was India.

In the words of captain Ajit Wadekar: 'The match was irrevocably settled by mid-afternoon. At Port of Spain, Durani had claimed Sobers and Lloyd to put us on the road to victory. At The Oval, the moment Chandrasekhar bowled Edrich and Fletcher off successive balls, I sensed that the game would be ours. Chandrasekhar's length, the crippling influence he exercised over the English batting was such that I could well dispense with our other star spinner. While Chandra ran amuck at one end, I brought Venkat on to keep runs down at the other ... England were hounded to their doom, as Solkar, in the close-in position, lent an added edge to the attack. It was one long procession as England's batsmen were unable to tell Chandra's top spinner from his leg-break ... Chandra's figures of 18.1–3–38–6 deserved to be engraved in letters of gold. By destroying England's batting, he had raised hopes of victory.'

While repeating that the spell at The Oval was the best he had seen Chandrasekhar bowl, Viswanath dismissed the myth that Chandra did not know what he was doing. According to Viswanath, there is no such thing as a mystery bowler. If a batsman is unable to pick the ball from the bowler's hand, it remains a mystery to him. Standing at slip, Viswanath said, he could understand everything Chandra was trying to do. 'It was a special day. Rhythm, pace, variation, everything seemed perfect. We often use the term 'unplayable' rather loosely. This was one spell that was truly unplayable,' Viswanath said.

Most journalists covering the game hailed Chandra as the best in the world, and for Wadekar and the team, he had opened up the game. From being 71 behind in the first innings and staring at a 300-plus run chase, India was left with a target of 174 to beat England in England for the very first time in history. At stake was not simply a Test win, but a series win that could take Indian cricket to unprecedented heights. It was India's moment of reckoning, set up beautifully by Chandra, Venkat, Solkar and Engineer.

There is an uncanny similarity between the 1971 Oval win and India's win in the 2011 World Cup at home. While in 1971, it was captain Wadekar who was sleeping in the dressing room, in 2011, it was Tendulkar who was pretending to sleep at the Wankhede stadium, as mentioned by Virender Sehwag in his interactions with us. It was only after Abid Ali had hit the winning runs and Ken Barrington had congratulated the Indian skipper that Wadekar stepped out to the balcony to soak in the moment in 1971. Forty years later, Tendulkar left the Wankhede dressing room to rush to the ground only after M.S. Dhoni had hit the most commented-upon six ever. Neither Wadekar nor Tendulkar watched history being made. While many dedicated the victory in 2011 to Tendulkar, Wadekar was the toast of the country in 1971, having turned a new leaf as captain.

'It is difficult to really express what each of us were going through. There were hundreds in the dressing room, and don't ask me how many bottles of champagne were emptied!' Viswanath recalled fondly. He confirmed that even Sunil Gavaskar, who rarely drank, sipped some of the celebratory champagne. When the players walked out to the balcony to soak in the atmosphere, the ground was a spectacle to behold. The tricolour was everywhere and Indian fans were chanting all sorts of slogans. Earlier, someone had brought an elephant from the nearby Chessington Zoo to The Oval, which was considered a good omen by the Indians on what happened to be Ganesh Chaturthi. Back home, the whole country was on the streets celebrating and preparations were afoot to give the team the welcome of their lives. Secretary Chandgadkar had promised a red-carpet welcome spanning the full stretch between the Santacruz airport to the Cricket Club of India in Bombay, and it was now time to make good on his promise.

Chapter 11
...And After

The night after winning India's only silver medal at the Rio 2016 Olympic Games, the shuttler P.V. Sindhu and her coach, Pullela Gopichand, had a conversation about sleep. Sindhu, who had only started relaxing after months of rigorous training and discipline, was reminded by Gopichand that she would do well to get some sleep, for once back in India, the duo would hardly get any time to rest in the midst of all the euphoria in the country. Gopichand was right. After landing in India, neither he nor Sindhu got any sleep for the next thirty-six hours. Sindhu was whisked away from one felicitation to another and, by the end of it all, was left knackered. 'In the middle of one of the functions, I could see Sindhu start to doze off,' recollected Gopichand, smiling. 'It was all starting to catch up with her. She needed to sleep and did not have any energy left to give yet another speech! All I hoped for was that the media should not see her fading.' He laughed before adding, 'Not once am I complaining. To see thousands as happy as they were and to know that you had a role in making them happy is a feeling nothing else can replicate. For both Sindhu and me, these celebrations are memories to cherish.'

The celebrity status that enveloped Sindhu in the weeks following her Olympic medal was reminiscent of the frenzy around India's title-winning 2007 and 2011 World Cup campaigns that brought the entire country out onto the streets to celebrate. The night of 2 April 2011 was like no other. The moment M.S. Dhoni hit the winning six at the Wankhede stadium in Mumbai, fans started dancing along Marine Drive, which runs alongside the stadium, and lined the entire stretch from the ground to the team hotel, the iconic Taj Mahal Palace and Tower. Earlier in the day, when the Indian team had left for the stadium ahead of the final, not a soul was to be seen on the roads. Security had been tightened and fans were not permitted to throng the vicinity. Barely seven hours later, though, that same area cut a starkly different picture as India sealed the chase against a resolute Sri Lankan side. Teeming with thousands of delirious supporters, either side of the approach to the stadium took on an avatar previously unseen—firecrackers went off as traffic nearly came to a standstill; frolickers scurried around holding aloft the tricolour; the beat of the dhol gathered pace as the night wore on, adding to the cacophony of conches and rhapsodies of triumph.

Sachin Tendulkar's wife, Anjali, has rather strange memories of these celebrations. Typically superstitious about watching her husband play, she refused to go to the Wankhede stadium for the final. It was only after India had won that Tendulkar had asked her to join in the celebrations.

As her car was approaching the Wankhede stadium, jubilant fans stopped the vehicle, intending to jump on top of it to celebrate. However, seeing her inside and recognizing her immediately, they stopped short of doing so and allowed the car to enter the stadium's VIP parking lot. Soon after Anjali was dropped off and the driver was back on the road, fans jumped on the car and started dancing on the roof. When Tendulkar saw the car the next morning, he was shocked to spot dents all over his BMW. But because this was a part of the jubilation that came with a home World Cup win, not only did Sachin not say a word to the driver, says Anjali, but he even consoled her by saying that she should rather look at the damage as 'happy dents', which would forever remind them of the immensity of the night.

For Tendulkar, the 2011 World Cup remains the best memory for two reasons. First, in an unrivalled international career spanning twenty-four years, twenty-two were an exercise in waiting—and arduously build up—to become a world champion. Second, it was a dream come true for his ten-year-old self, who had taken up the game in earnest after watching the 1983 World Cup final on television. 'I had danced on the streets of Mumbai when we won the Prudential Cup,' said Tendulkar. 'Not that I understood everything, but what I did realize was that we had achieved something very special. The whole city was celebrating and, as someone who loved cricket, I, too, wanted to win the World Cup someday. It was a dream I always had and finally, in 2011, the dream turned into reality.'

And when it did, a billion people celebrated with him. In the team hotel, the lobby was teeming with thousands of fans and the security had a harrowing time controlling them.

Excitement peaked as the team bus reached the hotel and the staff greeted the players with a cake in the lobby. Despite repeated requests, some fans managed to break through the curbs and hounded the players for selfies and autographs, a common sight during moments of public euphoria. For the record, it had taken the team bus close to two and a half hours to reach the hotel from the Wankhede stadium, a journey that had taken only fifteen minutes in the morning.

For us journalists, it was a challenge. For Boria, it was even tougher as he worked in television, which is a real-time 24/7 medium. He was expected to break news, get player interviews and drive coverage, which, in the midst of chaos, isn't easy. That's when you come up with innovative troubleshooting ideas, popularly known as 'jugaad' in India. Boria, who is good friends with Gary Kirsten, managed to get the Indian coach to carry his camera inside the hotel. Gary saw no reason to say no, and the security personnel wouldn't want to stop the Indian head coach. With the camera and other equipment inside the hotel, shooting multiple exclusive interviews over the next twenty-four hours was no problem.

If the 2011 World Cup celebration was the nation's night out, the open-top bus parade in Mumbai following the 2007 T20 World Cup win was far bigger than any political rally ever witnessed. Millions were on the street to catch a glimpse of Dhoni's team as they returned from South Africa, having beaten Pakistan in the inaugural 20-over World Cup. As the parade snaked through packed streets, the crowd continued to grow as people attempted to catch a glimpse of the heroes. It so happened that as the team bus was heading towards the Wankhede, Tendulkar, who was not part of the winning squad, was on his way to the MCA for a hit at the nets.

In his words, 'I actually passed the bus and clapped for the boys with the thousands who had gathered on the streets. They called me on the bus, but it was not my moment, and it would have been unfair of me to join them. They deserved every moment of what came their way, while for me, it was time to get to practice.'

While the 2007 and 2011 celebrations are part of our living memory, 1971 seems very far away. Fifty years is a long time in human memory, and in this chapter, we attempt to recreate for our readers what it was like in September 1971 when the victorious Indian team touched down first in Delhi and then in Bombay, having accomplished a sporting miracle.

The Celebrations

The celebrations had in fact begun in earnest in London barely hours after the victory. In a rare occurrence, the entire team went out for an Indian meal in the evening, with every player letting his guard down after days of intense concentration. While the series was not yet over and a few first-class games remained, the evening of the win at The Oval was a mixture of relief and joy. The players enjoyed their favourite Indian dishes, while for some, wine and champagne were the best way to unwind.

When the team finally left for home, there was an element of anticipation. 'We were aware of special arrangements being made, but none of us really knew what was happening back home in India. The BCCI secretary had mentioned earlier that we would be given a red-carpet welcome which would start at the Santacruz airport and continue to the Cricket Club of India,' Viswanath recalled. 'I have to tell you that except the red-carpet bit, everything else he had promised was fulfilled. Every cricketer who played in that series will remember the welcome, and it was no less than what you have seen in 1983 or 2011.'

The first destination upon returning to India was Delhi, where a special meeting had been arranged with Prime Minister Indira Gandhi and Education Minister Siddhartha Shankar Ray who, as mentioned earlier, was in charge of looking after sports in the country in the absence of a separate ministry at the centre. Ray, a very well-known lawyer, was an active participant in cricket matches organized for the members of Parliament and continued to help cricketers late into his career. He even represented Sourav Ganguly in the ICC hearing in 2005, when he was suspended for over-appealing and other alleged forms of misconduct.

The Air India flight touched down in Delhi forty-five minutes late, and the patience of the crowd gathered at the airport was tested further as the players took a while to collect their baggage. It turned out to be an anti-climax of sorts when passengers who were not part of the Indian touring party were allowed to disembark first, and it was only after everyone had left that Ajit Wadekar emerged wearing his India blazer, with all the other players trooping in behind him. Things did not go as planned because a number of players reported missing bags, which further held up the celebrations. In an interesting move, the Palam airport staff had hired a troop of bhangra dancers to ramp up the excitement. As the players started walking out, they were first smeared with gulal, while loudspeakers were blaring out music in the background. With an unprecedented number of journalists and photographers in attendance, Wadekar and his boys had to pose for an hour for the shutterbugs before they managed to leave the airport.

In the afternoon, a celebration was arranged at the Feroz Shah Kotla Ground (renamed the Arun Jaitley Stadium in 2019), an event which had been opened up for fans. Contemporary reports indicate the terraces of the stadium were full, with all in attendance excited to see and hear Wadekar and the boys. While the board officials were effusive in their praise, Wadekar, even at the felicitation, was a voice of reason. He bemoaned the lack of fast bowlers and lamented what could have been. With an able fast bowler in the team, India could have run through the English tail with much greater ease. In all the three Tests, getting the lower order out proved to be an issue and Wadekar was keen on addressing it ahead of India's next assignment. He was responding to Siddhartha Shankar Ray's claim that the series win against England meant the Indians were now at the top of the cricket world. While they had beaten both the West Indies and England on their home turf, Wadekar was quick to remind fans that they still needed to beat Australia to be considered the world's best cricket team. And the inclusion of a good fast bowler was key to accomplishing that. Wadekar also used the opportunity to remind everyone of the efforts undertaken by the team to raise money for the Bangladeshi refugees and urged the BCCI to organize matches in India to do more for the people in need. Replying to Ray's appeal to help the Bangladeshi cause, Wadekar was quick to point out that the team was committed to doing everything it possibly could to help the refugees who had lost lives and livelihoods due to the brewing political uncertainty over Bangladesh.

The team met with Prime Minister Indira Gandhi in the evening before attending two more hastily arranged functions in the national capital. In both these functions, Wadekar singled out Vijay Merchant for praise and stated that his contribution to the victory was his way of repaying the faith reposed in him. This was a public acknowledgment of the Merchant–Wadekar proximity, which was at the core of all that transpired in 1971.

The high point of the evening was Wadekar's recollections of how he had slept off in the dressing room on the final day of the Test at The Oval. Unable to deal with the pressure, going off to sleep was his way of insulating himself from the goings-on. Having spoken to his teammates at lunch and after instructing Viswanath to exercise restraint, Wadekar tried to shut himself up in the dressing room and only woke up at the end of the game. Much to the intrigue of the fans, Wadekar said this was his way of trying to keep calm under pressure and was a tried-and-tested formula.

In the context of the celebrations, Delhi was just a trailer. It was not part of the original agenda and had been hastily put together to make sure the team had an audience with the prime minister, who had wished them well on their return from the West Indies. The real story was to unfold in Bombay the next morning and the build-up had already started. A headline in the *Times of India* even announced that the landing time of the team had been pulled ahead by forty minutes and the revised time of arrival was now 9.15 a.m. The time was put out to help fans make their way to the airport since a massive crowd was expected to gather to welcome the players. The crowd was expected to be far bigger than the one that was present to greet the team at the end of the West Indies tour. And this time round, the celebrations were much more structured. In April, people had had to spend an entire night at the airport to welcome their heroes, since the flight from New York landed in the wee hours. On this occasion, things looked better. Updates from the media helped keep the fans up to date with the team's arrival plans while the police and airport staff worked tirelessly to put a four-tier graded system in place to meet and greet the players. In addition, state officials asked fans who weren't able to make it to the airport to line the streets on the way to the CCI. The homecoming was fast turning into a spectacle that Indian cricket had never witnessed before. It aptly demonstrated the growing brand value of Indian cricket. While the cable TV boom of the 1990s was still some years from manifesting, the spectacle organized in Bombay helped unlock the potential of cricketers to emerge as the nation's premier brands.

Mumbai Matinee

The felicitations started at the Santacruz airport with the police band playing 'Welcome the conquering heroes' to the tune of the tutari, a local instrument similar to the trumpet. The flight was parked at Bay number 4 in front of the main lounge for domestic flights, allowing the maximum number of fans to witness the festivities. As reported by the *Times of India*:

> There were five types of enclosures at the airport. Three of them for invitees, relatives and the press was in front of the lounge. Alongside there was an enclosure for those paying the airport admission fee

of Re 1. This enclosure could accommodate 3,000 people. The fifth enclosure was on the terrace and was free of charge.

Once the flight was parked at the designated stand, the team was received by S.K. Wankhede, the minister for sports, and the mayor of Bombay, who, thereafter, led the players to an elevated platform, specially created for the occasion, in the middle of the tarmac. Each player was garlanded and rose petals were showered on them before the captain and the manager were asked to say a few words.

The felicitation ceremony went on for about forty-five minutes, following which the players were permitted to meet their families, special invitees and a section of the press. Interactions with the family, however, were limited to thirty minutes, and every player was asked to wrap up pleasantries on time because individual Cadillac cars had been lined up for them to start the regal victory parade. Captain Wadekar, manager Adhikari, S.K. Wankhede and the mayor of Bombay were at the head of the procession all the way from Santacruz to the Cricket Club of India.

While the route was long and traversed nearly half of Bombay, largely so that most fans could be a part of the celebrations, several regulations were put in place to ensure the smooth passage of the cavalcade. At no point was any member of the public allowed to garland the players, and announcements were being made at regular intervals to stop fans from doing so. Instead, the public was asked to build arches all along the route. Outlining the plan, BCCI secretary M.V. Chandgadkar appealed to the public to not mob the players at any point in the journey, since any intrusion could potentially spoil the party.

The following account of the celebration, published in the *Times of India* on 14 September 1971, paints a moving picture of what was witnessed in Bombay a day earlier:

> All activities in the bustling metropolis seemed to have momentarily ground to a halt as over 10,000 fans turned up to greet the players at Santacruz airport and an estimated 1.5 million people witnessed the motorcade over its 20 kilometre route to the CCI ... Indeed for those countless fans who could not watch the historic triumph at The Oval, the return of the players seemed to be the next best thing. They mustered in strength at every vantage point and expressed their joy in a variety of ways—through colourfully brought out posters and arches, by bursting crackers and blowing trumpets and by showering the players with rose petals and gulal. The most touching scene was when even the sightless waved to the players as they passed the workshop for the blind at Worli.

The report went on to state that a huge number of school students, all dressed in uniform, stood along the route, as did a massive number of officegoers and other professionals. In fact, one of the highlights was when the entire staff of the State Bank of India near the Lotus Cinema came out on the road to greet their colleagues in the team. It was a dramatic reunion, with all the employees chanting slogans and celebrating the achievements of captain Wadekar, who was a member of the State Bank of India family.

Once the cavalcade reached the CCI, the players were asked to rest for a while and were requested to reconvene for the gala evening reception at 6 p.m. Fans had been let into the CCI to watch the function from the North Stand, and reports indicate that scores of men and women had come to be a part of the occasion. The following was reported:

> Over 10,000 fans gave the Indian cricket team a standing ovation at the Brabourne Stadium on Monday evening. The ovation came towards the end of a reception jointly organized by the BCCI, the BCA and the CCI ... The players were cheered lustily as they arrived in dark suits and 'electric violet' ties. 'We want Wadekar' chanted the fans. Solkar and Chandrasekhar, two outstanding performers in the England tour, were the other favourites of the crowd. The players were received with traditional arati, garlanded, eulogized and lavished with gifts which included diamond studded gold pins, vacuum flasks, radios and complimentary copies of *Sportsweek* for the rest of their lives.

A key talking point at the reception yet again was the very open mutual admiration that Wadekar and Merchant had for each other. While Wadekar said that the twin victories were a tribute to Merchant, given all that he had done for Indian cricket, and was a parting gift before he retired from his position as the chairman of the selection committee, Merchant called the England win the highest achievement in India's cricket history. 'Never in Indian sporting history have so many been given so much happiness by so few,'

Merchant said. He went on to add that he could now retire knowing Indian cricket was stronger than ever and the team was in the able hands of Wadekar. It was in the course of this speech that Merchant, for the first time, acknowledged that it was a contested call to appoint Wadekar as captain ahead of the West Indies series earlier in the year. This was an open public admission of how controversial the decision had been and drew attention to the kind of pressure Merchant had been under. While each time Merchant had defended his actions and stood up in support of his decision, it was a revelation that he had been under enormous pressure all this while. Had India not won in England, things could have turned ugly for Merchant. He would have been in the firing line for the calls he had taken and even Wadekar's West Indian honeymoon would have turned into a thing of the past. Some people were waiting to say that the West Indies was a mediocre side, and a failure in England would have reinforced the belief that the Indian side was still not good enough to compete against the best in the world. Merchant, more than anyone else, was aware of this, and it was a relief more than anything else when he stated that Wadekar had proved his decision right.

This was how the matter was reported in the *Times of India*: 'Vijay Merchant confessed he was technically wrong in giving Ajit Wadekar his casting vote. Normally, it should have gone in favour of the reigning captain. "Wadekar, however, has proved me right," he said.'

Finally, what must have pleased Merchant no end was Pataudi's statement that was published in the media, where he praised Wadekar and the team for the English series win, calling it one of India's best in history.

Memories of a Lifetime

Every player we spoke to remembered the Bombay reception with fondness. None of them had seen anything like it and they unanimously agreed it was no less than what we saw in 2007 or 2011. While Bishan Singh Bedi highlighted the human aspect of the celebration, Viswanath couldn't stop raving about the grandness of the event. 'Each one of us were treated like royalty,' said Viswanath. 'From the moment we landed in Bombay to the point we reached the CCI, I don't think any one of us had seen anything like this. There were thousands of fans on both sides of the road and each one was happy. You could feel the passion, and to know that you had a part to play to make each of them feel so happy was a sentiment that can rarely be matched. It had exceeded expectations.' For him, the highlight of the day was the fleet of Cadillacs that was arranged for the occasion. 'It was straight out of a Hollywood movie,' he said. 'You hadn't seen so many of these cars before, and each one of us had a car to ourselves. To stand and wave to the fans when they were throwing flowers at you—it all seemed unreal. We were performers and such public adulation was not something we had experienced before. It was also evidence of what cricket meant to fans in India and that's what gave me the maximum satisfaction.'

For those who weren't able to make it to the roads to see the cavalcade drive past, Shivaji Park was the preferred site of celebration. It was also where Ajit Wadekar had learnt his first lessons in the sport, and to commemorate this, a few youngsters garlanded a portrait of the Indian captain there as a recognition of his achievements.

Wadekar, by his own admission, enjoyed the Shivaji Park felicitation a lot more than many of the others organized in the next few days. He regaled his audience, a staggering 60,000-strong crowd that had come to celebrate him, by narrating anecdotes from his growing-up years while repeatedly stressing the importance of hard work and discipline. The crowd went into raptures when he said, 'I played marbles as a boy, and that's how I was able to run out Jameson with an accurate throw. I had to steal guavas from a tree and had to run fast to elude the dog and the Gorkha. That made me a good fielder. Travelling third-class on the footboards [of local trains], I had to be quick to dodge the poles on the way. That's probably why I can be nimble and agile in the slips. Playing cricket on the street, I used to break the windowpanes of Prabodhankar Thackeray [father of Balasaheb Thackeray, the founder of the political party, Shiv Sena]. That's how I developed the thick-skinned nature needed for international cricket.'

While a lot of what was spoken was said in a lighter vein, Wadekar was earnest in stating that it was not the time for India to rest on its laurels and claim that they were the world's best cricket team. There were areas of concern that needed to be addressed and he was keen on doing so rather than basking in the afterglow of the success in England. Aside from urging his batsmen to be more consistent, he reiterated his desire for a genuine fast bowler. While India had the best spin-bowling contingent in the world, the absence of a quick bowler was a major weakness that the opposition could exploit in the following series. To beat teams like Australia on their home turf, a good fast-bowling attack was a necessity, according to Wadekar.

At the gathering, every player present was asked to say a few words, and Eknath Solkar, a real crowd favourite, said that the next team India wanted to beat was Australia, following which they were looking to play against a combined World XI.

While researching this episode, what also struck us as interesting were all the events that were cancelled or rescheduled in Bombay because of the Indian team's arrival in the city. Many who had pre-booked tickets to the cinema decided not to go and joined the celebration instead. Some who had medical appointments moved them to another day, not wanting to miss out on the action. All that mattered in Bombay on 14 September 1971 was the return of the victorious Indian cricket team.

In trying to reach out to fans who were part of this celebration, we got lucky. During a webinar on the best moments in the history of Indian cricket moderated by Jamie Alter in April 2020, which was the height of the COVID-19 pandemic, Indian politician Shashi Tharoor was one of the panellists along with Boria. When the latter started describing the significance of the 1971 win in India's cricket history, we were pleasantly surprised to learn that Tharoor, who was a high-school student in Bombay at the time, had been part of the celebration. He was among the thousands of fans who stood on the road to watch the cricketers drive past. 'I was in Class eleven at the time and, I have to tell you, it was a truly grand occasion. Scores of us were on the road to see the cricketers and the spirit of the whole event was a tribute to what the victory meant to us in India,' Tharoor said during the webinar.

In the absence of any significant monetary rewards for any of the players—something they rue to this day—the spirit and passion among fans in Bombay is what they most fondly associate with 1971. 'While I don't want to sound bitter, it is a fact that the 1971 team has not been rewarded in any way by the BCCI. If you compare it with 1983 or 2011, we continue to be neglected and ignored,' Viswanath said. He is right to a degree, because many of the players' families continue to face serious financial issues, while the players from 1983 are relatively well off. The fact that Abid Ali is struggling to make ends meet and is unable to get himself the best medical treatment is a painful reflection on how we treat our sportsmen. To many stakeholders in the game, 1971 was as important a win as 1983 or 1985 and, without this initial breakthrough, Indian cricket would have never reached the highs it did in the 1980s and 1990s. As we celebrate the fiftieth anniversary of the glory of the 1971 achievements, it is only fair to expect the BCCI to take serious stock of what the Indian team achieved back in the day and do the needful to commemorate the occasion. While we can't replicate the passion and fervour that fans displayed in Bombay half a century ago, we can indeed make the players and their families feel special by doing something worthwhile for each one of them. If this book helps in drawing attention to this pressing need, we will feel vindicated.

Epilogue

2021: The Circle Is Complete

After losing to the hosts in Adelaide in the first Test of the 2020–21 tour of Australia, having been bowled out for 36 on the morning of 19 December 2020, India held a team meeting around midnight. 'We were determined to get past that one bad hour and a lot of ideas were on the table,' recalls Ajinkya Rahane, who had taken over the captaincy reins for the remainder of the tour from his designated counterpart, Virat Kohli, under the most challenging circumstances. 'That's when Ravi [Shastri] bhai said we could think of 36 as a badge. Would it be a badge of disgrace or a badge of honour? That was for us to decide in the remaining Test matches. The way we played thereafter, I can safely say that the 36 all out was the beginning of the turnaround.'

These recollections of Rahane, the stand-in captain for three of the four Tests on that tour where India capped off with an epic come-from-behind 2–1 victory in the longest format, reminded us of the team meeting on the 1971 tour of the Caribbean in captain Ajit Wadekar's room. It was in this meeting that the mercurial Salim Durani declared to the whole team that he would get the wickets of Sir Garfield Sobers and Sir Clive Lloyd the next day. He eventually did achieve what he set out to do, helping script a historic Indian win in Trinidad. These two wickets, hugely important under those circumstances, were badges of honour that Durani wore all his life thereafter.

In many ways, the trail of India's series triumphs overseas, which began in the West Indies in February–March 1971, entered a new phase later that year with the series-clinching win against England at The Oval, and came a full circle with the victory against Australia in the series decider at the Gabba in Brisbane in January 2021. Prior to 1971 and 2021, India had never won in either The Oval or the Gabba. The similarities don't end there, though. Apart from the preparation on the field and off it, and the self-belief that has come to define the current Indian team's approach to the game, their success in Australia also threw into relief the resilience of the squad and the depth of its talent. Both these factors were pivotal in India emerging victorious despite seemingly insurmountable odds, the foremost of those being the injury-enforced gradual depletion of the squad. A similar streak of this never-say-die spirit had shone forth through the successes of Wadekar's 1971 team that fought back miraculously at The Oval against Ray Illingworth's Ashes-winning English team, after having conceded a crucial 71-run first-innings lead in the series decider.

'I had trouble wearing gloves, so I put them on hours before I might have been needed to go out [to bat] ... If I could save the game for India, it would mean a lot to me and my team,' Ravindra Jadeja, one of the architects of the Boxing Day Test victory at the Melbourne Cricket Ground (MCG) in 2020–21, remembers thinking to himself. Less than a fortnight later, in the third Test at the SCG, off-spinner R. Ashwin, another star of the series, stood in the dressing room for three hours before going in to bat in the second innings, with the scales tipped heavily in favour of an Australia win. Along with Hanuma Vihari, Ashwin played a key role in helping India draw that game and kept the series alive. 'Ashwin did not sit because if he did, he wouldn't be able to get up,' recalled Bharat Arun, India's bowling coach. Vihari, who himself battled a torn hamstring through the best part of his second-innings knock, vividly remembers the drama that unfolded during his partnership with Ashwin. 'The Australian fast bowlers were bowling short to him [and into his body]. I went up to Ash and said he would find it easier if he bent his knees a little more. He said that with the kind of back spasms he was experiencing, if he bent any more, he wouldn't be able to stand up,' Vihari remembered. Despite the pain, the pair soldiered on and put on an unbeaten 259-ball stand for the sixth wicket to keep Australia from taking an unassailable 2–1 series lead before going into the decisive fourth and final Test at the Gabba.

The similarities between India's 2020–21 series victory against Australia and the '71 win against England are most pronounced in the way India breached Fortress Gabba. At The Oval, England had won the toss and scored a respectable 355 in the first innings. In Brisbane, too, Australia opted to bat first, making 369. In response, India were reduced to 186 for 6 before their No. 7 and No. 8 batsmen, Washington Sundar and Shardul Thakur, scripted a spectacular turnaround against a world-class Australian attack. At The Oval, Wadekar's men slumped to 125 for 5 in their first dig before Eknath Solkar and Farokh Engineer rebuilt the innings. The two added 97, a partnership that kept India in the game. Just like at the Gabba, where the Australians threw everything at Washington and Thakur, the English, led by John Snow and John Price, launched a fierce attack on the visitors at The Oval but didn't reap much rewards by way of wickets.

On display at both venues was the immense self-confidence of the Indian teams. In Brisbane, on the last day of the Test, Arun went up to stand-in captain Rahane in the dressing room to check if he felt the need to send in instructions to the batsmen in the middle. 'All Rahane said was to sit back and watch the fun,' recalls Arun. Wadekar was a step ahead and was fast asleep in The Oval dressing room after he got out early on the last day. However, this is not to say that Wadekar wasn't stressed about the result. He was, and the nap was his way of trying to calm himself. In that sense, Rahane could be considered relatively calmer than Wadekar, because all that the former did as India's second innings neared its close was bite his nails off as Rishabh Pant and Washington launched an all-out attack against Pat Cummins and Nathan Lyon.

Washington, on his Test debut, told Pant during their partnership that he was comfortable taking on Cummins, the spearhead of the Australian attack who sat atop the ICC Test bowlers' rankings at the time and would go on to be adjudged the Player of the Series. Washington insisted that he would go for the runs while Pant, the senior batsman of the two, should hang back and bat till the end. Not for a moment was Washington overawed by Cummins.

At The Oval in 1971, with India chasing 173 for a series victory, it was Farokh Engineer who played a role similar to Washington's. His brisk 28, which included three 4s, was arguably the final nail in the English coffin. Engineer, as we have discussed, was included in the touring party to England after much drama, having been left out of the squad that toured the West Indies earlier in the year. Washington, who was originally picked as a net bowler for the Test leg of the 2020–21 tour to help the Indian batsmen prepare against off-spinner Lyon, may not have made the playing XI in the series decider had it not been down to the spate of injuries that grounded several first-choice India bowlers.

The parallels become uncannier when the dismissals of Gundappa Viswanath and Washington Sundar are compared. In both cases, victory for India was within touching distance when each of them got out. Having helped brought India 10 runs shy of a win, Washington got out trying to reverse-sweep Lyon. Viswanath, on his part, went for a glory shot and was caught by Alan Knott off Brian Luckhurst, with India needing just three to win. Neither dismissal elicited much of a reaction from the opposition. While Lyon just walked up to his teammates knowing the game was beyond them at that point, the English had already thrown in the towel as India were just a stroke away from making history, with the winning runs eventually coming off Syed Abid Ali's bat.

Glory Days

From The Oval to the Gabba, separated by half a century, Indian men's cricket journeyed from one epochal phase to another. Wadekar and his team were the first to walk this path of glory before Kohli and Rahane's troops left their imprint on the historic trail. The twin series wins in 1971 and the triumph on the 2020–21 tour of Australia make for two of India's greatest-ever shows of dominance, as well as two of their greatest underdog stories of all time.

When Wadekar and his men won in England, a lot was said of their feat. What assumed greater pertinence over the years, though, was all that was left unsaid at the time. A middle-class Indian banker marshalling a group of professionals to outperform the West Indies and England in their own backyard within the span of a few months seems like a tale straight out of fantasy. The breaks with royalty and the Raj hangover were complete. It was as though a new India was speaking out to the world. Fast forward to Brisbane, and in Rishabh Pant was manifested a custodian of a new, resurgent India, who would be speaking the same language as his predecessors from the twin series wins of 1971, perhaps only louder and more fearlessly. Each time the Australians threw a challenge at him, Pant had a well-rounded, well-timed retort. On the final day of the Gabba Test, when Lyon bowled one which turned a mile and beat Pant, a less plucky batsman would have taken some time to recover and resorted to circumspection. Not so Pant. He danced down the track the very next ball and deposited Lyon over the long-on boundary. In doing so, he made a statement in unequivocal terms—India were in the ascendency and Fortress Gabba was on the cusp of being breached.

The moment that actually completed the transformation, though, happened after the series had been decided. During India's victory lap, Mohammed Siraj, the Hyderabad pacer who had lost his father, an auto driver, a month earlier while he was on national duty in Australia, was handed the tricolour as he led the victorious team's march along the boundary rope. The scene was emblematic of a united India that is proud of its diversity. Siraj, a twenty-six-year-old Muslim man, metamorphosed in those moments into the torchbearer of a resilient India that stands shoulder to shoulder to meet—and overcome—adversity head-on. By leading his colleagues to the victory lap, Siraj was giving a wordless, fitting reply to the spectators who had hurled racist insults at him and his teammate Jasprit Bumrah during the third Test at the SCG. In addition, he was also underlining to his compatriots the world over that cricket—and sports at large—remains one of the most powerful unifying forces, a supreme leveller, and that the game doesn't distinguish between a Hindu and a Muslim, the rich and the poor or those hailing from the metros and non-metros. The 1971 series wins were no different than the 2020–21 victory in Australia as far as upholding the tenets of a unified India goes. The victory parade in Bombay organized for Wadekar and his men upon their return from India's first-ever series win in England commemorated Indian cricket's ability to break through class and power hierarchies. Wadekar had worked hard to align Indian cricket with meritocracy and, in the fifty years since he first excelled overseas as captain, his legacy helped birth more success stories in the sport. Rahane and his teammates' epoch-defining accomplishments in Australia lend credence to this claim. It would therefore not be too far-fetched to assume that on 19 January 2021, when the Indian team celebrated their Australia exploits late into the night in their Brisbane hotel under bio-secure restrictions imposed by the COVID-19 pandemic, the late Ajit Wadekar would have worn a smile of contentment, watching his successors from his designated seat in his heavenly abode. As captain, Wadekar had made India believe they could win overseas and he must have been thrilled to see Rahane, who like him was a No. 4 batsman from Mumbai, lead India into a new chapter in history through a spirited turnaround on foreign soil.

If India today look like the team to beat, it's hard to pinpoint one important reason behind their supremacy in world cricket. An abundance of raw talent and bench strength explains only a part of their dominance, as does early strategic planning and institutionalized processes put in place for the discovery of talent. Well-timed exposure for national prospects, a robust infrastructure at the grassroots and sizeable professional rewards, too, tell only one part of the story. There's no denying that all of these factors play a role in shaping outcomes, but the work ethic and professionalism on view among the current team also warrants counting among the ingredients of its success. This is perhaps the only difference between 1971 and 2021. In time, the benefits of '71 were lost and India plummeted to an ignominious 42 allout the next time they toured England in 1974. Player unity suffered and some of those cracks remain conspicuous to this day. The standout feature of the 2021 team, however, was their ability to move on quickly—be it from the most crushing disappointment (the Adelaide defeat) or fairytale success (the Brisbane victory)—to the next assignment. England visited India soon after the epic Brisbane victory on a twelve-match tour, kicked off by a four-Test series that got underway on 5 February, less than three weeks after the Brisbane Test ended. It was a match that India would go on to lose. The second Test, also played in Chennai, saw a comprehensive Indian victory. Indian cricket fans the world over may have wished to linger on the triumph Down Under, but Team India had swiftly switched focus, moving into a new bio-bubble in Chennai. 'Just as we moved on from the 36 all out, it was important to move on from the series victory as well. That's now history,' said Bharat Arun matter-of-factly.

In closing, we must acknowledge the final common chord between India's victorious overseas exploits in 1971 and 2020–21. This strand involves the central actor in the drama of 1971, who, scoring a record 774 runs at an average of 154 in his debut series in the Caribbean, gave Indian cricket teeth and muscle and, in a sense, taught generations of Indian batsmen that followed to play fast bowling. In 2021, he was there again on the tour of Australia, in a different capacity, braving the pandemic and a fourteen-day hard quarantine. The only Indian commentator Down Under describing the exploits of Rahane and his men from the scene of action, it was fitting that Sunil Gavaskar would witness, from close quarters, the Indian team scripting the historic 2–1 Test series victory and lifting a trophy that takes half its name from him. On 19 January, as the 2020–21 Border–Gavaskar Trophy came to a formal close, Indian cricket well and truly had come full circle.

In Their Own Words

Mansoor Ali Khan Pataudi

We had the opportunity of interviewing Tiger Pataudi multiple times. Here, we have reproduced selected answers from the interviews. The first interview was conducted in 1988.

Q: Even after so many years, debates persist about your removal from the captaincy in 1971. It is said that Vijay Merchant, by exercising his casting vote against you, took revenge against your late father, who had toppled him to become the captain for the England tour of 1946 ...

A: I do not agree. In fact, much earlier than when Merchant used his casting vote, I had got a hint that I might be replaced.

Q: Really? When?

A: Yes. I had differences with the chairman over team selection. On one occasion, there was a big disagreement—

when I preferred Viswanath in Kanpur over his chosen candidate. The chairman's logic was that the South Zone selector had not watched him and so he couldn't play. I found that outrageous. The way Merchant was reacting to my suggestions made me feel something unpleasant was going to happen sooner rather than later. The other reason was that I had run into poor form and wasn't scoring heavily.

Q: But someone who had led the country for nine long years with distinction could easily have been informed well in advance. This would have helped you withdraw from the tour without having to go through the ignominy of a removal.

A: I think you are asking for a bit too much. Historically, such gestures are alien to us. Either they will give you the appointment letter or will sack you unceremoniously. In both cases, they will see no need to speak to you. In the Western world they would ask whether you are willing before conferring the knighthood upon you. Here, do they ask you before awarding a Padma Shri or Padma Bhushan? They do not. You take it or leave it. No one is bothered.

Q: What did you make of Merchant as a person?

A: He was involved with various organizations. I quite liked some of his philanthropic activities.

'MY ONLY REGRET IS THAT I WISH I HAD [HAD] ONE MORE EYE TO PLAY WITH.'

Q: If you look back on your career, are there any major disappointments or regrets?

A: My only regret is that I wish I had [had] one more eye to play with. Then my graph would have been ...

Q: More consistent?

A: Not just consistent—it would have gone higher.

Q: We have always found it remarkable that you managed to negotiate the fastest bowlers with one eye. Will you explain how you managed to do that?

A: It was difficult. Extremely difficult. I had immense problems in judging the length of the ball, which led to my dismissal a couple of times. It was so disappointing. But I had to come to terms with it. Another reason for disappointment was that I could not field in the close-in positions. But there was little I could do about it and it was best to accept the limitations.

Q: In your later years when you saw Tendulkar getting hailed as a teenage batting genius, did you ever feel jealous? Did you ever feel that if you had had both eyes, you could have been as good as Sachin?

A: No. I have never felt jealous seeing someone else excel. I only felt frustrated with myself. I did not need others to aggravate my disappointment or helplessness with myself.

'AROUND THAT TIME, THERE WAS NO CONCEPT OF PROFESSIONALISM.'

Q: You walked out of two important tours, leading to widespread speculation. In 1971, you opted out. Even in

1974, despite repeated persuading from the captain, you did not agree to go on the tour.

A: You have to understand that around that time there was no concept of professionalism. We used to compete for fun. We got paid five hundred rupees per Test match. As a result, I may have given preference to other work. Today, it would have been unthinkable, as you earn a lot of money as a player. Yes, Ajit did want me to travel with the team to England, but I could not.

Q: But once Ajit won in the West Indies and also in England, you must have had second thoughts.

A: That was my team. The three spinners, Solkar, Viswanth, Sardesai, Jai ... they were all my players. Once or twice the thought did strike my mind that Ajit, you borrowed my team and won. I did think it was my land and you reaped the harvest. But then I thought that in a war, the lucky general is chosen to lead the army. Ajit had that luck.

Q: So you did feel a sense of regret.

A: Please ask Ajit who sent him the first telegram in the West Indies following the victory. You will hear mine was the first one.

'I WAS THE FIRST TO CONGRATULATE AJIT AFTER THE WIN.'

Q: The controversial captain selection happened at a time when the media was not so strong. Yet, many stories were written about your removal. Some even said something seemingly outrageous—that Merchant was communal.

A: No, I do not think Merchant was communal. Till today, I do not know what was the actual reason. But the fact remains he made me miserable at the selection committee meetings. Every time he would choose a bad team, the onus finally rested on me. I would get all the blame. So, selection committee meetings always remained unpleasant. I was never the sort who would promote youngsters for the sake of promoting them. My take has always been that the best eleven should play for the country, irrespective of their age. But I could never convince the selection committee. In the 1969 home series against New Zealand and then Australia, they fielded four-five young cricketers who were completely ill-equipped to play for the national team. Why were they played? Because the chairman felt they were fresh and young. As luck would have it, they could not progress much in the later years.

Q: Who were these players?

A: No names please.

'I WAS NEVER GIVEN THE TEAM OF MY CHOICE.'

Q: Fair enough. But can you reveal your preferences and tell us who all you wanted?

A: I wanted a few seniors. I was never given the team of my choice. The irony was that the same seniors were picked for the 1971 series, and each of them went on to play a huge role in the Windies series win. Now, I would like to ask why were they suddenly brought back when I wasn't there? Did the chairman realize their value only when I got replaced?

Ajit Wadekar

*This interview was conducted in mid-2015 at Ajit Wadekar's
Worli Sea Face residence in Mumbai.*

Q: India suffered a 3–0 series whitewash at the hands of
hosts England in 1974. How did the team end up losing the
paradise after three successive series triumphs?

A: The tour had started on a bad note. The problems had
begun with our own board. In a way, they were responsible.
Without asking us, they agreed to a playing condition
change that was quite detrimental to the side. They agreed
to a stipulation of not more than five fielders on the on-
side. This hugely affected the fortunes of our team. Both Pras
[Erapalli Prasanna] and Venkat [Srinivas Venkataraghavan]
were used to [bowling] to six fielders on the on-side. They
were shattered. I was very angry and told the board officials
that although we were not wearing a black badge, we were
actually playing in protest.

Q: A number of seemingly unpleasant incidents took place off the field as well.

A: Yes, we had our share of unpleasant incidents. I think the then high commissioner of India, Mr B.K. Nehru, was partly responsible for the heightened discomfort. It was baffling how arrogant he was. In 1971, we had Mr Appa B. Panth occupying the same chair, and he was very cooperative. Mr Panth was concerned about the well-being of the team. No one in the media knows this, but we had huge problems in 1971 after landing in the UK. The English had given us such tiny rooms that I had to call up the then finance minister of India, Mr Yashwantrao Chavan, to sanction additional foreign exchange. He immediately resolved the matter.

'No one in the media knows this, but we had huge problems in 1971 after landing in the UK.'

Q: What triggered the problems with Mr Nehru?

A: I thought the problems started at the ground itself when he was about to enter our dressing room. I stopped him and said, 'You can't go in here. This is strictly players' territory.' The following evening we were late to the high commissioner's party, and that annoyed him no end.

Q: But why would the team be late for an official gathering they were to attend?

A: Look, we had a State Bank of India function to attend before that and then while driving down to the high commissioner's residence, the driver took the wrong route. We lost a few minutes there and eventually arrived late. The moment we entered his place, the high commissioner told me flat to my face that I must leave. I have never encountered such a curt person in my life. I immediately left, as did the team once they heard what was said to me. When we were seated in the bus Donald Carr came and requested us to return. [Srinivas] Venkataraghavan also spoke to the team and we finally decided to go back in, but no one spoke to the high commissioner. We merely—and silently—completed a formality.

Q: It is a bit uncommon for a diplomat to behave so rudely. What could have been at the heart of conduct such as his?

A: Our infamous innings of 42 all out had happened the same day, only hours earlier. That may have triggered it. I honestly could never figure what led him to lose his temper.

Q: There was also the much-talked-about Sudhir Naik shoplifting episode. What exactly had happened?

A: Naik was too nice a guy to attempt something like this. Left to ourselves, we could have handled his issue much better, but then the Indian High Commission absolved themselves of all responsibility. It was so sad that even though Naik had 250 pounds in his pocket, he got accused of shoplifting. I played him in the third Test as he was crying like a child, and I actually feared for his safety. I feared that he may commit suicide.

Q: Looking back on the episode—and the allegations—all these years later, what, in your view, lay at the genesis of the accusations?

A: It was a careless mistake on the part of Sudhir. But he was absolutely innocent. Some overenthusiastic employees at Marks & Spencer felt they could capitalize on it.

Q: Why did you retire immediately after returning from England in 1974?

A: I was shocked when the West Zone selectors stripped me of my captaincy. I was only thirty-two at the time and was shattered thinking about my future. I spoke with my wife, Rekha, who said, 'If your self-respect is getting bruised, step down.' I actually felt hurt because despite failing in Test matches I got runs in the tour games. How could the West Zone selectors, led by Polly Umrigar, overlook those knocks? I felt they should have defended me in my hour of crisis and not run away.

Q: The twin victories of 1971 are a significant part of your legacy, but the defeat in England three years later remains a low point in your career.

A: The tour was a non-starter. I told you at the start that the board had agreed to the change in playing conditions. And the selection committee did not listen to me either; I did not get the team I wanted. I had specifically asked the selection committee to give me an extra medium-pacer. I had even categorically mentioned that I wanted either Umesh Kulkarni or Ramakant Desai in the mix.

Q: But Desai had quit international cricket by then and was only playing on the domestic circuit...

A: He was still very good, and I would have convinced him to come out of retirement.

Q: After the '71 tour, Prasanna accused you of having developed a subservient attitude towards manager Adhikari.

A: Adhikari was of great help. Apart from managing the team, he used to give us fielding practice. Had there been any other manager, I may have ended up giving fielding practice.

Q: A lot was made of your decision to drop Prasanna and play Venkataraghavan in 1971. Pataudi, however, did just the opposite.

A: I already had two millionaires in the team: Chandra and Bedi. In order to strike the right balance, I needed someone who would have been of all-round utility, someone who could check the flow of runs from one end, field close-in and bat decently. Even someone like Bedi found logic in that argument. Mind you, Venkat bowled some very decent spells, especially against Gary Sobers. Again, instead of England, had we toured Australia, Pras would have played [because] the Australians were suspect against top-quality off-spin.

'PRAS ALWAYS HELD A GRUDGE AGAINST ME FOR NOT PLAYING HIM IN THE '71 TOUR. I DON'T BLAME HIM.'

Q: To date, Prasanna does not seem to have forgiven you for that decision.

A: I am aware of that. Pras always held a grudge against me for not playing him in the '71 tour. I don't blame him; he was the No. 1 spinner at the time. But as I said earlier, since Bedi bought his wickets from the other end, I required someone who could contain the batsmen and wouldn't attack much.

Q: Did Prasanna and Venkataraghavan share a cordial relationship?

A: [They were] not the best of friends, obviously, but I saw them smoking from the same pack of cigarettes. And yes, they *did* talk to each other (*laughs*). By the way, I was the only person—dead or alive—who could joke with Sir Venkat (*laughs*).

Q: In the capacity of a Team India captain and later as their head coach, you worked with several Indian spinners. Who were the top five among them?

A: The best spinner has to be Anil Kumble; I have no doubt about that. After Kumble it has to be Chandra, as he was an absolute match-winner. Pras would be No. 3; then comes Bishan, and finally Venkat.

Q: Since we are comparing eras, how would you rate Sunil Gavaskar alongside Sachin Tendulkar?

A: Both were very, very special. They had unbelievable mental strength, resolve and courage. For me, Sunny is the Raj Kapoor of Indian cricket—someone who founded the empire. Sachin is the Amitabh Bachchan—the brightest star ever. Only I am above Gavaskar (*laughs*).

'SUNNY IS THE RAJ KAPOOR OF INDIAN CRICKET; SACHIN IS THE AMITABH BACHCHAN.'

Q: What do you mean by that?

A: I mean, only I stay on top of Sunny. In our building, Sportfields, Gavaskar lives on the eighth floor and I am on the floor above, which happens to be the top floor (*laughs*).

Q: Is it true that you were sleeping when the historic winning stroke was hit at The Oval?

A: Yes, I had dozed off out of worry and fatigue. Ken Barrington, the assistant team manager for England, woke me up, saying, 'This is a magical moment and you shouldn't be sleeping now.' I must admit, it was very nice of him to do so.

Q: Some members of the '71 squad tell us that for all practical purposes, [Dilip] Sardesai was the vice-captain of the side.

A: Untrue; he wasn't the vice-captain. I used to consult him, yes. Then again, I used to consult other senior players as well.

'It's been so many years since the tour, but I can still visualize Jamaica, I can still visualize Sardesai and Solkar batting.'

Q: Is it true that Vijay Merchant did not want Sardesai in the squad for the West Indies tour?

A: Yes, he wanted [Chandu] Borde. But I had always had faith in Dilip, who was given a raw deal by Tiger [Pataudi] in Australia. I knew he would be suspect for the first three overs, but if he got past the initial difficult period, he could whip up a big innings. It's been so many years since the tour, but I can still visualize Jamaica, I can still visualize Sardesai and Solkar batting, their partnership pulling us back from the brink of disaster. It turned things around for us.

Q: Your bowlers played a significant role in helping you enforce the follow-on.

A: Yes, and Gary was almost speechless when I said I would be enforcing the follow-on. He recovered quickly to say, 'How is it possible?' I asked him to check his rulebook. In a five-day Test, one day got washed out. So, in a four-day match, the target for the follow-on also came down to 150.

Q: The jury is still out on the kind of relationship you shared with Pataudi. Most say it had its share of ups and downs.

A: That is not true. We were friends. He used to confide in me regarding strategic discussions. At times this would be done overlooking the vice-captain, Chandu Borde. Also, many perhaps do not remember that I was the runner for him in the Melbourne Test of 1967, which gave us Tiger's timeless knock—he batted with almost one leg and scored that magical 85. I had earlier gotten out for 99. But his innings was unbelievable. Coming back to your question, I do not know who told you what about us, but our relationship was smooth. In Melbourne, we even went out fishing for a fairly long period of time.

Q: Some say that you only reaped the rewards of the seeds sown by Pataudi.

A: I have heard it so many times, and that I was a lucky captain (*scoffs*). Despite winning three back-to-back series, I was still only lucky?

Q: You seem to be very bitter that your consistency as a leader was not appreciated appropriately.

A: No, it's dissatisfaction. I look at it in a completely different way—my dissatisfaction remained that as a captain, I couldn't score too many runs.

'DESPITE WINNING THREE BACK-TO-BACK SERIES, I WAS STILL ONLY LUCKY?'

Q: Some say that the Raj hangover loomed so large that people, the Indian cricket media included, could not come to terms with the fact that a middle-class man like you could be an achiever.

A: What can I say? At times, I felt certain writers had a bias against me. Maybe what you are saying is correct.

Q: Would India still have won in 1971 had Pataudi led the team?

A: [I] don't think so ... We were getting stale. The team was going nowhere and we needed a change at the helm.

Q: Did Tiger have a hunch about what was going to transpire?

A: I thought he had some inkling, because he had told me that if I became the captain, I should consider picking him in the side. I said the same thing to him. But if you ask me honestly, despite this seeming apprehension about losing, the captaincy, Tiger never seriously thought he could be replaced. His aura was such; I can't blame him for thinking that nobody was good enough to replace him.

Q: That Pataudi eventually did not tour must have come as a relief to you. Could leading him have been hugely uncomfortable for you?

A: No, I was quite used to the SBI [State Bank of India] culture—when a man below your rank gets a promotion, you may take some time to adjust, but the promoted employee must adjust faster than you. Corporate banking tricks say one should never criticize the previous ruler openly. Do not that ever say a bad word about him. For all you know, people working for you may have additional sympathies for the former leader.

Q: Did you ever miss Pataudi the batsman on any of your three overseas tours?

A: I missed him in England in 1974. His presence would have lent experience. I did ask him to come, but he declined. As for my maiden series in the West Indies, I do not think I missed him much. Please remember that had Tiger agreed to come, there would have been no Sardesai. And no Sardesai would have meant no renaissance. (*laughs*)

Q: Did Pataudi ever show signs of being envious of you?

A: Can't say. Look, the first congratulatory telegram in the West Indies came from him. Tiger never said anything openly that might suggest he was jealous. Then again, Tiger was such a private person that even with a glass of beer in hand, he would not open up.

Q: What was your equation like with Motganhalli Jaisimha?

A: Jai was very nice, so it was easy to get along with him. When I visited his room in the West Indies to mention that I had to drop him from the second Test, he took it very sportingly. In a matter-of-fact tone, Jai said, 'I was coming to your room to tell you that if you feel like it, don't consider me.' What an attitude! Jai then opened a bottle of beer and we started drinking. Could you imagine a captain going to a player's room to break the bad news, and after hearing that, the player offers him a drink? Jai was a really big-hearted friend.

'I won't deny that handling Bishan was the most difficult part of my job.'

Q: Did you have problems handling Bedi and think he owed Pataudi his loyalty?

A: I won't deny that handling Bishan was the most difficult part of my job. In Trinidad, despite telling him time and again that he should bowl on the rough, he wouldn't. He wouldn't bowl faster either. Eventually [Salim] Durani made my task easy by removing [Clive] Lloyd and Sobers. I ran into another problem with Bishan at The Oval in 1971. He went wild when after getting [Derek] Underwood's wicket in the very first over, I removed him from the attack. The reasoning behind that decision was a left-hander in John Price had come out to bat. He would have handled Bishan better than a right-arm off-spinner or a leg-spinner. Eventually, Chandra got him, but I could still see Bishan fuming.

Q: Three years later, in London, you had an infamous spat with him.

A: (*Takes a moment*) It was a heated argument which should have been avoided. I actually got very upset when he accused me of not doing enough for the players. The reality was I tried my best to convince the board to reward the players financially, but failed.

Q: Did that lack of trust have a bearing on the overall performance of the team?

A: I would still say the new playing condition introduced by the English was the biggest reason [behind our failure].

Inclement weather was another factor. As for Bishan, at times he clearly disobeyed my instructions. During the Lord's Test, when the England batsmen started going all guns blazing, I asked him to bowl faster and try to control the run flow. Yet, he continued going for wickets and kept imparting flight to his deliveries. He got quite a few wickets in the innings, no doubt, but we ended up giving away over 250 runs. That was unacceptable to me.

Q: Your journey as captain had a touch of drama about it. A sensational start that gave way to consistent success over the next two years, and then suddenly there was the drop. How did you cope with the vicissitudes of captaincy?

A: I do not think that was a drop of any kind, considering I continued to serve Indian cricket in the capacity of a cricket manager and then as the chairman of selectors twice. I have no regrets as I could serve Indian cricket in different capacities for a fairly long time. The only thing that bothered me was the term 'lucky'. How can you get lucky thrice in a row?

C.D. Gopinath

Veteran cricketer C.D. Gopinath was part of the team selection committee in 1971 and remembers the infamous 'casting vote' meeting well. It was a privilege for us to be able to speak to the nonagenarian Mr Gopinath.

Q: You are the lone survivor of the Indian team that recorded the country's first-ever victory in Test cricket against Nigel Howard's MCC, way back in 1952. You are also a living witness of the historical 'casting vote' selection meeting in 1971 that removed Pataudi as the captain of the Indian team. Of course, that was long ago. Five decades have gone by. But are there still any memories left with you?

A: Oh yes (*laughs*). I have been part of so many selection meetings. I was also the chairman of the selection committee for close to five years. But I never saw anything similar to that meeting, where the name of the captain got debated over three hours.

Q: You apparently wanted Pataudi to remain.

A: Yes, I was strongly in favour of Pataudi. I thought India's interests in the West Indies would be served best by Pataudi. Jagdale was with me. But Merchant and Dani disagreed. It came to a standstill. There were two-three breaks in between. But that hardly helped as both parties had stuck to their views. Look, I never knew that Dutta Ray from East Zone wouldn't be there. Had he been there it wouldn't have come to this.

Q: They wanted Wadekar right from the word go?

A: Yes, the chairman did. And Dani went with him. Their logic was that the time had come for a change.

Q: Some reported that Chandu Borde was also in contention for the captaincy and lost out at the last minute?

A: Not true. Borde never figured in our discussions. It was a straight fight between Pataudi and Wadekar.

Q: Can you describe the scenario inside the meeting room?

A: As I said, we kept on debating inside Merchant's office room for hours. I think it began around 6 p.m. and continued up to 9 p.m.

Q: Where does Merchant's office figure in this? The meeting was at the CCI, wasn't it?

A: No, the captain selection happened in his office. It was almost a battle to see which party would give in first. I was certainly not going to concede and made it clear to the chairman.

'MERCHANT DID NOT WANT A CASTING VOTE SITUATION.'

Q: Was Merchant, as the chairman, a bit dictatorial?

A: I don't think he was. In fact, he was trying very hard to resolve this and come to a unanimous decision in favour of Wadekar. Merchant did not want a casting vote situation. I must say, he tried very hard. But I remained steadfast in my resolve and told him that I can't fall in line with his views. I said, please don't force me to give up my views. You go ahead and do what you can do legally.

Q: Subsequently the man you opposed turned the tables on the West Indies and England.

A: Yes (*laughs*). Wadekar did very well as the captain. And I knew I wasn't very popular for my strong views that I expressed at the meeting. But that's what I felt, and that was it.

Q: Apparently, Dilip Sardesai's inclusion was also debated at the subsequent team selection meeting where Wadekar was finally successful in convincing Merchant of said player's abilities.

A: I do not remember that. It may have happened. One thing you must remember is that the selection committee picks the team in advance. People who usually comment on the selection are mostly the ones who get wise after the event. It is easy to do that. Selectors do not enjoy that advantage.

Q: Once Merchant left, you took over as the selection committee chairman around 1972.

A: Yes, I did, and continued for the next five years.

'IN THOSE DAYS, PACERS WERE ONLY REQUIRED TO TAKE THE SHINE OFF THE BALL.'

Q: Reportedly, there was a problem again in 1974, where Wadekar, the captain, demanded two medium pacers for the tour of England. He had also specified who. But the committee led by you turned down the request.

A: (*laughs*) Again, I have to say that I don't recall clearly. But what I can tell you is the selectorial mindset prevailing in those days was quite unlike today's—pacers were only required to take the shine off the ball. After the first 3–4 overs, medium pacers had little role to play. Even someone as good as Dattu Phadkar got picked primarily for his batting. We did not have very good medium pacers in those days, so the combined selectorial thinking was that instead, pick two batsmen who will strengthen your batting if the need arises.

'THE THING THAT STRUCK ME ALMOST IMMEDIATELY WAS THAT [GUNDAPPA VISWANATH] LOOKED SO TECHNICALLY SOUND AND GOT SO MUCH TIME TO PLAY HIS SHOTS. THAT HAS ALWAYS BEEN THE HALLMARK OF GREAT BATSMEN, THAT THEY SOMEHOW FIND ADDITIONAL TIME TO PLAY THEIR SHOTS. I TOLD THE COMMITTEE THAT VISWANATH WAS A SOLID TALENT AND HE MUST BE TRIED.'

Q: You were the first one who spotted Gundappa Viswanath.

A: Yes, I did (*laughs*). I do not remember where I first watched him play. Could be a Duleep Trophy match or a Ranji game. But the thing that struck me almost immediately was that he looked so technically sound and got so much time to play his shots. That has always been the hallmark of great batsmen, that they somehow find additional time to play their shots. I told the committee that Viswanath was a solid talent and he must be tried. But they were not willing to listen and kept on saying that we have not seen him. How could we be convinced about his ability? I retorted that if we have not seen him, that can't be his fault. Then it was decided that the board would invite him to join the squad for the first Test match [in 1969], where the electors would watch him closely at the nets. Once the rest were convinced, he was taken for the second Test in Kanpur. In the first innings, he got a duck, and the rest we all know.

[*Viswanath would go on to score a century in the second innings of his debut Test match, and score over 6,000 Test runs in his illustrious career.*]

Bishan Singh Bedi

(as told to the authors)

We are reminiscing about an achievement that stands tall even fifty years after it became a reality—a truly memorable feat for Indian cricket. But as we jog our minds back to the twin victories of 1971, I would like to offer some views, some of which may seem like a bit of a hard talk, though they reflect what I genuinely felt at the time and continue to even now.

We should have won the series in the West Indies either 2–1 or 2–0. That did not happen because of our captain Ajit Wadekar's defensive captaincy; he was too scared to lose. Somehow, as a routine of sorts, he employed the 'safety-first' tactics, which irritated me no end. At our first team meeting in Kingston, the first time Ajit was addressing us as a group, he told us, 'Boys, we will go all out to draw this Test match.' [Erapalli] Prasanna, [Srinivas] Venkataraghavan and I looked at each other in surprise, wondering if Ajit had indeed just said what we thought he did.

I can understand that trying one's best to not lose the series opener could be the primary aim of some captains. But why shouldn't a team first attempt to win the match? Look, we went one up in Trinidad and had three more Tests to play. But Ajit decided that that was it for us; instead of gunning for further victories, we were to try to hold on to the win we had achieved in the first game. In Jamaica itself we had enforced the follow-on, which proved to be the turning point in the series. Did we try to go for a win? No. In the Barbados Test, we won the toss and asked them to bat first. Can you believe that we did not try to put them on a fourth-innings track? And they scored 501 in the first innings. I was fuming. We just avoided defeat by the skin of our teeth.

'WE SHOULD HAVE WON THE SERIES IN THE WEST INDIES EITHER 2–1 OR 2–0. THAT DID NOT HAPPEN BECAUSE OF OUR CAPTAIN AJIT WADEKAR'S DEFENSIVE CAPTAINCY.'

I will not subscribe to the theory that because the India of the 1970s was still reeling under the colonial hangover, someone like Wadekar, who represented the common Indian man, was looked down upon by his teammates. Absolute nonsense! [Mansoor Ali Khan] Pataudi, too, had his shortcomings, and I have had multiple arguments with him as well. But the beauty of Pataudi as a leader was that he wanted to win, irrespective of who the opposition was. It was he who started the process of winning and cultivated the team spirit that you talk about today—the seeds were sown by Tiger. He brought enormous confidence back in the dressing room. We may have won three series under Wadekar's captaincy, but I did not see too many scribes raving about his captaincy skills. Pataudi, by contrast, was very positive. He would never sledge, shout or scream. He never boasted about his individual achievements, nor would he use the handicap of having to bat with just one eye as an excuse for failure. Not only did he introduce an 'Indianness' to the system, but he also earmarked one day of the week for the team to talk among themselves in Hindi, the language most spoken across the country. No conversations in regional languages were allowed—no Marathi, no Bengali, no Gujarati. I have heard people say Tiger only liked people who spent time with him ... completely untrue! Tiger was too good a human being to fall for such petty things. You have to understand the context in which Tiger imposed his authority. The dressing room at the time was not always unified. I found the West Zone players were too wrapped up among themselves. I am yet to see a great leader emerge from the west. I remember during the Adelaide Test of 1977–78, when [Dilip] Vengsarkar completed his fifty, [Sunil] Gavaskar hollered from the dressing room, 'Well played, Dadar Union!' I was aghast. Dadar Union? What was he saying? It was parochial. 'Damn it,' I told him, 'we are playing for India.' Coming back to Ajit, 'the leader' in him we speak of never existed. He was a dear friend of mine, and his passing did affect me. But during his playing days, reality suggested he was a weak man. His communication abilities were very poor, and what irked me most was the fact that he appeared to be deeply worried about the consequences of defeat. I never refused to bowl on the bowler's footmarks, contrary to the allegations levelled against me. The problem with Ajit was that he was an establishment man. He never fought for the players. It was only at the insistence of Tiger that the players' remuneration was raised from a daily sum of INR 750 to INR 2,000. And it remained 2,000 rupees even when we won three consecutive series. Can you believe that? I do not wish to shower credit on myself, but the fact remains that Bishan Bedi, the captain, and Gavaskar, the vice-captain, sat down to negotiate with the board and got the match fee raised to INR 16,000. Plus the right to hold a benefit match and raise benevolent fund money. Initially, Tiger was instrumental in raising the sum. Ajit was a very good bloke possibly the best of the Bombay boys as far as socializing after the match was concerned. But he was a withdrawn kind of a person; very unsure of himself and rarely inclined to expressing himself courageously in front of people he did not know. I am sorry to say this, but he was not a great leader of men.

Mind you, he was a magnificent left-handed batsman. Magnificent is the only word I have for him. But for such an outstanding player to call it a day so abruptly was difficult to decipher. If you ask me, personally, I felt we did not plan well enough for the series in 1974, which resulted in the undoing of all that we had achieved three years earlier. We deserved to lose. Controversies kept erupting in its aftermath, making the tour a nightmare. As for myself, I had a huge disagreement with Ajit in 1974 at an Indian gentleman's house in England. We were given very poor clothing by the board and did not have decent sweaters to wear. To make matters worse, we were touring in the first half of summer and it was freezing cold. The kitting was really very poor. On the opening day of the tour, we were playing a match in Eastbourne, England, against Derrick Robins's XI. There, we met a Sikh gentleman who was into golf equipment manufacturing. He invited us to his place that evening and gifted a woollen sweater to each of us. He had also given some 30 pounds to each player. It was a substantial amount considering we were woefully short of foreign exchange. We were really grateful to him. Right from the beginning of the tour, Colonel Hemu Adhikari, our manager, had been negotiating with the board to increase our daily allowance. But to no avail. Towards the end of the tour, the board realized that it had to find a scapegoat for this disaster, and the scapegoat was readily available in Bishan Bedi. The board eventually did raise our allowance, but only for the last fifteen days. Yet, they were asking all of us to sign for the amount for the entire tour. Incidentally, the foreign exchange we received was in fact sanctioned by the education ministry of India as we did not have a sports ministry at the time. I felt what we were being asked to do wasn't acceptable by any means. Why should I sign for the entire tour when I had been given the increased amount only for the last fifteen days? They put all sorts of pressure on us. On the team, on myself, on the captain. That is how Ajit was manipulated into saying that I refused to bowl according to the field. Again, how ridiculous could it get? If I had not been bowling according to the field, you could have taken me off the attack—why was I asked to bowl over 64 overs at Lord's? I mean, he was the one who handed me the ball; I do not recall snatching it away from him.

Ajit had complained about me not bowling to my field to the all-powerful Purushottam Das Rungta, popularly known as Bhaiji, who said, 'Bedi is trying to put up a resistance. Let's catch him.' That was the reason I was dropped from the starting XI for the first Test against the West Indies in 1974–75.

I also remember the incident at the Sikh man's house vividly, even though so many years have elapsed. I did not want to talk about it earlier because Ajit was gone, and I felt raking up the past would be of little value. But now that I heard other team members have spoken about it, I thought I must present the story as it unfolded before me. We were having drinks at the Sikh man's place and a slight argument between Ajit and me broke out. Even before we realized, we lost our cool and started arguing a bit loudly. The lady of the house politely requested that we keep our volume down lest it cause inconvenience to the other occupants of the house. She suggested we resolve our differences at the hotel. At this point Ajit suddenly shouted at the lady. I feel embarrassed even talking about it all these years later. After all, he was my captain. I said, 'You ungrateful b*** … You're having a meal at her expense in her house, and you have the audacity to abuse her?'

I went down for breakfast the following day only to find a much-mellowed-down Wadekar. He hugged me and said, 'Paaji, let's forget this.' I was still livid, though, and said, 'Jitu, whatever happened last night, one of us will have to say sorry for it. And I can assure you it's not going to be me.' Colonel Adhikari and most of the team were at the table as we spoke. What had irked me no end was the fact that while I was accusing him of not having done enough for the team, he suddenly said, 'Oh, you want me to get into an argument with the board so that they get sufficiently displeased with me, remove me from captaincy and then you can walk into my shoes? Is that the strategy?' It is strange he would think of me that way, because I was not even vice-captain at the time; Venkat was. The man, as I told you earlier, was very insecure. Colonel Adhikari could bully Jitu as he pleased. Once, when the then high commissioner of India, Mr B.K. Nehru, had refused to let Wadekar into his house because he had arrived late, we had all rallied around our captain. All of us got back into the bus and refused to move because our captain had been insulted. At this point, Adhikari threatened Wadekar, saying, 'I will get your passport impounded.' So Wadekar started crawling. I stood up for Ajit and said that if he agreed to go inside, we would follow him, but none of us would hold a drink in the party. Solkar most likely could not understand what I had said. At the party, Solkar was found holding a glass of brandy and the Bombay boys immediately told him, 'Didn't you hear what Bishan said in the bus? What are you doing?' An embarrassed Solkar quickly put his drink down. I still hold it against the high commissioner. As a top diplomat, he should have handled the situation better. Colonel Adhikari wasn't of much help either. Instead of trying to help broker an understanding between the two parties, he was only busy saving his own skin.

'TO MY MIND, SUNIL GAVASKAR IS THE GREATEST BATSMAN INDIAN CRICKET HAS SEEN.'

Despite all the unsavoury incidents, the twin victories remain immensely special to date. The series announced the arrival of Sunil Gavaskar, who I felt was a complete batsman. And during my time as the Indian cricket manager, I saw Sachin Tendulkar blossom under my eyes. That was an equally special experience. In recent years, we have seen Virat Kohli become a star; he is indeed a jewel in Indian cricket's crown.

I do not want to take away anything from these achievers, but Gavaskar, in my view, was ultra-special. He had the temperament, technique, courage and a will to perform. All these qualities were ingrained in him so deep that you had no other option but to admire him and his skills. To my mind, he is the greatest batsman Indian cricket has seen.

Sunil Gavaskar

We spoke with Sunil Gavaskar multiple times in the course of writing this book. While we have used his quotes throughout the narrative, we felt it was important to also reproduce some of what he said in the form of an interview, giving our readers an insight into his mind.

Q: Do you feel disappointed that the heroics of 1971 have been largely forgotten?

A: No, I don't. The nature of human beings is such that they tend to remember only the recent things. So it is not disappointing at all, and fully understandable.

Q: Can you walk us through the magical winning moment in Trinidad, where you effected the winning stroke?

A: Oh, it was unbelievable—even after all these years. We were chasing only 124 in the fourth innings, and [Syed] Abid

Ali was promoted up the order as he was a fantastic runner. Abid would just chip and run. I thought I was pretty good as a non-striker to respond to quick singles. In Mumbai, we called this 'chipping', and running 'tiffin singles'. Abid came. The singles started happening and quickly, there were a few overthrows. In that desperate state, they were trying to run us out directly. It made our task easy.

Three years later in Manchester, Abid helped me a lot to complete my hundred. I remember taking some singles with him which would not have been possible with some other members of the team. Abid was a fantastic runner, a complete team man, a very sharp bowler and a dangerous batsman. He could cut and pull. And he was a real gutsy cricketer. What a fielder at short fine leg he was! Just amazing. We talk about Eknath Solkar in glowing terms. But trust me, Abid Ali was not too far behind.

Q: In Manchester, your 85-run partnership with him could not save India from defeat. But three years earlier, in the second Test at Port of Spain, your unbeaten 41-run stand with him accorded India a glorious moment of history.

A: Finally, it was Arthur Barrett who was trying to bowl a googly. It was too short and landed halfway down the pitch. I went back and pulled it over mid-wicket for a one-bounce boundary to win us the game. It was unbelievable! Then, walking back and Gary Sobers shaking hands with you—I never thought I would be within hand-shaking distance of Sir Garfield, the greatest ever! And here I was playing against a Sobers and a Rohan Kanhai. An absolute dream come true, it was.

'WALKING BACK [AFTER THE WIN] AND GARY SOBERS SHAKING HANDS WITH YOU—I NEVER THOUGHT I WOULD BE WITHIN HAND-SHAKING DISTANCE OF SIR GARFIELD, THE GREATEST EVER! AND HERE I WAS PLAYING AGAINST A SOBERS AND A ROHAN KANHAI. AN ABSOLUTE DREAM COME TRUE, IT WAS.'

Q: In countries like Australia and England, fans celebrate old cricketing achievements with renewed passion. They fondly talk about the 1948 team, about the achievements of W.G. Grace or go hysterical on Sir Don Bradman's birthday. Why would a victory that was described as the 'Renaissance of Indian Cricket' completely evaporate from public memory in our country?

A: The great Vijay Merchant had said it. He was the chairman of the selection committee, and while the team was getting felicitated in Mumbai after returning from the West Indies, he had said Dilip Sardesai was the 'Renaissance Man of Indian Cricket'. I guess if somebody like Vijay Merchant said it, you have to look at it in that light.

'THE GREAT VIJAY MERCHANT HAD SAID DILIP SARDESAI WAS THE "RENAISSANCE MAN OF INDIAN CRICKET".'

Q: You went on the West Indies tour as a complete rookie, literally unknown, and yet returned with the tag of the 'new superstar'. Some say that when you got back and scored some 70 runs in a relatively insignificant office tournament in Chennai, the stadium was packed to the rafters with fans who just wanted to watch you bat.

A: I actually was not even sure. Look, we had an ACC team that took on the State Bank in a local college ground in Chennai, a team that had so many big names of Indian cricket: Polly Umrigar, Ramakant Desai, Bapu Nadkarni and, possibly, Dilip Sardesai too. It was a star-studded outfit, so it did not strike me that they may have come to see me. But I, of course, remember the crowd. It was daunting as they were huge in number. The whole ground was jam-packed. Some people could not find seats and were standing.

Q: Can you walk us through what your mindset was like in the West Indies? Apparently, after scoring his double hundred, Sardesai pointed towards you in the dressing room and predicted you would also hit two hundreds in the series.

A: If I recall correctly, he had said that on arrival to the immigration officer. Subsequently, he repeated it at a party hosted by a Jamaican Indian. There again he stood up for me. Sardesai's confidence in me was incredible. It was also quite daunting to live up to. Then, when the whole team had gathered at the CCI before the departure, Vijay Merchant, while addressing the team, mentioned me separately by saying that he expected Gavaskar to be a huge success on this tour. I did not know how to handle that. Here I was. I had not even played the Duleep Trophy and yet, the chairman of the selection committee, who also happens to be one of India's all-time best cricketers, was predicting I would be successful on the tour. It was very comforting and uplifting, but unbelievable [at the same time]. Then, of course, there was the captain, who had immense faith in me to have ensured my place in the touring side. But honestly, it is not easy to recollect what exactly had happened fifty years ago, and I am no spring chicken. All I can tell you is that my cricket before leaving for the West Indies was a kind of step-by-step progression; say, from the Bombay school [of cricket] to the West Zone school; from the West Zone school to the India school. But here I was, only four Ranji matches old and with no Duleep Trophy experience, going to play against the West Indies. In between, a step was missing, and a very vital one—the Duleep Trophy. [In] Those days, all the top players turned out for Duleep matches. It was quite a severe examination of your skill and temperament. That was at the back of my mind when I left for the West Indies, [with] a little bit of uncertainty.

Q: Subsequently, the world-record tally of 774 happened in your debut series. Was it a huge cross to bear?

A: There is no denying the fact that expectations had turned sky high. Till then, they may have expected a good performance, but not so much. In a debut series, such a fabulous performance had been recorded only by Sir Don Bradman. So they expected something similar every time. But it was not possible to replicate it all the time.

Q: Did the three years you went century-less affect your mindset?

A: We played only two series in those three years. One against England in England. And then when we played them at home. After that, there was nothing. So there weren't any misgivings that I had lost it all. But yes, there were question marks even in my mind as I was not scoring enough even at the domestic level.

Q: At a recent cricket function, former tennis player and commentator Vijay Amritraj said you must have been under severe pressure following your early success. For a developing country riddled with insecurities, growing unemployment and self-doubts, your winning performances were perceived to be the only glimmer of hope.

A: Well, I never thought about it from that perspective. These are the things that really got talked about much later when I finished—what kind of pressure the country was under and all that. The most important factor was that I loved cricket immensely. I loved playing the game. I still love the game. Well, I was certainly aware of the expectations following my debut series, but nobody had vocalized it from this perspective.

'THE PROPOSITION THAT INDIANS CAN'T PLAY FAST BOWLING WAS STARTED BY THE BRITISH PRESS.'

Q: Imran Khan repeatedly said, and this was echoed by others, that before you, Indians could not play fast bowling well. At some stage, did you set out to change this perception?

A: The proposition that Indians can't play fast bowling was started by the British press. You show me a team, including England, that can play quality fast bowling. No team can master good fast bowling. Look at the success India have had of late. It is only because we have a pair of good fast bowlers. What about England against the West Indies in the 1980s? Did anybody ever say the English can't play fast bowling? When the Australians got hammered by the West Indies, did anybody say Australian batsmen can't handle fast bowling? I don't think so. You can tell that this was a myth created by interested parties against India. Nobody generalized the failures of other teams in this manner.

Q: What's your take on Merchant's historical casting-vote, which was debated for several years? How different were the two captains—Pataudi and Wadekar—in your opinion?

A: I don't know what the casting-vote situation was. At that stage I was wanting to make it to the Indian team, and the captaincy issue hardly occupied my thinking. All I remember was that nobody expected a change. People thought Tiger Pataudi would carry on. And, as it happens, whenever a casting-vote situation arises, the chairman takes all the blame. No one talked about the other two selectors who also voted for Wadekar, besides Merchant. As for Ajit's captaincy, I had played under him in Bombay. We hero-worshipped Ajit. Very seldom would a weekend pass without Ajit getting a hundred in club or office matches. It was a regular feature ... he was a tremendous batsman. He had a laid-back air about him but deep inside was very steely, otherwise he could not have scored all those runs. Same went for his captaincy. From the outside, he had this laid-back persona but was actually very sharp. He knew exactly what to do and when. Wadekar's management skills were superb. The way he looked after the younger players and scolded them whenever necessary was exemplary. When I broke my bat in Barbados, he gave me his brand-new bat. We always wanted to do something special for him. He had a unique way of captaining the team.

As for Pataudi, I only played two Test matches under him, so it would be unfair for me to comment. But there is no doubt that he was charismatic and had an aura about him. Tiger was a lovely guy. When he came back in the team during the 1972–73 series against Tony Lewis's MCC side, we got along really well.

'THE MEDIA'S RELUCTANCE TO GIVE AJIT HIS DUE WAS ONE OF THE SADDEST THINGS IN INDIAN CRICKET.'

Q: The media of the 1970s, despite the twin series wins, kept describing Wadekar as a 'lucky' captain. Did the tribe suffer from a colonial hangover in that they could not accept the fact that a commoner was leading the team to glory?

A: Absolutely. Their reluctance to give Ajit his due was one of the saddest things in Indian cricket. They gave him virtually no credit at all and called him lucky. Now, tell me, what was lucky about his wins? I fail to understand what was lucky about his captaincy. His team, like other Indian teams touring abroad in that era, had to bear the brunt of very biased umpiring. At the Lord's Test, Ray Illingworth was plumb leg before to Chandra [B.S. Chandrasekhar] and was given not out. If we had got him at that stage, India would have won the Test that ultimately ended as a rain-affected draw.

Q: In 1992, Wadekar was brought back as the cricket manager to reshape the game in India. He achieved success in that work. Some say you played a role in it.

A: No, I had no role at all. But all I can say is that despite Wadekar doing so well as the cricket manager, he was unnecessarily removed in 1996. Indian cricket those days had a culture, *ki usne itne din kiya, abhi dusra kisiko chance de do* (he did it for so long, now give someone else the chance). It had hardly anything to do with meritocracy; only regional considerations prevailed.

Q: Gundappa Viswanath told us about a team culture that Wadekar introduced—every evening there used to be a session in his room where anyone could walk in. This was where juniors and seniors participated merrily. Did it help bridge the gap between generations and foster team spirit?

A: Those hotel rooms were not five stars but more like the hotel rooms of old. Some of the players would sit on the sofa, some on the floor, some on the carpet. They would enjoy each other's company. These gatherings would help enormously in team-bonding. Even when the seniors were playing cards and you were sitting in the sidelines, the topic that was invariably discussed was cricket. There was never any deviation. A junior could learn so much from those cricketing stories.

Q: Despite the hattrick of victories, the mistrust between the West Zone players and others remained unabated. Did you find it unfortunate that it led to a strange environment within the team, where the captain (Wadekar) and a senior player (Bedi) almost came to blows in England in 1974?

A: Yes, it was [sad]. It is hard to know what was the genesis of the argument [or] how it started, but it was ugly with two seniors shouting and screaming at each other. This did not leave a good taste in the mouth. This east-north-south thing—I did not know. I do not remember having looked at someone as [being] from the east or north or south or central, whether he was a Sikh or a Christian or a Muslim or a Hindu. I only looked at how good they were as cricketers; I still do.

Q: According to eyewitness accounts, Wadekar kept accusing the team members of being 'Pataudi's men', and it angered Bedi considerably. Since this was at the beginning of the tour, the team's unity reportedly took a hit and it may have also affected the performances.

A: It was not very pleasant. This was possibly on the first day of the tour match. But I do not agree that our performance on the tour was influenced by this incident. Maybe the two people involved in the incident could not forget [it]. But the rest of us remained focused to play the best we could. You can't say we lost because of that. It was one of those incredibly wet English summers and we were just caught on that against a top-class bowling attack.

Q: Rohan, your son, shared with us that since the Sudhir Naik incident in 1974 (Naik was accused of shoplifting a pair of socks from Marks & Spencer), you have never stepped into a Marks & Spencer outlet. Is this true?

A: Yes, in the last forty-six years, maybe twice or thrice. That too for carrying the wife's bag (*laughs*). But I have never bought anything from there.

Q: Has it been a silent protest against the allegations levelled at Naik?

A: Absolutely. It was totally unfair. Sudhir was given the wrong advice to plead guilty, and that left a stain that was very hard to remove. I have known Sudhir all these years, from the time we played tennis-ball cricket against each other. I felt very strongly about him. We lived nearby. I didn't think he was ever capable of shoplifting. And after the incident, I asked Colonel Adhikari to allow me to share the room with him because I do not remember who it was, but the person said he was too embarrassed to share a room with Sudhir. I picked up a lot of calls coming to the room where the abuse started straight away. I tried to shield him from all that.

'AFTER OUR WIN IN TRINIDAD, THE WEST INDIES CAME BACK VERY HARD AT US.'

Q: Coming back to the twin victories of the West Indies and England in 1971—did they play a part in boosting India's confidence ahead of the wins at the MCG in 1981, the World Cup triumph in 1983 and the Benson & Hedges World Championship of Cricket win in 1985?

A: Oh yes, in that respect the '71 victory was huge. Mind you, after our win in Trinidad, the West Indies came back very hard at us. Sobers himself was under a lot of pressure at home because he had gone to play an exhibition double-wicket game in Rhodesia. He was under a lot of stress, as a result of which he was not only bowling faster but batting magically. So, there was an increased pressure on our team to maintain the lead and win the series. Once we succeeded in doing that, it gave the whole team a lot of confidence for the English tour. [The win in] 1981 was also a defining moment, as again there were multiple moments where the going got extremely tough. To start with, to get past the pathetic umpiring standards. In my very first year in international cricket, I had the good fortune of touring three countries—the West Indies, England and subsequently Australia—turning out for the Rest of the World. The standard of umpiring I saw in these countries was appalling. And, more importantly, it was so biased. But for some strange reason, our media— whenever they toured—never highlighted the umpiring standards that the team was subjected to. In comparison the foreign media, be it England or Australia, acted as if they were the extra support staff of the team. I never understood the reluctance of our media to highlight the dubious umpiring standards. They seemed so shy, as if it was a worry that if they wrote anything against [the umpiring], the home board would not accord them the necessary accreditation, or whatever reasons that I don't understand. I am not saying that you cook up stories. But what prevents you from pointing out realities? In 1981, right from the first game, the umpiring was ridiculous. Absolutely pathetic. We just managed to draw the second Test, which was preceded by some terrible umpiring decisions. At the press conference, I said all those who come to India and talk about Indian umpiring are nothing but whiners and moaners.

The next day, that was the headline. That time also nobody had objected to the umpiring decisions. Neither the media nor our own board. So when it came to the final Test, towards the end of the match we thought we were in a very good position. Despite Australia chasing a relatively small total of 142 in the fourth innings, it wasn't easy as the pitch had started deteriorating. So considering everything, it was a huge victory. At least we did not lose the series and won for the first time in Australia.

'IN MY VERY FIRST YEAR IN INTERNATIONAL CRICKET, I HAD THE GOOD FORTUNE OF TOURING THREE COUNTRIES—THE WEST INDIES, ENGLAND AND SUBSEQUENTLY AUSTRALIA— TURNING OUT FOR THE REST OF THE WORLD. THE STANDARD OF UMPIRING I SAW IN THESE COUNTRIES WAS APPALLING.'

Q: Now 1985.

A: In my view, the 1985 Indian team was probably the best ever Indian one-day side apart from the 2011 World Cup winning team. If you were to have a match between these two sides, 2011 and my 1985 team, it would be a fantastic game of cricket.

Q: Is there a common thread between 1971, 1983 and 1985? Should they even be compared?

A: No, you can't compare Test cricket and one-day cricket.

Q: How does it feel to be associated with some of the most defining moments in Indian cricket?

A: I feel fortunate. I feel blessed that I have been around at that time. Also the fact that I could rub shoulders with some of the giants of the game, both from India and outside.

Q: Finally, between the twin victories of 1971, which one was more special?

A: It has to be England, as the conditions were completely different. In the West Indies, you had bounce but little grass. Compared to that, England presented a bigger challenge. Definitely, the win in England was something to savour.

Syed Abid Ali

Q: You were at the centre of two of Indian cricket's greatest moments—first, in March 1971, in the second Test against the West Indies in Port of Spain, and five months later, in the series decider against England at The Oval. Fifty years on, how do you look back on those victories?

A: At The Oval, I hit the winning stroke and, at Port of Spain, I allowed Sunil [Gavaskar] to hit it. I had ample opportunities to finish the match at Port of Spain myself, but restrained myself from doing so. [Garfield] Sobers had bowled a full toss and I played it for a single, which allowed Sunil to get back on strike to Arthur Barrett. He was a little surprised and asked me, 'Why did you do it?' I said, 'Sunil, you have batted so well in this Test that you deserve it.'

'I ALLOWED SUNIL GAVASKAR TO HIT THE WINNING STROKE AT PORT OF SPAIN ... I SAID, "SUNIL, YOU HAVE BATTED SO WELL IN THIS TEST THAT YOU DESERVE IT."'

Q: Many believe that at 2.42 p.m. on 24 August 1971, when you cut England's Brian Luckhurst to the boundary for the winning runs at The Oval, Indian cricket achieved its independence.

A: Yes, that was certainly memorable. But what had irritated me then was the fact that Farokh Engineer came running to me from the non-striker's end to tell me to take a single. He wanted to hit the winning stroke. I found it strange and saw no need to listen to him. I thought it was important that an Indian was hitting the winning stroke. It did not matter whether his name was Abid or Farokh. Till date, I have not understood why personal glory was more important than the nation's pride.

'AT THE OVAL, FAROKH ENGINEER WANTED TO HIT THE WINNING STROKE.'

Q: Is there any other incident you often call to mind from the Test against England?

A: During England's second innings, [Dilip] Sardesai had dropped two easy catches. As luck would have it, both were off my bowling. I went to our captain, Ajit Wadekar, and told him, 'Please get [Kenia] Jayantilal in. He would any day be a safer option.' Accordingly, Sardesai soon started limping and went off the ground. Jayanti came in [as a substitute fielder] and took a very good catch in the outfield.

Q: The 1971 series victories against the West Indies and England marked a transition in Indian the cricket as captaincy changed hands. Did it have any impact on the team culture?

A: Even after so many years, I feel sad to state the truth—that the team, despite winning, was divided into two groups, the West Zone boys and the rest. This divide did no good to the team. After the team had returned, the *Times of India* had organized a sort of donation camp to raise money for the players. Mafatlal Mills had done something similar. Film star Dharmendra threw a party for the team. The rest of the team were kept out of all these [felicitations and celebrations] and only the West Zone boys were involved. I still don't understand why this happened. There is no denying the fact that the West Zone players had performed tremendously. But they also had people supporting them well enough. After all, eleven players were playing for one team called India.

Q: After three consecutive series wins, what led to the disastrous England tour of 1974, where India lost the Test series 3–0 and the ODI series 2–0?

A: You would not believe that we went to England a day later than what was earlier scheduled. An astrologer had told Ajit that if we delayed our journey by a day, we would do well. He had cautioned our captain that if we left on the scheduled date of departure, we would lose badly. Ajit was very weak about stars and planetary positions. He gave in and we departed a day later. When we eventually landed at Heathrow, there was only one man from the English board who had come to receive us at the airport. You know, I respected Ajit a lot. He was a good guy, but at this age of my life, I feel the truth had to be told at some stage.

'WE WENT TO ENGLAND A DAY LATER THAN WHAT WAS EARLIER SCHEDULED [IN 1974]. AN ASTROLOGER HAD TOLD AJIT THAT IF WE DELAYED OUR JOURNEY BY A DAY, WE WOULD DO WELL.'

Q: What about Lieutenant Colonel Hemu Adhikari, the manager? His role had raised a few eyebrows.

A: I found some of the West Zone players a little selfish in the way they conducted themselves and stuck to their own group. As the manager of the team, Colonel Adhikari did little to address that. He had caught one of the West Zone players red-handed, kissing a woman openly on the street. The concerned player was summoned and warned. But had he been from any other zone, he would have been sent back then and there, and not played for India again. Clearly, double standards were practised.

Q: The tour was forgettable for India, but you had a century partnership with Gavaskar in the first innings of the opening Test in Manchester.

A: Gavaskar was a very special player. He had immense concentration and unbelievable confidence in himself. In Manchester, when I came out to bat, he said, 'I want to get my first-ever hundred on English soil.' I said, 'Not to worry, Sunil. I will support you.' And I did.

'TIGER [PATAUDI] NEVER PLAYED FOR HIMSELF. I CAN'T IMAGINE TIGER PLAYING POLITICS WITH ANYBODY.'

Q: Had Mansoor Ali Khan Pataudi gone on that tour, do you reckon things might have been different?

A: Some difference would surely have been felt as Tiger [Pataudi] never played for himself. Tiger may have had some close people around him all the time, but I can't imagine Tiger playing politics with anybody.

Q: You seemed to have taken the 1974 hurt very badly.

A: How can you forget the humiliation which came after three series wins? All sorts of unfortunate incidents came our way. On the second day of the tour, a gentleman called Stuart Surridge came over to see us in London. He played cricket and also owned a cricket goods shop. He got some of us to sign a bat contract. We were given two bats each. Soon, we discovered these were rotten bats. I quickly procured a Gray-Nicolls bat and used it at the nets. Stuart's son noticed this and got angry. He confronted me by saying, 'Why are you playing with this bat? You have signed a contract with my dad.' Then his father surfaced at Lord's and threatened, 'I will take you to court.' I said, 'Go ahead.' Such incidents took away the morale of the side. It was disastrous right from the word go.

Q: Did the failure of 1974 somewhat dull the highs of 1971?

A: Yes. What we eventually realized was that despite the hat-trick of wins, it [1971] never made us a composite side.

Erapalli Prasanna

Q: The euphoria about the twin wins of 1971 got somewhat marred by the controversy surrounding your exclusion from the playing eleven in England. In your autobiography, *One More Over*, you lambasted the management.

A: The hurt is nearly fifty years old, but it still burns. I thought I was treated very harshly. At The Oval, how I wish I had had a role to play! How could they not play me there? Tiger [Pataudi] told me later on that he was very surprised that I was not played. What I still find baffling is that based on my performances in the tour games, both John Arlott and Jim Laker wanted me to play for their counties. Yet, they were fed all sorts of wrong information about me that my shoulder was gone, my bowling arm was gone, etc. All of this was the handiwork of the team management.

Q: We are very surprised to hear this, considering the fact that you shared a very warm relationship with the late Ajit

Wadekar even after retirement. You even went to Mumbai to attend his memorial.

A: We remained very good friends. But while he was the captain, Jitiya allowed himself to get ruled by the manager of our team, Colonel Adhikari. I exposed the duo in my book and till today have no regrets on that count.

Q: Did you ask them why you weren't playing?

A: They had a very strange system. Half the time they wouldn't communicate with me directly. At times they communicated through Govindraj. Maybe they felt guilty about the whole thing.

Q: Once again, considering the deep personal connect you had with Wadekar, the comments are surprising.

A: I am telling you, Ajit presented himself as a very weak person in the presence of Colonel Adhikari. Bishan [Bedi], for one, did not endorse this at all. He fought with Ajit at the breakfast table over my exclusion.

'I WAS SHOCKED TO HEAR THAT TIGER [PATAUDI] HAD GOT REPLACED [AS CAPTAIN]. WITH AJIT [WADEKAR] COMING IN AS THE CAPTAIN, THERE WAS A SEA CHANGE. I SUDDENLY FELT WE WERE A LITTLE DEFENSIVE. I COULDN'T ALWAYS DO WHAT I WANTED TO DO.'

Q: But in 1974, when India toured England again, the same team management did play you.

A: Yes, I was played in the second and third Test. You can say I was made the sacrificial goat. The place was handed over to me as a consolation prize. I thought that after losing the first Test, fearing a further backlash, they added me to the team. It had no connection with cricketing logic.

Q: They say Adhikari was a strict disciplinarian.

A: What discipline? All this talk means little to me as once I spotted him drinking at 11 p.m. in the hotel bar. As manager, he was so opposed to the players' interests that when I became manager of the Indian team, for the World Championship of Cricket in 1985, I did exactly the opposite of what Adhikari used to do.

Q: Was there a divide between Wadekar and Pataudi loyalists?

A: Yes, and the captaincy change had created a confusion in the bowlers' minds. I was shocked to hear that Tiger had got replaced. With Ajit coming in as the captain, there was a sea change. I suddenly felt we were a little defensive. I couldn't always do what I wanted to. In Jamaica in 1971, I asked for and only then got a forward short leg for Sobers. The seniors were stunned. Then in the 1972–73 series against the MCC, I remember a moment where Ajit, after handing me the ball said, '*Pakar ke pakar ke.*' I said, 'What pakar ke? Let me try and win the Test for you—and I did. You know, had Chandra been there in '71 in the West Indies, we would have won the series 3–0! And Ajit did say this a number of times: that we are all Pataudi's men.

'Had Chandra [Bhagwat Chandrasekhar] been there in '71 in the West Indies, we would have won the series 3–0!'

Q: But as a captain, Wadekar was successful.

A: Well, Jitiya was the epitome of the West Zone philosophy of cricket. It said, play it safe. Play it hard. Don't give away easy runs.

Q: Why were you so fascinated by Pataudi? Are you sure it was not the Raj hangover?

A: What are you saying! Tiger could think five steps ahead. He believed in logic. The media had asked him about his preference for me over Venkat [Srinivas Venkataraghavan] and he had explained it beautifully. He had said that Venkat had a chance of getting his wickets mostly in two places. Forward short leg and in the slips. With Pras, you can expect to get a wicket in silly point, mid-off, mid-on, deep fine leg, forward short leg and the slips. The whole ground is basically at his disposal for a wicket-taking opportunity. Now you tell me, who should you play?

Q: But Pataudi could not achieve what Wadekar did.

A: I differ with you there. In any case, our first overseas triumph was under Tiger in New Zealand. To me the golden era of Indian cricket began from there and 1971 was only a significant extension.

Q: Some say that Pataudi was standoffish and distant.

A: Not at all. In fact, before meeting him I had certain notions that nawabs are snooty and [he] will invariably wear a huge turban (*laughs*). They will be six feet tall. How wrong I was! In reality, it was so pleasant to discover that this prince did not have an attitude. He never imposed himself on the team.

Q: To you, what were the defining moments of the 1971 win against the West Indies?

A: There were quite a few. Gavaskar's batting, of course. How the spinners encountered Sir Gary was also important in the overall context. In Jamaica we had scored 300 in a day. We were very happy that finally we had been able to handle the West Indies' attack. In Jamaica, in the tour opener, I had bowled my heart out for 30 overs. Sobers came up to me after the day's play and said, 'Well bowled.' Those days he used to drive a white Jaguar. Before he left, he told Ghulam Ahmed, who happened to be there, 'Take good care of this boy.' I was touched. But for me, the real defining moment of the series was Salim Durani's spell in the Trinidad Test. 'Uncle Salim', as we used to lovingly call him, was as good an all-rounder as Kapil Dev or Vinoo Mankad. I wish he could play the IPL for the modern generation to understand his worth. I used to marvel at his confidence and ability. For some reason he was never promoted by Tiger. I felt it was wrong.

Q: Viswanath confirmed to us that he [Durani] claimed he would get both Sobers and Lloyd out, which he did.

A: Of course he did. As a matter of fact, this happened in front of us all. Uncle Salim told me and Jai [M. Jaisimha] the evening before, over drinks, that 'Ask Jitiya to give me the ball and I shall remove both Sobers and Lloyd.' Jai went and told Ajit and the rest is history. He was an amazing cricketer.

> '[WADEKAR] WAS THE EPITOME OF THE WEST ZONE PHILOSOPHY OF CRICKET. IT SAID, PLAY IT SAFE. PLAY IT HARD. DON'T GIVE AWAY EASY RUNS.'

Q: Before we close, please answer this. Post all these accusations and allegations, how much did your personal relationship with Wadekar suffer?

A: Initially it did, but we remained good friends throughout. We have had so many drinking sessions together. So many get-togethers. Yes, it is a fact that he allowed himself to get dictated to by Adhikari but deep inside he had loads of respect for me and it was reciprocal. I still feel very sad that he suddenly passed away.

Bhagwat Chandrasekhar

Q: Please take us through that all-important day at The Oval.

A: When I wasn't picked for the West Indies tour months before the English one, I was very disappointed. The Oval, I thought, was a vital Test match for me. If I hadn't done well, I may have been dropped yet again. The John Jameson run-out in the second innings was the turning point. Then I got John Edrich and subsequently Fletcher. I was turning back towards my run-up when [Dilip] Sardesai shouted, 'Isko Mildred dal.' Mildred, incidentally, was a horse which had recently won a race. What he meant was, try and bowl faster. The next delivery got Luckhurst.

'I WAS TURNING BACK TOWARDS MY RUN-UP WHEN SARDESAI SHOUTED, 'ISKO MILDRED DAL.' ... WHAT HE MEANT WAS, TRY AND BOWL FASTER. THE NEXT DELIVERY GOT LUCKHURST.'

Q: India in their previous tours had not won any of the 19 Tests they had played in England since the inaugural Test in 1932. This was a watershed win in every sense.

A: Yes, the win was very special. People talk a lot about my 6 for 38, but I must say a huge amount of credit is due to the late Eknath Solkar. I am very grateful to Solkar for holding on to some of those unbelievable catches. Solkar at forward short leg was a great help to each of the spinners.

Q: How different were the captaincy styles of Pataudi and Wadekar? You had won matches for both.

A: Tiger [Pataudi] was more attacking. Wadekar in comparison was more orthodox.

'People talk a lot about my 6 for 38 [at The Oval] but I must say a huge amount of credit is due to the late Eknath Solkar. I am very grateful to Solkar for holding on to some of those unbelievable catches.'

Q: There is a saying that Pataudi used to set the field on his own and most of the time did not ask the bowlers what they wanted.

A: Yes, there is truth in that, but I was quite happy with the close-in fielders he gave me. Slips, forward short leg, leg slip. He had very good game sense. At Eden Gardens in 1974–75, we were in a difficult situation against the West Indies. I started the day badly and bowled two expensive overs. While I was going back to third man, knowing I would be replaced, Tiger called me and said I would continue. Next over I got

Lloyd, Kalicharan and then Julian. Tiger, I always felt, had a gambler's instinct.

Q: It was often said that forget the batsmen, even Chandra did not know what he was bowling.

A: Absolute rubbish. Of course I knew what I was bowling; this was some people's way of undermining my achievements.

'TIGER [PATAUDI], I ALWAYS FELT, HAD A GAMBLER'S INSTINCT… HE HAD VERY GOOD GAME SENSE.'

Q: At that pace it must have been very difficult for keepers to stand up to you?

A: It was. And I would give lot of credit to Farokh [Engineer] and Kiri [Syed Kirmani] as they kept brilliantly to me. With that pace I was also able to spin the ball. So, it must have been difficult. But both managed it admirably.

Q: From the high of 1971, India fell by the wayside in 1974. What, according to you, went wrong?

A: It happens in cricket. You can't keep winning all the time. But yes, something went wrong somewhere; but I think for your book you should focus more on the good rather than the bad!

Q: What has been your best cricketing memory?

A: The Oval is the best memory for sure. We had not only won the Test but also the series. I still have that special ball with me.

Q: Did you ever go to The Oval to relive those memories?

A: Yes, I did, a few years ago. I remembered bowling that spell from the Vauxhall end. Memories were flooding back. The ground has changed a lot, but the memories remain fresh.

Q: Did anyone recognize you?

A: No. I just walked around along with a friend of mine.

Q: It must have been very nostalgic?

A: Yes, it was.

'The Oval is the best memory for sure. I still have that special ball with me.'

Srinivas Venkataraghavan

Q: Old-timers talk about the enormous contribution of Eknath Solkar towards the success of the four spinners. How good was Solkar?

A: He was phenomenal. If you had him, it was like we had two extra fielders.

Q: Looking back, how special was 1971?

A: 1971 was a watershed year. When we first landed in the West Indies, no one gave us a chance. They said that a club side has come. In Montego Bay, Lawrence Rowe and Alvin Kalicharan both were playing in one of the early tour games. I took Kali early and Bish [Bishan Singh Bedi] got Rowe. Because of the failures they did not get a look in at the Test series. I thought that was one of the defining points of the tour.

'1971 was a watershed year. When we first landed in the West Indies, no one gave us a chance.'

Q: Any other defining points?

A: The turning point, according to me, came in Jamaica when Ajit [Wadekar] asked Sobers to follow on. I had suggested the same to Ajit as the Test had got reduced to four days, so the follow-on margin had also come down from 200 to 150. Sobers hadn't noticed it. He checked with the umpire and Sang Hue informed him that 150 was indeed the follow-on margin.

Q: Overall, how would you describe the series?

A: We played very well throughout and they were clearly caught napping. We had an opportunity to win and go 2–0 ahead in the series. But the captain decided to bring down the shutters. We didn't want to take a chance and I don't blame him.

'The turning point came in Jamaica when Ajit [Wadekar] asked Sobers to follow on.'

Q: Sunil Gavaskar shone remarkably in the series. What are your memories of him?

A: The way Sunil approached the game, and the way he approached batting overall, was stunning. I remember watching him for the first time in Madras in a university tournament. He had created an impression. In fact, it is inexplicable why Sunil did not get more runs in England in the next series. Maybe the expectations were too high.

Q: A word on the late Dilip Sardesai's performance?

A: Sardesai in the West Indies was a revelation. The resurgence of his batting made us believe that we could beat the West Indies in the West Indies. Contrary to what some people said, I felt Sardesai was a very good batsman against fast bowling. Before this series, the West Indies was a mental block for us. We not only overcame that but if the ICC had a rating system, then post The Oval Test we would have been ranked number one in the world.

Q: What was the difference between the two leaders you played under, Pataudi and Wadekar?

A: Tiger was charismatic. But Ajit was down to earth and pragmatic. He was prepared to speak to even the junior-most member and offer his inputs. Wish I had the same luck as Ajit on the 1979 tour of England. Despite Sunil's double hundred in the second innings, we very narrowly missed the target. The thought haunted me for a long time that had either Kapil or Viswanath stayed a little longer we could have easily won.

'THE RESURGENCE OF [SARDESAI'S] BATTING MADE US BELIEVE THAT WE COULD BEAT THE WEST INDIES IN THE WEST INDIES.'

Q: We have heard a lot of stories about manager Hemu Adhikari. How far are these true?

A: No matter what anyone tells you, Hemu Adhikari was very good. I have fond memories of him.

Q: You had a constant battle with Prasanna to get into the final XI. Almost every time he got dropped there was a controversy.

A: Go back and check the stats. I only played because of my performances. Even after fifty years the record stays.

Q: Did these controversies hurt?

A: Yes, to a great extent. But they also pushed me to do better. In the West Indies I had topped the bowling averages. In The Oval Test I got the maximum number of wickets in the first innings. I was also involved in a vital 50-run partnership with Abid in our first innings.

'AJIT [WADEKAR] WAS DOWN TO EARTH AND PRAGMATIC. [I] WISH I HAD THE SAME LUCK AS AJIT.'

Q: You were always known as one of the best thinkers of the game. Looking back, how do you analyse the disaster of 1974?

A: The playing conditions were changed before the series had begun, without informing the team. It was shocking and reduced the effectiveness of our spin attack. Then the weather remained cold throughout. Wickets were seam friendly. Mind you, England was a good side and had some excellent seamers. Yet, I still feel we could have drawn two out of the three Tests. Sadly, things turned out much worse.

Kenia Jayantilal

Many in India believed that Kenia Jayantilal should have played a lot many more games. In the only game he played in 1971 in the West Indies, he got out for zero to a very good catch, and then Sunil Gavaskar took over the opener's slot from the next Test. In Gavaskar's case, Sir Garfield Sobers dropped a very easy catch of his, and the rest is history. That's why you always need an element of luck in sports—Jayantilal clearly did not have it.

Q: The West Indies tour was your first one with the Indian team. Can you walk us through the experience?

A: The initial reactions our arrival generated were pretty negative. Their media and the local cricket authorities behaved as if a club side had come from India. The inclusion of many fresh faces in the side was possibly the reason.

Q: You got just one innings in Test cricket and never played again. How hard was that for you to accept?

A: Very difficult. You know, luck plays such a huge role in a one-ball sport like cricket. Sir Garfield Sobers, in the first Test, took an out-of-this-world, one-handed catch to dismiss me. Yet, he dropped Sunil's relatively easy catch standing in the same position.

Q: Why couldn't you find a place in the remaining Tests, considering that you only got one opportunity to prove yourself?

A: After I got a good score in the tour game against Guyana, Rohan Kanhai came up to me and said, 'You are playing in the next Test.' When that did not happen, Kanhai tried his best to console me.

Q: He had become that friendly with you?

A: Yes, for a player as big as Rohan Kanhai, he had no airs. He used to join us in our drinking sessions. Interestingly, Kanhai used to understand a bit of Hindi, so we were clearly told by the seniors that irrespective of what you say, in the presence of Kanhai, do not talk strategy, even in Hindi.

'WADEKAR RELIED TOO MUCH ON SARDESAI. AT TIMES, I FELT SARDESAI WAS THE VICE-CAPTAIN AND NOT VENKAT.'

Q: How frustrating was it to sit out even in the next tour?

A: It was very frustrating. I thought at some stage, captain [Ajit] Wadekar would be convinced of my claims. But he relied too much on [Dilip] Sardesai. At times, I felt Sardesai was the vice-captain and not Venkat [Srinivas Venkataraghavan].

Based on Sardesai's suggestion, Ajit kept playing Ashok Mankad, who was practically failing in every Test.

Q: A few members in the team felt there was a powerful West Zone lobby that existed within the setup. How far was this true?

A: Yes, there used to be a lobby and they clearly seemed very happy in each other's company.

Q: You and Mansoor Ali Khan Pataudi played in the same team for Hyderabad. What was it like playing with him?

A: Oh, Pataudi was a class apart. Most of the time he wouldn't even ask the bowler for his field preferences and go on to set the field himself. His understanding of the game was so solid. I remember one tough Ranji game against Madras on their home turf—Venkat and V.V. Kumar were bowling at their best. Pataudi came out to bat and I was at the other end, looking tentative. The ball was turning square. Pataudi told me coolly, '*Apna game khelo* (Play your own game),' and went about his business. I found that highly impressive.

'PATAUDI WAS A CLASS APART. HIS UNDERSTANDING OF THE GAME WAS SO SOLID.'

Q: What was the experience of travelling to England on your second overseas tour like?

A: England presented completely different conditions. It was wet and seam-friendly. I remember in the Manchester Test, Sardesai played on the front foot to a delivery, pitching outside the off-stump, and the ball moved just enough to dislodge the leg-stump. Though I did not play in any of the

Test matches, I had a feel as a substitute fielder in the Oval Test. Sardesai was instructed by the captain to start limping so that he, an average fielder, could go out, and I, the twelfth man, could come in. I did take [Basil] D'Oliveira's catch in the outfield. I felt that at least was some contribution from me towards the win.

Salim Durani

Q: Despite a match-winning partnership in England, you weren't picked for the 1971 English tour. Did you find that strange?

A: Strange is an understatement. It was a massive disappointment and has stayed with me ever since. I ended my career without playing in [1971 in] England.

Q: The explanation given was that you and Motganhalli Jaisimha did not get enough runs on the Caribbean tour.

A: I would think we got dropped because [Vijay] Merchant had this vision of grooming youngsters. He should have considered the reality—that we were going to England, where experience mattered. As for not getting runs, yes, I disappointed myself, but I did get a hundred in the four-day game against Jamaica before the first Test. This has happened with me so many times that—I performed and immediately got dropped. Once, in a Brabourne Test match, I got 55 and then they dropped me. In the 1972–73 series in Kolkata, I got decent runs in both the innings. Yet, they dropped me from the next Test. But this exclusion hit me the hardest. Even my mother and the family were shattered.

Q: Some people say that your captains, including Mansoor Ali Khan Pataudi, were never very vocal in terms of supporting you at the selection meetings.

A: I know some said that after I did not find a place in the '67 tour of England. But I won't agree with that. Tiger [Pataudi] was a fine man, a good captain and he wasn't the type who would backstab.

Q: What were your initial thoughts when you landed in the West Indies with Ajit Wadekar's team, armed with the experience of the previous tour in 1962?

A: The most important difference was that the quality of their bowling had deteriorated considerably. That was one reason why they did not stand a chance of beating us. You can't call [Vanburn] Holder or [Grayson] Shillingford fast bowlers by any stretch of the imagination.

'By 1971, THE QUALITY OF THE WEST INDIES' BOWLING HAD DETERIORATED CONSIDERABLY.'

Q: Followers of Indian cricket continue to talk about your back-to-back wickets in the Trinidad Test. Can you walk us through the background?

A: I was casually talking to Jaisimha about how confident I was about removing them, and it was Jai who went and

asked Ajit to get me to bowl. I had noticed that the wicket in
the second innings had turned a bit slow, so you needed to
bowl faster. There was a spot created outside the off-stump
that I had noticed earlier. I decided to capitalize on that.
[Garfield] Sobers, after getting out, just couldn't believe [it].
He went away muttering, 'Oh, Jesus!'

Q: You played against Sobers in a number of Test matches.
How good was he?

A: He was incredible! I hear IPL commentary—commentators
talking about raw talent, fresh talent. I only wish the IPL had
seen Sobers!

'GAVASKAR WAS SENSATIONAL. HE SHOWED SUPREME
CONFIDENCE IN HANDLING THE WEST INDIAN BOWLERS.
FOR A BEGINNER, HIS READING OF THE PITCHES WAS TOP-
CLASS AND GAME ANALYSIS SIMPLY BRILLIANT. GAVASKAR IS
THE GREATEST OPENING BATSMAN I HAVE EVER SEEN.'

Q: How good was Sunil Gavaskar on his maiden tour?

A: Gavaskar was sensational. He showed supreme confidence
in handling the West Indian bowlers. For a beginner, his
reading of the pitches was top-class and game analysis
simply brilliant. Personally, Polly Umrigar's 1962 hundred is
the best knock I have ever watched an Indian play. On that
tour, the West Indian wickets were very fast and Wesley Hall
was at his prime. Still, Umrigar was hooking and pulling. But
if I keep that one particular innings aside, Gavaskar is the
greatest opening batsman I have ever seen.

Abbas Ali Baig

Q: You were considered an important member of the 1971 team to England since you came in for an out-of-form Jaisimha. It was expected that you would figure in the final XI as you had so much experience of English conditions. That eventually Abbas Ali Baig didn't get to play a single Test was considered surprising.

A: Well, what can I say? In a tour game preceding the first Test, I had scored 60 and thought my chances of making it to the final XI had improved. The fact that manager Adhikari praised my fielding abilities was another pointer. But almost immediately I had this strange feeling that if everything remained the same, in an equal fight, Ajit [Wadekar] would prefer a West Zone player. As I said, Colonel Adhikari admired my fielding and always gave me additional fielding practice. But despite everything, the deadlock continued.

'I HAD THIS STRANGE FEELING THAT AJIT [WADEKAR] WOULD PREFER A WEST ZONE PLAYER.'

Q: Was there actually a West versus South undercurrent in the team?

A: Look, on tours we would frequently get to see the Bombay boys going out for food separately. At times one felt that if all of us were trying to bring glory to the country and had the same intensity, why should there be different camps in one team?

Q: Your competition for the opening slot was against Ashok Mankad, who finished with a paltry 42 runs from the series. His average was just 11. You knew Wadekar well enough. He used to call you 'Baigi' lovingly. What stopped you from approaching him directly?

A: I could never ask him that. I did not know him that well, and moreover, I would never do som for that's not how I played my cricket.

'TIGER WAS RESERVED BUT VERY CHEERFUL. PEOPLE HAD THIS MISCONCEPTION OF HIM BEING ARROGANT. HE CERTAINLY WASN'T.'

Q: How different was the team under Tiger [Pataudi]?

A: Oh, Tiger's world views were completely different.

Q: But he was considered very standoffish and unapproachable. Wadekar was a people's captain.

A: That's grossly wrong. Tiger was reserved but very cheerful. People had this misconception of him being arrogant. He certainly wasn't.

Q: Apparently you were his dancing partner at family dos.

A: We used to have a lot of fun. Tiger used to sing as well.

Q: Really?

A: You know, in those days we used to be on long train journeys and Tiger, after some time, would invariably ask his Man Friday Kishan to pull out the harmonium. He would sing some numbers and then put a dupatta around his head to dance to the tune of the famous *Barsaat* song, 'Hawa me udta jaye'.

Q: Was he a good singer?

A: Oh no. It was more in fun (*laughs*).

Q: Do you think, perception-wise, you suffered in the 1971 dressing room as you were considered Pataudi's man?

A: Well, I did miss Tiger's presence in the dressing room. People who ran the team did not take me into confidence.

Q: But once the team returned you were a part of the celebrations?

A: Of course I was. We all went on that open motorcade. There was no denying the fact that it was a landmark win.

Farokh Engineer

Q: Nearly fifty years after India's tour of the West Indies, new stories about the selection of the captain continue to emerge. You were a senior member in the squad by the time the tour began. Do you have anything to add to the casting vote drama?

A: Of course, I do. In 1971, I was asked to lead the side to the West Indies. I was called by the Indian cricket board. I met Vijay Merchant and Keki Tarapore at the CCI. Merchant said something that did not seem very charitable. He said, 'I find you and [Mansoor Ali Khan] Pataudi too flamboyant.' Merchant was somewhat like his batting—dour, safe, conventional.

> 'IN 1971, I WAS ASKED TO LEAD THE SIDE TO THE WEST INDIES.'

Q: Old world?

A: Exactly—old world. Initially I was told I would be co-opted in the selection committee while picking the team. Now, I was in for a shock when the duo started cross-questioning me. Merchant said, 'How will you play for India? You play cricket in England.' I reminded him that I did play domestic cricket in India. They somehow seemed extremely cynical at whatever I said. I started wondering why on earth did they call me if they had so much negativity? Finally, I got up from my seat, highly irritated, and told them, 'You wasted your time. You wasted my time. You also wasted money for an international ticket.' Indian cricket in those days was full of such unpleasant dramas and I was subjected to it again.

Q: What was the second such instance?

A: In 1975, the night before the Delhi Test, board official Ram Prakash Mehra told me that I was leading. Tiger [Pataudi] had to sit out because of an injury. Being the seniormost, I ought to have led. But Raj Singh alerted me the next morning that something sinister was happening behind my back. Venkat [Srinivas Venkataraghavan] wasn't in the team, but at the Chidambaram Stadium [in Chennai] said he [Venkat] will lead. To accommodate the new captain, Chandra [B.S. Chandrasekhar], who got five wickets in the earlier match, got dropped. It was diabolical.

Q: Why were such incidents happening to you time and again?

A: I got short-changed by the BCCI because I never knelt before the administration.

'I COULD READ CHANDRA EVEN IN MY SLEEP. I KNEW EXACTLY WHEN HE WOULD BOWL A GOOGLY.'

Q: People say Chandrasekhar was unplayable at The Oval. How difficult was it to stand up to him, especially when he bowled those fast-ish deliveries?

A: I could read Chandra even in my sleep. I knew exactly when he would bowl a googly. I must also tell you that for the twin victories, [Eknath] Solkar deserves a lot of credit. As a close-in fielder, he was sensational.

Q: It is believed that you adopted a special strategy for Allan Knott in the second innings at The Oval by not allowing him to touch the bails.

A: Yes, Knotty was a big threat. He could have taken the match away, so we had to put him under pressure quickly. I knew he had this superstition of touching the bails once he came out to bat. So, the moment he reached the middle, I guarded the stumps. He kept on saying, 'Rookie, rookie,' and I gave the impression that I had not heard him by looking elsewhere. It was a small, little thing, but it can really get to you—as it did there.

Q: When Abid Ali cut Brian Luckhurst to create history at The Oval, you were at the other end.

A: Yes, when Abid came out to bat, we were by no means out of the woods. I told him to play safe as after us, only [Bishan Singh] Bedi, Chandra and Venkat remained. The first ball that he faced from [Derek] Underwood, Abid missed. By chance, Knotty missed the easiest of stumpings. Next over, first ball from Luckhurst, I took a single. Next ball, Abid edged it and it went for a four. Lucky fellow, Abid (*laughs*). He just played two balls and rewrote history.

'FOR THE TWIN VICTORIES, [EKNATH] SOLKAR DESERVES A LOT OF CREDIT. AS A CLOSE-IN FIELDER, HE WAS SENSATIONAL.'

Q: After India won the series against England in '71, there was a huge motorcade celebration in Mumbai. How come you were not a part of it despite being a winning member?

A: Because I had to go back to Lancashire to fulfil my county obligations. The next day, I had a match against Yorkshire, which always was huge. That day, when I went out to bat, the crowd gave me a standing ovation. It was so touching. I remember the entire day's play and the previous evening, and how packed the schedule was. After the win, we celebrated at an Indian restaurant called Mumtaz, very close to Lord's. I was in such a hurry that I couldn't finish the dinner. I packed my chicken tandoori and rushed off. I reached Manchester at 2 a.m., and the next morning at 10, I was out in the middle.

Q: Despite the success on the previous tour, India was found wanting in 1974. How would you explain the debacles, especially the stigma of being bowled out for 42 in the second Test at Lord's?

A: Look, in '74, the ball seamed so much that you needed a different technique to handle [the challenge]. Having been used to the English conditions, perhaps I was better prepared and that possibly explains why I topped the batting averages. As for the disastrous 42-all-out saga, we batted well in the first innings. In the next game, we were caught on a dry pitch. As for my dismissal, I was given out wrongly [in the second innings]—LBW Arnold. I had a thick inside edge and Dickie Bird later apologized to me. But the damage was done.

Q: How good was the bond between Ajit Wadekar and Pataudi? One of them said they had a solid friendship.

A: Friendship? Really? If so, I am not aware. Rather, I would say the Wadekar versus Tiger tension was a bit of an issue within the team.

Rusi Jeejeebhoy

Q: You went on the 1971 tour of the West Indies but did not feature in a single Test.

A: They did not play me as the management thought [Pochiah] Krishnamurthy was a better batsman. But I played and kept wickets in most of the tour matches.

Q: Can you walk us through any interesting anecdotes from the tour?

A: There are plenty. In one of the team meetings, the inexperienced me got up to ask a simple question: why is it that we can get rid of their main batsmen but struggle against the tailenders? The spinners did not take it very kindly. Another incident worth mentioning is that at customs, the officials used to regularly joke with Dilip Sardesai. I remember at the Barbados airport they told him, 'Hey, Sardee man, you may play well and beat the West

Indies, but you can never beat Barbados.' Another anecdote I remember even after so many years was that before we left for the West Indies, Vijay Merchant, while addressing the team, had said, 'We all know the famous saying that when in Rome, do as the Romans do. But don't try to replicate the same in the West Indies. When in the West Indies, don't do what the West Indians do.' He meant, don't follow their lifestyle. Looking back [on his words], I suspect he had some information that previous Indian teams to the Windies had suffered on this account. But I must say, the local [West] Indians were very warm towards us. After the series win, they took us to some factory outlet in Trinidad and said, 'Take as much as you can.'

> 'BEFORE WE LEFT FOR THE WEST INDIES, VIJAY MERCHANT, WHILE ADDRESSING THE TEAM, HAD SAID, "WE ALL KNOW THE FAMOUS SAYING THAT WHEN IN ROME, DO AS THE ROMANS DO. BUT DON'T TRY TO REPLICATE THE SAME IN THE WEST INDIES. WHEN IN THE WEST INDIES, DON'T DO WHAT THE WEST INDIANS DO."'

Q: Players we interviewed from the tour mostly talked about two Mumbai batsmen on the tour: Sunil Gavaskar and Sardesai. What were your impressions from observing their excellence from close quarters?

A: I thought three Mumbai players excelled on the tour, not two. You are leaving one Eknath Solkar out. I think, without Solkar's all-round contributions, the efforts of a Sardesai or Gavaskar would have been in vain. Solkar was such an important figure in the overall scheme of things. Ekki was very courageous; he was prepared to give his life for captain Wadekar. In those days, there was no physio or doctor accompanying the team. In the event of an emergency, you did not get ready attention. Considering the scenario, in that respect, Abid Ali was also very courageous. At the end of the day, when he and Solkar took off their shirts, you could see all sorts of bruises on their bodies.

Q: Did you try to learn anything from the West Indian greats?

A: I only watched them in half disbelief (*laughs*). Rohan Kanhai, for instance—I had got very friendly with him. Once, he took me to a nightclub. I returned around midnight and he stayed back till 3 a.m. While I was there, he complained of a mild fever. However, the next morning, he got back to score a Test hundred. I found that unbelievable. I realized that their genes were different.

Q: You returned around midnight, you said. The team curfew must have been pretty relaxed.

A: We did not have curfews. Manager Keki Tarapore had told us first thing on the tour: 'You are all adults; you know how to handle yourselves. You also know your limits. I would request you to stay inside those limitations.'

Q: How did you find Wadekar, the captain?

A: He was the PRO [Program Relationship Officer] of State Bank and knew how to manage people. The best part about him was that he spoke to the players individually, so nobody felt neglected.

'IN THE BARBADOS TEST, WHILE GAVASKAR WAS ON HIS
WAY TO ANOTHER HUNDRED, NO ONE MOVED AN INCH
INSIDE THE DRESSING ROOM TILL HE ATTAINED THE THREE-
FIGURE MARK.'

Q: Gavaskar shone magnificently on that tour. What are your memories about his performances?

A: Gavaskar displayed immense powers of concentration over a long period of time. He was phenomenal. Sobers had dropped him a few times. Once it was a sitter while the great man was standing at short mid-wicket. I remember, in the Barbados Test, while Gavaskar was on his way to another hundred, no one moved an inch inside the dressing room till he attained the three-figure mark. After he got a hundred in the last Test at Port of Spain, so many people came inside the ground and shook hands with him. Some of them also put dollars in his pocket. He returned to the dressing room with his pockets full of those notes. He had got a one thousand dollar note as well and the team was most curious. Finally, it was found out that the thousand dollar note was a fake one (*laughs*).

Syed Kirmani

(as told to the authors)

I was the baby of the team in 1971. At the time, I was a wide-eyed teenager who was seeing the world through his wicketkeeping gloves. I still have that India cap of mine. In fact, I was delightedly surprised that I actually made the team. Later on, I was told when my name came up for selection, that there was a tie between myself and Mohinder [Amarnath]. Vijay Merchant's casting vote decided the outcome. Perhaps not many know about this second casting vote of the same season.

On that 1971 tour [of England], I came in close contact with both Farokh Engineer and Allan Knott. Knott was my role model and I asked him all about his fitness regime. I was Engineer's roommate on that tour. It was another matter that I almost ended up enjoying a room all by myself (*laughs*). On that tour, in the Test matches Engineer kept, and for the county matches, I shared [wicketkeeping duties] with P.

[Pochiah] Krishanamurthy. Even though I was nowhere in contention to make it to the final XI, the win at The Oval was so magical. Even an hour after Abid Ali had hit the winning shot, we were not moving from The Oval balcony.

In the '83 World Cup, I won the Golden Gloves award. That, and the win, remain my proudest cricketing moments. I could prove to the world that I was the best wicketkeeper. It removed the agony of the 1974 tour, which was dreadful. I have still not been able to find the reasons for such a disastrous tour. Incidentally, I had toured England in 1967 as part of the Indian schoolboys' team. Even on that tour, Hemu Adhikari was the [team] manager. I respected Adhikari a lot. In front of him, even the seniors like [Dilip] Sardesai or a [Abbas Ali] Baig remained frightened. Adhikari was a no-nonsense man—a side to his personality that had endeared him to me.

'THE WIN AT THE OVAL WAS SO MAGICAL. EVEN AN HOUR AFTER ABID ALI HAD HIT THE WINNING SHOT, WE WERE NOT MOVING FROM THE OVAL BALCONY.'

Gopal Bose

(as told to the authors)

Some of our readers might think: why include a Gopal Bose piece in a book primarily about the twin victories of 1971? This is because one of Indian cricket's biggest regrets is that the benefits of 1971 were all lost in 1974, when India collapsed to a stunning 42 all out and also lost the subsequent Test by an innings. Bose, who was a member of the 1974 side, helps give us some context regarding what went wrong and what all resulted in the undoing of the 1971 legacy.

The cracks were not visible at all in December 1973 when I had first joined the Indian team. The team under Ajit Wadekar resembled a picture-postcard happy family while touring Sri Lanka. It possibly remained united and happy as the big [name] spinners were not around to throw a leadership challenge to the captain. But in England, in April 1974, from the very first day of the tour, things went haywire. The [team] dinner was at some Mr Lalwani's place, if I remember correctly. There, all of a sudden, a heated conversation began between [Bishan Singh] Bedi and Wadekar. It turned so vicious that the children [in the household] were asked to go upstairs. Obviously, this was happening under the influence of alcohol. But it had a terrible effect on the team. Wadekar quite openly started accusing [us]: 'You are all [Mansoor Ali Khan] Pataudi's men.' This led to a very strong argument, and a physical fight was just about avoided. What happened subsequently was much worse as Bedi threatened to go back. My roommate on that tour was Sunil Gavaskar. He tried to pacify Bedi but didn't succeed. Bedi demanded a public apology, else he would go back home. So the following morning, Wadekar, in the presence of the entire team, apologized to Bedi.

'[WADEKAR] COMPLETELY LOST CONTROL OF THE TEAM [IN 1974].'

After that, he completely lost control of the team. Still a ball wasn't bowled on the tour but the team went rudderless. That Wadekar did not get runs in the Test matches aggravated his misery. And you could see, [both] on and off the field, he had no control over Bedi, who almost bowled at his will. I have had full faith in and respect for Wadekar, who I always found to be very fair. I did not see any parochial or zonal considerations in him, otherwise why would he prefer a Gopal Bose at the expense of a Ramnath Parker? But the situation completely went out of his hand, resulting in the poor performance all through the series.

Raymond Illingworth

Q: Nearly fifty years on from India's victorious tour of England, can you recollect any memories of what transpired in the 1971 series?

A: Yes, I can.

Q: How disappointing was it to lose the series against a side that was, on paper, considered a pushover?

A: Look, the result ought to have been 2–1 in our favour. Had the weather not intervened, we would have gone up 2–0 by the time [the Test at] The Oval had begun. But I agree that in the last Test, India played really well. They deserved to win that one.

Q: What, according to you, was the turning point in the series?

A: Well, I would say the rain and, subsequently, Chandra's [B.S. Chandrasekhar] bowling (*chuckles*).

Q. How good was Chandra?

A: Chandra was unplayable at The Oval. [The] pace with which he bowled was almost impossible to handle, though some of our batsmen made cardinal technical mistakes while playing him; they mostly went on the front foot when they should have stayed back. It looked as if some of us got mesmerized.

Q: What are your other memories from the Oval Test?

A: I would say the Indian performance at the Oval Test was very commendable. They came back from a first-innings deficit to battle it out splendidly. India's close-in catching was very good. What still disappoints me is the fact that we lost the Test in perfect English conditions.

'CHANDRA WAS UNPLAYABLE AT THE OVAL.'

Q: The most controversial element in the series was perhaps the collision between Sunil Gavaskar and John Snow at Lord's. What did you make of it?

A: A lot was made of that incident. I was of the opinion that Snow bumped onto him quite accidentally and Sunil had turned sideways. In the process, the bat had dropped out of his hand. It was a nasty fall, but such things happen routinely in today's cricket. No one takes notice. I feel the charge against Snow had little basis.

Q: If that was your personal impression of him, and the incident, why did you drop him from the second Test?

A: I dropped him not because I wanted to drop him but the MCC wanted him to go. I still remember how fired up Snow was when he got back for the last Test and removed Gavaskar early in both innings.

Q: How difficult was it to handle Snow?

A: Not difficult at all. People like Snow and [Geoff] Boycott were intense characters and only needed understanding from their leader.

Q: Was Gavaskar the finest Indian batsman you have seen?

A: No. To me, [Sachin] Tendulkar was clearly the finest from India.

Intikhab Alam

Intikhab Alam captained the Pakistan team to England in 1971 and could well have become the first Asian captain to beat England in England. We felt it relevant to get his thoughts on playing England and what he thought of the Indian win a month later

Q: You led Pakistan in the 1971 away series against England, just before India played them. Do you remember the series well?

A: Oh, that series still remains a major cricketing regret. As the Pakistan captain, I did experience a bit of success—we won our first series overseas under my leadership. As the coach, [I] was a part of our two World-Cup-winning teams. But that has not erased the major cricketing regret of mine about the 1971 series. We were so near and yet we could not do it. Had we not lost the third Test at Headingley by 25 runs, we would have been the first Asian team to win a series in England.

Q: The target for the series-deciding third and final Test was only 231, and Pakistan was bowled out for 205 in the fourth innings. Does the wound still run deep?

A: Yes, because we dominated throughout the series, and because of bad batting in one innings, [we] ended up losing the series. As we could not cross the final hurdle, everything went away. I also learnt an important lesson in life—irrespective of how well the team plays, unless you win, no one will stand beside you.

Q: The batting collapse at Headingley undid your gains through the hard-earned draws in the previous two matches.

A: Yes, it did, and I still remember the bus ride from Headingley to London, which was almost four hours long. Hardly anyone spoke. Even fifty years later, I can recall it—it was almost like attending a funeral.

Q: What did it teach you?

A: It taught me to quickly find out the reason for failure, which, in this case, was primarily bad batting and the fact that we did not have a quality medium-pacer. Imran [Khan] made his debut in the series, but he was very raw [at the time]. I also learnt that in case of such a disaster, it was advisable not to address and accuse the batsmen collectively. You must speak to them one on one. This was a lesson I used to great advantage in my post-retirement years as the Pakistan coach.

'I WOULD LIKE TO BELIEVE THAT WE LAID THE FOUNDATION FOR AN INDIAN WIN.'

Q: Did you know Ajit Wadekar at the time?

A: No, we met later. He was very nice and friendly.

Q: Under him, a few months later, India achieved the success you could not.

A: Yes, they did. But remember, we toured in the first half of the English summer, which was tougher to negotiate. I would also like to believe that we laid the foundation for an Indian win. We knocked the door and rattled them. Then, India opened it successfully.

Zaheer Abbas

Zaheer Abbas batted brilliantly in Pakistan's tour of England in 1971, just ahead of the India tour. His batting was a lesson for the Indian batsmen and Zaheer was distinctly unlucky not to be on the winning side.

Q: You shone spectacularly in the 1971 tour of England. It must have been enormously difficult to get a double century in the first half of the English summer.

A: In cricket, one's frame of mind is very important. Even though it was my maiden English tour, I felt very confident.

Q: What did the senior players advise?

A: Advise? *(laughs)* Most of them had predicted my downfall. Some of them openly said, 'You have a high backlift and your bat comes down from the slips. You can›t get, runs in England.'

Q: How did you score runs, then, defying the odds?

A: Before the first Test, I had scored four hundreds in the tour games. Just before the Test, I was batting [in the nets] in Manchester. It felt so good that I instantly told myself I would get a hundred in the first Test and so, let me keep this bat for the Test and get another bat [for the practice session]. I was that confident. You won't believe I had told Mushtaq Mohammad, '*Meri lottery nikal aayi hai* (I have won the lottery).' That's how important frame of mind is for a batsman.

Q: Your 274 in the Birmingham Test is still talked about.

A: Trust me, when I was batting on 50, I told non-striker Mushtaq again, '*Maine goro, key khilaaf pehla pachaas kar liya, abhi sab kuch kar sakta hoon* (I've got my first fifty against the English, I can do everything now).' He was a little surprised, but I knew what I was talking about.

'In those days, neither India nor Pakistan had any standing. They were not expected to win in England.'

Q: In the same year, an Indian, Sunil Gavaskar, was also making heads turn. He had also scored a double hundred about two months ago in another part of the world.

A: Yes, we both made our names in that particular year *(laughs)*. That was the time when I got friendly with Sunil Gavaskar and, till today, we are very close.

Q: Was there a bit of disappointment that Pakistan was so close to defeating England but India ultimately walked away with the honours?

A: Not really. In those days, neither India nor Pakistan had any standing. They were not expected to win in England. So the Indian win had opened it up for Asia. I actually watched India's Oval win from the gallery. There was never any jealousy involved. In fact, after the match, I walked into the Indian dressing room to offer my congratulations. I felt so proud. There were always very friendly feelings between us. I was so close to the Indians that when I threw a party in Karachi to celebrate my hundredth 100, I invited a few Indian cricketers.

Kapil Dev

Kapil Dev may not have played in 1971, but was one who grew up hearing of the twin victories in the West Indies and England. Also, many feel that there would be no 1983 had there been no 1971. As India's World-Cup-winning captain in 1983, we decided to speak to Kapil about his memories of 1971—and must say were startled by what he said.

Q: India's historic series wins in 1971 came about when you were only twelve years old. Do you have any memories of those victories?

A: To be honest, hardly any. I never kept track of cricket records. I was always involved in the action; always preferred playing and not watching. Even today, if you ask me, 'Will you watch Test cricket or play a round of table tennis?' I would happily choose table tennis every time.

Q: Did you have an inkling at the time that India had scripted two historic series wins in the same year?

A: Look, sitting there in [my hometown] Chandigarh, the news did reach us that India had won in England and that [B.S.] Chandrasekhar's brilliance with the ball had made it happen. But beyond that, nothing.

Q: Did you know the name of the winning captain?

A: No chance. I just knew we had some good spinners [in our team], but that was it. Only Chandra I had heard [of] because of the victory.

Q: That sounds unbelievable.

A: Yes, I know (*laughs*), but [it's] true. When I went to play my first Ranji [Trophy] game in 1975, my elder brother asked me, 'Can you name all the cricketers currently playing for India? [If you can,] I will get you whatever you want.' I obviously did not know, but told him, '*Yeh sab baatein chodo. Main khelta hu, dekhta nahi* (Forget all this. I play cricket, I do not watch it).' I had no clue about their names (*laughs*).

'[Ajit Wadekar] was Indian cricket's first representative of a successful common man captain, and I have tremendous regard [for him] because of that.'

Q: You met Ajit Wadekar years later in the '90s, when he was the Indian team's cricket manager. Then, in the late 2000s, in your capacity as the chairman of the Indian Cricket League's executive board, you roped him into refereeing a match in a domestic T20 tournament. What did you think of his leadership abilities?

A: He spoke so softly. A nice man he was. Very decent. The thing that still strikes me the most is that a common man [like him] took over from royalty and won. He was Indian cricket's first successful common man captain, and I have tremendous regard [for him] because of that.

Q: Did he ever discuss with you the twin series wins of 1971?

A: Never. I felt the '71 heroes were all very humble and never said I did this or I did that.

Q: In the subsequent years, you must have heard stories from some of the team members who were involved in those two series.

A: Not really. Sunil [Gavaskar] told me a few stories. That was it.

Q: Had you heard of Dilip Sardesai or of his heroics on the tour of the West Indies?

A: No, I gathered all that years later. I only knew one batsman's name: [Gundappa] Viswanath (*laughs*). That name had struck a chord with me very fast. Our friends used to talk about him and be in awe of his maiden hundred against Australia. We used to wonder how a *char footiya aadmi* (a man who is all of four feet) could be so good against express fast bowling. He has got to be a genius!

Q: What about Gavaskar and the record 774 runs he scored in his debut series on the tour of the West Indies?

A: I knew nothing [about that], and you know what? The name Sunil is so common [in India], it did not register. Viswanath was relatively uncommon, so it stuck.

Q: When did you get to know about Gavaskar?

A: Later on (*chuckles*). He was the second wonder as he kept piling runs. I remember discussing with my friends whether short batsmen have a huge advantage against fast bowling [because] the bouncers usually sail over their heads. Whereas if you are tall, it comes straight onto your face.

Q: In your view, would India's maiden World Cup win in 1983 have been a reality without the era-defining twin series triumphs in 1971?

A: I can't answer this. I think you should ask Sunil. He is better qualified for a reply.

Q: Fifty years on, how do you rate those victories?

A: They were huge. Winning abroad in those days was a remarkable achievement. The team had no fast bowlers, nor did it have athletic cricketers. Despite these limitations, we did win in 1971.

'Winning abroad in those days was a remarkable achievement.'

Q: After retiring from the game, Wadekar lamented the absence of an all-rounder like you in the sides he led and believed that it could have averted the drubbings India was handed in 1974. Did he ever share these thoughts with you?

A: I don't remember. However, just think about it–a team winning abroad, in front of foreign umpires, where 50–50 decisions always went in favour of the home team—to counter that and win made the effort timeless. These days it has become 100 per cent easier with neutral umpires.

Appendix

Scorecards

India v. West Indies, 1971
First Test

At Kingston, 18, 19, 20, 21, 22, 23 February 1971
Result: Match drawn

INDIA

First Innings

S. Abid Ali c Camacho b Shillingford 6

K. Jayantilal c Sobers b Shillingford 5

*A.L. Wadekar c Fredericks b Holder.. 8

D.N. Sardesai c Findlay b Holder 212

S.A. Durani b Barrett 13

M.L. Jaisimha b Holder 3

E.D. Solkar b Sobers.. 61

S. Venkataraghavan c Findlay b Sobers 4

†P. Krishnnamurthy b Noreiga 10

E.A.S. Prasanna b Holder.. 25

B.S. Bedi not out 5

B 9, l-b 6, n-b 20 35

1-10, 2-13, 3-36, 4-66, 5-75, 6-212, 7-222, 8-260, 9-382,   387
10-387

First Innings – Holder 27.4–9–60–4; Shillingford 26–2–70–2; Sobers 30–8–57–2; Noreiga 31–7–69–1; Barrett 35–6–86–1; Lloyd 4–1–7–0; Carew 5–2–3–0

293

WEST INDIES

First Innings		Second Innings	
R.C. Fredericks c Abid Ali b Prasanna	45	c Krishnamurthy b Bedi	16
G.S. Camacho c Wadekar b Prasanna	35	c Abid Ali b Venkataraghavan	12
R.B. Kanhai c sub (D. Govindraj) b Venkataraghavan	56	not out	158
C.H. Lloyd run out	15	run out	57
*G.S. Sobers c Abid Ali b Prasanna	44	c Krishnamurthy b Solkar	93
M.C. Carew c Wadekar b Prasanna	3		
A.G. Barrett c Solkar b Venkataraghavan	2	(6) c Abid Ali b Solkar	4
†T.M. Findlay b Bedi	6	(7) not out	30
V.A. Holder b Venkataraghavan	7		
G.C. Shillingford b Bedi	0		
J. Noreiga not out	0		
B 4	4	B 9, l-b 5, n-b 1	15
1-73, 2-90, 3-119, 4-183, 5-202, 6-203, 7-205, 8-217, 9-217, 10-217	217	1-18, 2-32, 3-147, (5 wkts) 4-320, 5-326	385

First Innings – Abid Ali 9–2–30–0; Solkar 2–0–9–0; Bedi 31.5–12–63–2; Prasanna 33–12–65–-4; Venkataraghavan 18–5–46–3

Second Innings – Abid Ali 5–2–11–0; Solkar 22–4–56–2; Prasanna 21–5–72–0; Bedi 24–5–63–1; Venkataraghavan 37–8–94–1; Durani 14–0–42–0; Jaisimha 13–1–32–0

Toss won by West Indies
UMPIRES   D. Sang Hue and R. Gosein

India v. West Indies, 1971
Second Test

At Port of Spain, 6, 7, 8, 9, 10 March 1971
Result: India won by 7 wickets

WEST INDIES	
First Innings	*Second Innings*
R.C. Fredericks b Abid Ali............ 0	run out 13
G.S. Camacho c Solkar b Bedi.... 18	(6) b Venkataraghavan 3
R.B. Kanhai c Solkar b Prasanna 37	(2) c Venkataraghavan b Bedi............................... 27
C.H. Lloyd b Abid Ali 7	c Wadekar b Durani 15
C.A. Davis not out 71	(3) not out 74
*G.S. Sobers b Venkataraghavan . 29	b Durani............................. 0
A.G. Barrett c Solkar b Prasanna.. 8	b Venkataraghavan........... 19
†T.M. Findlay b Bedi.................... 1	c Solkar b Venkataraghavan. 0
V.A. Holder c Krishnamurthy b Bedi......................... 14	b Vnekatraghavan 14
G.C. Shillingford c Solkar b Prasanna 25	c Durani b Venkataraghavan 1
J.M. Noreiga b Prasanna 0	c Solkar b Bedi 2
B 2, l-b 2 4	B 18, l-b 7, n-b 1 26
1-0, 2-42, 3-62, 4-62, 5-108, 214 6-132, 7-133, 8-161, 9-214, 10-214	1-73, 2-150, 3-152, 261 4-169, 5-169, 6-218, 7-222, 8-254, 9-256, 10-261

First Innings – Abid Ali 20–4–54–2; Solkar 3–0–12–0; Gavaskar 1–0–9–0; Bedi 16–5–46–3; Prasanna 19.5–3–54–4; Venkataraghavan 13–0–35–1

Second Innings – Abid Ali 5–2–3–0; Solkar 7–2–19–0; Prasanna 16–5–47–0; Bedi 29.5–11–50–2; Venkataraghavan 36–11–95–5; Durani 17–8–21–2

INDIA	
First Innings	*Second Innings*
A.V. Mankad b Shillingford........ 44	c sub (S.A. Gomes) b Barrett....................29
S.M. Gavaskar c Lloyd b Noreiga..................................... 65	not out 67
S.A. Durani c and b Noreiga 9	b Barrett..............................0
D.N. Sardesai c Shillingford b Noreiga.................................. 112	c Findlay b Barrett..............3
*A.L. Wadekar c Kanhai b Noreiga..................................... 0	
E.D. Solkar c and b Noreiga....... 55	
S. Abid Ali c Shillingford b Noreiga 20	(5) not out........................21
S. Venkataraghavan st Findlay b Noreiga..................................... 5	
†P. Krishnamurthy c sub (S.A. Gomes) b Noreiga........................ 0	
E.A.S. Prasanna not out 10	
B.S. Bedi c Holder b Noreiga........ 4	
B 18, l-b 2, n-b 8 28	B 2, l-b 2, n-b 1 5
1-68, 2-90, 3-186, 4-186, 5-300, 6-330, 7-337, 8-337, 9-342, 10-352 352	1-74, 2-74, 3-84 125 (3 wkts)

First Innings – Holder 19–8–37–0; Shillingford 20–3–45–1; Sobers 28–7–65–0; Noreiga 49.4–16–95–9; Barrett 37–13–65–0; Davis 3–1–11–0; Lloyd 1–0–6–0.

Second Innings – Holder 2–0–12–0; Shillingford 6–2–13–0; Noreiga 18–4–36–0; Sobers 15–5–16–0; Barrett 8.4–0–43–3.

Toss won by West Indies
UMPIRES   R. Gosein and S. Ishmael

India v. West Indies, 1971
Third Test

At Georgetown, 19, 20, 21, 22, 23, 24 March 1971
Result: Match drawn

WEST INDIES	
First Innings	*Second Innings*
R.C. Fredericks c Abid Ali b Venkataraghavan 47	lbw b Solkar 5
M.C. Carew c Mankad 41	c Durani b Bedi 45
R.B. Kanhai c Krishnamurthy b Bedi............................. 25	
C.H. Lloyd run out 60	c Krishnamurthy b Bedi...... 9
C.A. Davis lbw b Solkar............. 34	(3) not out 125
*G.S. Sobers c Venkataraghavan b Bedi............................... 4	(5) not out 108
†D.M. Lewis not out 81	
K.D. Boyce c Gavaskar b Venkataraghavan 9	
G.C. Shillingford c Bedi b Venkataraghavan...................... 5	
L.R. Gibbs run out 25	
J. Noreiga run out 9	
B 11, l-b 9, n-b 3 23	B 5, l-b 6, n-b 4 15
1-78, 2-119, 3-135, 4-213, 5-226, 6-231, 7-246, 8-256, 9-340, 10-363 363	1-11, 2-114, 307 (3 wkts, dec.) 3-137

First Innings – Abid Ali 13.2–5–42–0; Solkar 17–3–34–1; Venkataraghavan 59–14–128–3; Bedi 55–18–85–2; Durani 14–3–51–1

Second Innings – Abid Ali 14–2–55–0; Solkar 16–4–43–1; Bedi 26–9–55–2; Venkataraghavan 20–10–47–0; Mankad 5–0–33–0; Durani 16–2–47–0; Wadekar 3–0–12–0

INDIA	
First Innings	*Second Innings*
A.V. Mankad b Noreiga 40	not out 53
S.M. Gavaskar c Carew b Sobers 116	not out 64
*A.L. Wadekar b Sobers 16	
G.R. Viswanath b Boyce 50	
S.A. Durani lbw b Sobers 2	
D.N. Sardesai run out 45	
E.D. Solkar run out 16	
S. Abid Ali not out 50	
S. Venkataraghavan lbw b Shillingford 12	
†P. Krishnamurthy run out 0	
B.S. Bedi b Boyce 2	
B 5, l-b 6, n-b 15, w 1 27	B 4, n-b 1, w 1 6
1-72, 2-116, 3-228, 4-244, 5-246, 6-278, 7-339, 8-370, 9-374, 10-376 376	(no wkt) 123

First Innings – Boyce 20.4–5–47–2; Shillingford 21–2–76–1; Sobers 43–15–72–3; Gibbs 39–17–61–0; Noreiga 42–9–91–1; Carew 2–0–2–0

Second Innings – Boyce 2–0–12–0; Shillingford 2–0–13–0; Lloyd 3–0–20–0; Noreiga 10–0–30–0; Gibbs 1–0–4–0; Sobers 5–1–14–0; Fredericks 4–0–9–0; Davis 3–0–15–0

Toss won by West Indies
UMPIRES   C.P. Kippins and R. Gosein

India v. West Indies, 1971
Fourth Test

At Bridgetown, 1, 2, 3, 4, 5, 6 April 1971
Result: Match drawn

WEST INDIES	
First Innings	*Second Innings*
R.C. Fredericks b Abid Ali............ 1	b Venkataraghavan........... 48
†D.M. Lewis b Bedi..................... 88	b Abid Ali.......................... 14
R.B. Kanhai c Mankad b Venkataraghavan..................... 85	c Krishnamurthy b Solkar............................ 11
C.A. Davis c Venkataraghavan b Abid Ali.................................... 79	(8) not out....................... 22
*G.S. Sobers not out 178	c Bedi b Abid Ali 9
C.H. Lloyd c Mankad b Bedi 19	(4) c Venkataraghavan b Abid Ali......................... 43
M.L.C. Foster not out 36	not out 24
J.N. Shepherd did not bat	c Solkar b Venkataraghavan. 3
B 10, l-b 4, n-b 1 15	B 2, l-b 3, n-b 1 6
1-4, 2-170, 3-179, 4-346, 5-394 501 (5 wkts dec.)	1-17, 2-36, 3-112, 180 4-126, 5-132, 6-133 (6 wkts dec.)

Inshan Ali, V.A. Holder, U.G. Dowe
did not bat.

First Innings – Abid Ali 31–1–127–2; Solkar 19–4–40–0; Jaisimha
10–2–32–0; Bedi 54–15–124–2; Venkataraghavan 57–12–163–1

Second Innings – Abid Ali 21–3–70–3; Solkar 14–0–73–1; Venkataraghavan 7–0–25–2; Bedi 1–0–6–0

INDIA	
First Innings	*Second Innings*
A.V. Mankad c Lewis B Holder.... 6	c Shepherd b Inshan Ali...... 8
S.M. Gavaskar c Holder b Dowe.. 1	not out............................ 117
†P. Krishnamurthy c Inshan Ali b Dowe 1	
*A.L. Wadekar c Lewis b Sobers .. 28	(3) c Lloyd b Sobers 17
G.R. Viswanath c Lewis b Sobers.. 25	(4) c Shepherd b Sobers...... 0
D.N. Sardesai lbw b Holder 150	c Fredericks b Shepherd.... 24
M.L. Jaisimha b Dowe 0	(5) lbw b Dowe 17
E.D. Solkar c Lewis 65	(7) not out........................ 10
S. Abid Ali run out 9	
S. Venkataraghavan b Shepherd . 12	
B.S. Bedi not out 20	
B 6, l-b 6, n-b 18 30	B 2, l-b 8, n-b 17, w 1....... 28
1-2, 2-5, 3-20, 4-64, 5-69, 6-70, 347 7-256, 8-269, 9-285, 10-347	1-35, 2-71, 3-79, 221 4-132, 5-192 (5 wkts)

First Innings – Holder 25.4–7–70–2; Dowe 23–7–69–4; Shepherd 24–4–54–1; Sobers 20–9–34–2; Inshan Ali 20–4–60–0; Foster 11–3–28–0; Davis 2–0–2–0

Second Innings – Holder 8–4–13–0; Dowe 11–5–22–1; Inshan 18–1–65–1; Shepherd 20–7–36–1; Sobers 23–8–31–2; Foster 14–7–10–0; Davis 3–2–1–0; Lloyd 4–0–13–0; Fredericks 1–0–1–0; Kanhai 1–0–1–0

Toss won by India
UMPIRES   H.B. de C. Jordon and D. Sang Hue

India v. West Indies, 1971
Fifth Test

At Port of Spain, 13, 14, 15, 16, 17, 18, 19 April 1971
Result: Match drawn

INDIA	
First Innings	*Second Innings*
S. Abid Ali c Davis b Sobers 10	lbw b Sobers........................3
S.M. Gavaskar c Lewis b Holford.................................. 124	b Shepherd 220
*A.L. Wadekar c Sobers b Shepherd 28	c Shepherd b Noreiga.......54
D.N. Sardesai c Lewis b Holford.. 75	c and b Foster...................21
G.R. Viswanath c Lewis b Shepherd................................ 22	b Sobers 38
M.L. Jaisimha c Carew b Dowe.... 0	lbw b Shepherd 23
E.D. Solkar c sub (R.C. Fredericks) b Dowe 3	c Sobers b Noreiga 14
S. Venkataraghavan c Carew b Shepherd 51	b Noreiga..........................21
†P. Krishnamurthy c Lewis b Noreiga............................. 20	c sub (S.A. Gomes) b Noreiga.............................2
E.A.S. Prasanna c Lloyd b Holford.................................. 16	not out 10
B.S. Bedi not out 1	c Sobers b Noreiga 5
L-b 1, n-b 9 10	B 2, l-b 8, n-b 6 16

1-26, 2-68, 3-190, 4-238, 360 1-11, 2-159, 3-194, 4-293, 427
5-239, 6-247, 7-296, 8-335,   5-374, 6-377, 7-409,
9-354, 10-360   8-412, 9-413, 10-427

First Innings – Sobers 13–3–30–1; Dowe 29–1–99–2; Shepherd 35–7–78–3; Davis 10–0–28–0; Noreiga 16–3–43–1; Holford 28.3–5–68–3; Foster 2–0–4–0

Second Innings – Sobers 42–14–82–2; Dowe 22–2–55–0; Shepherd 24–8–45–2; Noreiga 53.4–8–129–5; Holford 27–3–63–0; Carew 7–2–15–0; Foster 12–4–10–1; Davis 10–2–12–0

WEST INDIES	
First Innings	*Second Innings*
M.C. Carew c Wadekar b Prasanna 28	run out 4
†D.M. Lewis c Krishnamurthy b Bedi 72	(9) not out 4
R.B. Kanhai run out 13	(4) b Abid Ali 21
C.A. Davis c Solkar b Venkataraghavan 105	(8) c Viswanath b Venkataraghavan 19
C.H. Lloyd c Venkataraghavan b Prasanna 6	(3) c Wadekar b Venkataraghavan 64
*G.S. Sobers b Prasanna 132	(5) b Abid Ali 0
M.L.C. Foster b Abid Ali 99	(6) run out 18
D.A.J. Holford st Krishnamurthy b Venkataraghavan 44	(7) c Bedi b Solkar 9
J.N. Shepherd c Abid Ali b Venkataraghavan 0	(2) c and b Abid Ali 9
U.G. Dowe lbw b Venkataraghavan 3	not out 0
J.M. Noreiga not out 0	
B 14, l-b 8, n-b 2 24	B 9, l-b 8 17
1-52, 2-94, 3-142, 4-153, 5-330, 526 6-424, 7-517, 8-522, 9-523, 10-526	1-0, 2-16, 3-50, 4-50, 165 5-101, 6-114, 7-152, 8-161 (8 wkts)

First Innings – Abid Ali 31–7–58–1; Solkar 11–1–35–0; Bedi 71–19–163–1; Prasanna 65–15–146–3; Venkataraghavan 37.3–5–100–4; Jaisimha 1–1–0–0

Second Innings – Abid Ali 15–1–73–3; Solkar 13–1–40–1; Venkataraghavan 5–1–11–2; Prasanna 5–0–23–0; Bedi 2–1–1–0

Toss won by India

UMPIRES   D. Sang Hue and R. Gosein

India v. England, 1971
First Test

At Lord's, 22, 23, 24, 25, 26, 27 July 1971
Result: Match drawn

ENGLAND	
First Innings	*Second Innings*
G. Boycott c Engineer b Abid Ali 3	c Wadekar b Venkataraghavan 33
B.W. Luckhurst c Solkar b Chandrasekhar 30	b Solkar 1
J.H. Edrich c Venkataraghavan b Bedi 18	c Engineer b Bedi 62
D.L. Amiss c Engineer b Bedi 9	run out 0
B.L. D'Oliveira c Solkar b Chandrasekhar 4	b Bedi 30
†A.P.E. Knott c Wadekar b Venkataraghavan 67	c Wadekar b Venkataraghavan 24
*R. Illingworth c Engineer b Bedi 33	c Wadekar b Venkataraghavan 20
R.A. Hutton b Venkataraghavan . 20	b Chandrasekhar 0
J.A. Snow c Abid Ali b Chandrasekhar 73	c Chandrasekhar b Venkataraghavan 9
N. Gifford b Bedi 17	not out 7
J.S.E Price not out 5	c Abid Ali b Venkataraghavan 0
B 8, l-b 12, n-b 5 25	L-b 5 5

1-18, 2-46, 3-56, 4-61, 5-71, 304
6-161, 7-183, 8-223, 9-294, 10-
304

1-4, 2-65, 3-70, 191
4-117, 5-145, 6-153,
7-153, 8-174, 9-189,
10-191

First Innings – Abid Ali 15–3–38–1; Solkar 8–3–17–0; Venkataraghavan 28–8–44–2; Chandrasekhar 49–10–110–3; Bedi 39.3–18–70–4

Second Innings – Abid Ali 9–1–20–0; Solkar 6–3–13–1; Venkataraghavan 30.5–11–52–4; Chandrasekhar 23–7–60–2; Bedi 30–13–41–2

INDIA	
First Innings	*Second Innings*
A.V. Mankad c Gifford b Snow.... 1	c Knott b Snow 5
S.M. Gavaskar c Amiss b Price 4	c Edrich b Gifford 53
*A.L. Wadekar c Illingworth b Gifford...................................... 85	c Boycott b Price 5
D.N. Sardesai c Illingworth b Gifford...................................... 25	(6) b Illingworth.................. 1
G.R. Viswanath c Knott b Hutton 68	c Amiss b Gifford 9
†F.M. Engineer c Illingworth b Hutton... 28	(4) st Knott b Gifford 28
E.D. Solkar c Knott b Gifford..... 67	not out 6
S. Abid Ali c Luckhurst b Snow.... 6	c Snow b Illingworth........ 14
S. Venkataraghavan c Hutton b Price 11	c Hutton b Gifford............. 7
B.S. Bedi c Price b Gifford............ 0	not out 0
B.S. Chandrasekhar not out 0	
B 7, l-b 9, n-b 2 18	L-b 7, n-b 1 8

1-1, 2-29, 3-108, 4-125, 5-175, 313
6-267, 7-279, 8-302, 9-311, 10-
313

1-8, 2-21, 3-87, 145
4-101, (8 wkts)
5-108,6-114, 7-135,
8-142

First Innings – Price 25–9–46–2; Snow 31–9–64–2; Hutton 24–8–38–2;
Gifford 45.3–14–84–4; D'Oliveira 15–7–20–0; Illingworth 25–12–43–0

Second Innings – Price 4–0–26–1; Snow 8–0–23–1; Hutton 3–0–12–0;
Gifford 19–4–43–4; Illingworth 16–2–33–2

Toss won by England
UMPIRES   C.S. Elliot and D.J. Constant

India v. England, 1971
Second Test

At Old Trafford, 5, 6, 7, 8, 9, 10 August 1971
Result: Match drawn

ENGLAND	
First Innings	*Second Innings*
B.W. Luckhurst c Viswanath b Bedi.............................. 78	st Engineer b Solkar 101
J.A. Jameson c Gavaskar b Abid Ali 15	run out 28
J.H. Edrich c Engineer b Abid Ali ... 0	b Bedi............................... 59
K.W.R. Fletcher lbw b Abid Ali 1	not out 28
B.L. D'Oliveira c Gavaskar b Abid Ali.................................... 12	not out 23
†A.P.E. Knott b Venkataraghavan 41	
*R. Illingworth c Gavaskar b Venkataraghavan................... 107	
R.A. Hutton c and b Venkataraghavan..................... 15	
P. Lever not out 88	
N. Gifford c Engineer b Solkar.... 8	
J.S.E. Price run out 0	
B 6, l-b 12, n-b 2, w 1................. 21	L-b 5, n-b 1 6
1-21, 2-21, 3-25, 4-41, 5-116, 386 6-168, 7-187, 8-355, 9-384, 10-386	1-14, 2-167, 3-212 245 (3 wkts dec.)

First Innings – Abid Ali 32.4–5–64–4; Solkar 21–5–46–1; Chandrasekhar 30–6–90–0; Bedi 40–10–72–1; Venkataraghavan 35–9–89–3; Gavaskar 2–0–4–0

Second Innings – Abid Ali 26–2–95–0; Solkar 5–0–23–1; Gavaskar 12–3–37–0; Chandrasekhar 2–0–5–0; Venkataraghavan 16–3–58–0; Bedi 5–0–21–1

INDIA	
First Innings	*Second Innings*
A.V. Mankad c Knott b Lever....... 8	b Price................................. 7
S.M. Gavaskar c Knott b Price ... 57	c Knott b Hutton.............. 24
*A.L. Wadekar c Knott b Hutton 12	b Price................................. 9
D.N. Sardesai b Lever................. 14	not out........................... 13
G.R. Viswanath b Lever 10	not out........................... 8
†F.M. Engineer c Edrich b Lever. 22	
E.D. Solkar c Hutton b D'Oliveira . 50	
S. Abid Ali b D'Oliveira................ 0	
S. Venkataraghavan c Knott b Lever... 20	
B.S. Bedi b Price 8	
B.S. Chandrasekhar not out 4	
B 1, l-b 4, n-b 2 7	B 2, n-b 2 4
1-19, 2-52, 3-90, 4-103, 5-104, 212 6-163, 7-164, 8-194, 9-200, 10-212	1-9, 2-22, 3-50 65 (3 wkts)

First Innings – Price 22–7–44–2; Lever 26–4–70–5; D'Oliveira 24–11–40–2; Hutton 14–3–35–1; Illingworth 7–2–16–0

Second Innings Price 10–3–30–2; Lever 7–3–14–0; Hutton 7–1–16–1; D'Oliveira 3–2–1–0

Toss won by England
UMPIRES   A.E. Fagg and T.W. Spence

India v. England, 1971
Third Test

At Kennington Oval, 19, 20, 21, 22, 23, 24 August 1971
Result: India won by 4 wickets

ENGLAND	
First Innings	*Second Innings*
B.W. Luckhurst c Gavaskar b Solkar 1	c Venkataraghavan b Chandrasekhar 33
J.A. Jameson run out 82	run out 16
J.H. Edrich c Engineer b Bedi 41	b Chandrasekhar 0
K.W.R. Fletcher c Gavaskar b Bedi 1	c Solkar b Chandrasekhar 0
B.L. D'Oliveira c Mankad b Chandrasekhar 2	c sub (K. Jayantilal) b Venkataraghavan 17
†A.P.E. Knott c and b Solkar 90	c Solkar b Venkataraghavan 1
*R. Illingworth b Chandrasekhar.. 11	c and b Chandrasekhar 4
R.A. Hutton b Venkataraghavan 81	not out 13
J.A. Snow c Engineer b Solkar 3	c and b Chandrasekhar 0
D.L. Underwood c Wadekar b Venkataraghavan 22	c Mankad b Bedi 11
J.S.E Price not out 1	lbw b Chandrasekhar 3
B 4, l-b 15, w 1 20	L-b 3 3

310

1-5, 2-111, 3-135, 4-139,   355   1-23, 2-24, 3-24,
5-143, 6-175, 7-278, 8-284,   4-49, 5-54, 6-65,   101
9-352, 10-355   7-72, 8-72, 9-96,
                                     10-101

First Innings – Abid Ali 12–2–47–0; Solkar 15–4–28–3; Gavaskar 1–0–1–0; Chandrasekhar 24–6–76–2; Venkataraghavan 20.4–3–63–2

Second Innings – Abid Ali 3–1–5–0; Solkar 3–1–10–0; Bedi 1–0–1–1; Chandrasekhar 18.1–3–38–6; Venkataraghavan 20–4–44–2

INDIA	
First Innings	*Second Innings*
S.M. Gavaskar b Snow 6	lbw b Snow 0
A.V. Mankad b Price 10	c Hutton b Underwood 11
*A.L. Wadekar c Hutton b Illingworth 48	run out 45
D.N. Sardesai b Illingworth 54	c Knott b Underwood 40
G.R. Viswanath b Illingworth 0	c Knott b Luckhurst 33
E.D. Solkar c Fletcher b D'Oliveira 44	c and b Underwood 1
†F.M. Engineer c Illingworth b Snow 59	not out 28
S. Abid Ali b Illingworth 26	not out 4
S. Venkataraghavan lbw b Illingworth 24	
B.S. Bedi c D'Oliveira b Illingworth 2	
B.S. Chandrasekhar not out 0	
B 6, l-b 4, n-b 1 11	B 6, l-b 5, n-b 1 12
1-17, 2-21, 3-114, 4-118, 5-125, 284 6-222, 7-230, 8-278, 9-284, 10-284	1-2, 2-37, 3-76, 174 4-124, (6 wkts) 5-134, 6-170

First Innings – Snow 24–5–68–2; Price 15–2–51–1; Hutton 12–2–30–0; D'Oliveira 7–5–5–1; Illingworth 34.3–12–70–5; Underwood 25–6–49–1

Second Innings – Snow 11–7–14–1; Price 5–0–10–0; D'Oliveira 9–3–17–0; Illingworth 36–15–40–0; Underwood 38–14–72–3; Luckhurst 2–0–9–1

Toss won by England
UMPIRES   C.S. Eliot and A.E.G. Rhodes

Acknowledgements

Looking back, it was an interesting coincidence that we were to meet for lunch to discuss this book the day India went into lockdown. The meeting was cancelled and little did we know that we wouldn't be able to meet in person for weeks. But what the lockdown did was help us dive deep into the project. *1971* kept us mentally sane. If Gavaskar and the rest of the team could achieve the unthinkable in 1971, so could we in 2020, while dealing with COVID too. Dozens of zoom calls and WhatsApp calls with Bishan Bedi, Sunil Gavaskar, Gundappa Viswanath and others set the tone, and we are grateful to each one of them for their time.

We have been fortunate in our careers to speak with almost all the cricketers who made 1971 possible (some of whom aren't with us anymore). Their inputs have been hugely valuable in trying to put together the backstory.

Over the years, Boria has painstakingly built the Fanattic Sports Museum in Kolkata. The one thing that is still missing in the museum is a library. It is interesting that he has the library in his house and in his home that comprises of hundreds of volumes of *Sportsweek*, the *Times of India*, *Sport and Pastime* and more. Needless to say these came to our rescue during the lockdown. As journalists, we had a vehicle pass to meet each other when needed and a ready library at hand to spend hours in. It helped us turn adversity into opportunity!

Our special thanks to Udayan Mitra, our publisher at HarperCollins India. Over the years, Udayan has become a close personal friend. He remembers the victories of 1971 from his childhood and it was only natural that he would treat this book as his own.

Thank you, Umakanta Roy, for the hours you spent looking through the archives with us. And Souvik Naha, thanks or all your help in looking up missing newspapers during the lockdown; some of what you sent us was invaluable.

Aisha, now seven, who kept asking what Boria was doing with the yellowing pieces of paper and why he wouldn't let her use them to hone her reading skills—hope you enjoy the book and read the stories.

About the Authors

Boria Majumdar, a Rhodes Scholar, is the author of multiple books on Indian sport and its history, and the co-author of Sachin Tendulkar's autobiography, *Playing It My Way*. His most recent publications include *Eleven Gods and a Billion Indians* (2018) and *Dreams of a Billion: India and the Olympic Games* (with Nalin Mehta, 2020). He is Senior Research Fellow at the University of Central Lancashire and Consulting Editor, Sports, for the India Today Group. Find him @BoriaMajumdar on Facebook, Twitter and Instagram

Gautam Bhattacharya, currently the Joint Editor of Kolkata's leading daily *Sangbad Pratidin*, has been a longstanding cricket writer and commentator, and is the author of several books. In a career spanning four decades, apart from reporting cricket across the globe, he has had the rare privilege of interviewing some of the all-time greats of the game. He is the co-author of Sourav Ganguly's book, *A Century Is Not Enough*.